Occupational and Environmental Medicine

Protecting Health at Work and in the Community

Tee L. Guidotti, MD, MPH, Editor

BLOOMSBURY ACADEMIC
NEW YORK • LONDON • OXFORD • NEW DELHI • SYDNEY

BLOOMSBURY ACADEMIC
Bloomsbury Publishing Inc
1385 Broadway, New York, NY 10018, USA
50 Bedford Square, London, WC1B 3DP, UK
29 Earlsfort Terrace, Dublin 2, Ireland

BLOOMSBURY, BLOOMSBURY ACADEMIC and the Diana logo are trademarks of
Bloomsbury Publishing Plc

First published in the United States of America 2023

Library of Congress Cataloging-in-Publication Data
Names: Guidotti, Tee L., editor.
Title: Occupational and environmental medicine : protecting health at work
and in the community / Tee L. Guidotti, editor.
Other titles: Occupational and environmental medicine (Guidotti)
Description: New York : Bloomsbury Academic, [2023] | Includes
bibliographical references and index.
Identifiers: LCCN 2023002777 | ISBN 9781440877117 (hardcover ; alk. paper)
| ISBN 9798216172154 (ebook) | ISBN 9781440877124 (ePDF)
Subjects: MESH: Occupational Medicine | Environmental Medicine | BISAC:
MEDICAL / Allied Health Services / General | LAW / Medical Law & Legislation
Classification: LCC RC964 | NLM WA 400 | DDC 616.9/803—dc23/eng/20230323
LC record available at https://lccn.loc.gov/2023002777

ISBN: HB: 978-1-4408-7711-7
ePDF: 978-1-4408-7712-4
eBook: 979-8-216-17215-4

Typeset by Amnet ContentSource

Printed and bound in the United States of America

To find out more about our authors and books visit www.bloomsbury.com and sign up
for our newsletters.

This book is dedicated to the memory of J. Frederic Green (1934–2020), past president of ACOEM (1995–1996). Fred was a visionary leader who brought a new generation of leaders into OEM and transformed the college into an effective and forward-looking medical institution. He began his career as a surgeon, served in the navy, and was for 25 years corporate medical director of the John Deere Company in Moline, Illinois. Fred's personal recollections reflected the history of OEM in the first half of the twentieth century, from an initial emphasis on acute injury care and an emphasis on heavy manufacturing through employer-initiated health-care innovations to the changing role of medical departments, which led to the rise of wellness and health promotion. His presidency was noteworthy for careful mentoring of future leaders; careful and selective engagement in political advocacy for worker protection; and enhancing OEM organizations, meetings, and educational opportunities. He dedicated his later efforts to strengthening and defending ACOEM as the vehicle for developing and advancing OEM.

Contents

Preface

This book is *not* a textbook. It is a book *about*, not a book *of*, occupational and environmental medicine (OEM). The reader will come away with an appreciation for this exciting and opportunity-filled field, but this book will not turn a physician into a specialist in OEM or a manager into an expert on what an OEM physician does. It is an introduction to what the medical specialty and field of practice is about and what it can do. Readers who are looking for a textbook of OEM are directed to another work from the same publisher, written by the editor of the present volume, *The Handbook of Occupational and Environmental Medicine* (Praeger/ABC-CLIO, 2020, 2nd ed.) or to other texts designed for learning the field in depth.

The intended readership includes physicians outside our field, potential resident candidates, medical students, employers, department chairs and others who need to understand us better, and the interested general public. There are several American textbooks of OEM available, even more international titles, and a plethora of books on individual aspects of OEM. The reader is encouraged to explore! But this book does not provide substantive references in the text other than citations for essential rules and regulations as they appear. There are two reasons for this. First, it is not a textbook or a monograph; it is only an introduction. Although every effort has been made to ensure accuracy, both historical and medical, this book is not intended to be a primary source on any technical or interpretive issue, which the presence of reference citations would encourage. It is an introduction and a distillation of current thinking, some of which is not spelled out in the literature. The second is that resources in this field change, especially online, and doing a search is better than relying on a book that predictably will go stale on some topics within a short time.

This book was originally commissioned by the publisher, ABC-CLIO, for its series Essentials of . . . —concise introductions to topics in the social, behavioral, and now, the health sciences. The format of these books is standardized. Initially, this format felt rigid and inflexible, because OEM is so different from the other fields covered in the series. In OEM, we tend to think in concrete terms, not in the abstract. We do not usually think in terms of theories, schools of thought, or core controversies. However, accommodating the Essentials format forced a creative rethinking. This book offered the opportunity to think about the field on a more abstract, integrated way, about fundamental agreement and disagreement, how we approach problems, and how we may approach problems from different points of view. Thus, OEM physicians who read this book may find a perspective that is not so much different from their daily practice as explanatory.

This book is the product of teamwork, tied together with trust. The American College of Occupational and Environmental Medicine (ACOEM) joined the effort and agreed to help support the development of the book. Following ACOEM's regular procedures for special projects, a docket was created. All ACOEM members were sent notice of the opportunity to participate. Some jumped on the opportunity with alacrity. Others were invited for their particular expertise or to fill gaps in coverage. ACOEM leaders were invited, several times, to contribute and to review the text in progress. The objective was to ensure that the text reflected something approaching a consensus view, although not necessarily a formalized position representing the college.

Certain chapters require comment.

Chapter 1, "A Brief History," is unvarnished and honest but necessarily incomplete, in the sense that the history of OEM is long, complicated, and at times, ambivalent. A comprehensive history of the field, particularly its role as a positive force in the Progressive Era, has yet to be written.

Chapter 2, "Schools of Thought," describes how OEM fits into medicine, preventive medicine, and public health and the various centers of emphasis and innovation that have emerged. OEM physicians are generally not accustomed to thinking of their field as having "schools of thought," but it most certainly does.

Chapter 3, "Theory and Practice," describes foundational concepts in prevention science and occupational health protection that lie at the heart of the field and help the reader to understand it but are often not made explicit because OEM tends to be more practice based than theory based. This is in sharp contrast to general preventive medicine, public health, and community medicine, which are more strategic in orientation and very much theory driven. The Essentials format, based as it is on social and behavioral sciences, is not the way most OEM physicians would view their field, but it is a legitimate way to view its underpinnings.

Chapter 4, "Relationships"; Chapter 6, "Corporate Sector and Private Practice"; Chapter 7, "Practice Settings"; and Chapter 8, "Academic Occupational and Environmental Medicine," describe the rich diversity and connectedness of OEM, which in many ways relates more closely to society and the economy than to advances in clinical and biomedical science.

Chapter 5, "Profiles," features individual OEM physicians who have achieved but who also illustrate the particular niches or practice opportunities described in the chapter. This chapter should therefore be considered a companion to chapter 7—a collection of examples (far from comprehensive) of the types of practice OEM physicians engage in. We anticipate that many readers will be particularly interested in knowing more about practitioners of environmental medicine. This field is still coalescing (see chapter 2), and there are few examples of OEM physicians in mainstream medicine who have clinical practices exclusively or even predominantly in environmental medicine, aside from academic institutions. However, as some of the profiles indicate, and as described throughout the book, environmental health concerns are central to the field, and many OEM physicians in academic and government agency practice are deeply engaged in them.

Chapter 9, "Case Studies," comprises fictionalized cases (based on true patients) and is not to be construed as an accurate medical casebook. To repeat, this is not a textbook of medicine. Details of diagnosis and treatment are left vague for a reason. However, the cases illustrate the nature of cases OEM physicians see and provide a flavor for practice in the field.

Chapter 10, "Core Controversies," carrying over another element of the Essentials format, may surprise readers who were expecting an emphasis on labor management relations and how that affects occupational health issues, partisan politics, OSHA or EPA regulations, or disputed workers' compensation claims. This book takes the view that these specific issues are expressions of core controversies on such issues. The controversies that truly lie at the core of the field have to do with intrinsic tensions, contradictions, and sources of strength. Understanding these is foundational, because they underlie issues of the moment. Arguments over risk assessment of a particular hazard, adoption of a particular regulation, or ethical aspects of one issue come and go, but it is critical to understand the deep tensions described in the chapter to appreciate the field.

Chapter 11 provides an overview (only) of important research that has shaped OEM and that OEM physicians have led. However, it should be understood that occupational and environmental health, not to mention toxicology, epidemiology, and risk science, are much broader than OEM and that OEM physicians depend on research from many fields in which they do not necessarily lead.

Chapter 12 is one view of emerging areas of new research and the agenda for future investigation. It provides examples of important work in progress, but it cannot be comprehensive or anticipate the results. This chapter also reminds us that OEM is global. Its author, a fellow of ACOEM and active in the college, is a distinguished senior scientist in Taiwan and so has wide perspective. This reminds us that although ACOEM is the American college, it is global in membership and connects worldwide, through its international section, its participation in and support of the International Occupational Medicine Society Collaborative, and its support of the International Commission on Occupational Health.

Chapter 13 is a notebook of ideas and proposals that have been put forward about the future of OEM. It is in no way definitive, nor is it a consensus view, but it captures musings from serious observers of the field. It is for discussion only and not to be considered a position statement or official document of ACOEM.

We thank the insightful and expert assistance given by the authors, Marianne Dreger and the staff of ACOEM for indispensable assistance, and the staff of ABC-CLIO for making this unusual opportunity available. We also thank the numerous colleagues who supported the endeavor but were not able to participate due to their priority duties during the COVID-19 pandemic, which not only severely interfered with the timely production of the book but also highlighted the urgency and importance of OEM. Special thanks to Drs. Beth Baker, Pamela B. Hackert, Douglas W. Martin, and Annyce Mayer for input and being willing to help.

ACOEM assisted in the production of this book, as described above. Many leaders of the college participated as authors, contributors (of profiles or case studies), and reviewers. A task force of ACOEM officers reviewed the final manuscript before publication and made constructive suggestions. The final decision on edits and modifications rests with the editor. Individual passages in the text do not necessarily reflect the views of the editor or ACOEM or all the individual authors—who have been entirely free to disagree.

The author is a former president of ACOEM who has held positions as professor of occupational and environmental medicine at several institutions, particularly the University of Alberta (Canada) and the George Washington University (Washington, DC). After writing extensively on global OEM, this book was a return to focus again on the United States and to explore anew the enormous potential for addressing occupational and environmental health issues and building better and stronger communities through OEM.

Tee L. Guidotti

CHAPTER ONE

A Brief History of Occupational and Environmental Medicine in the United States

Tee L. Guidotti, Manijeh Berenji,
and Judith Green McKenzie

Conditions in the New World were harsh, and industrialization was primitive. There was a serious shortage of workers and much to be done in the new mines, canals, factories, and cities. The historical development of occupational medicine in the United States was initially a continuation of European practice adapted to local economic necessity. Scientific environmental medicine arose out of the public reforms of the nineteenth century.

During the first century of the American republic, physicians and surgeons were recruited by employers in dangerous industries to reduce the consequences of hazardous conditions by treating injuries. They began to develop a specialized area of practice, not yet a true specialty. In the country's second century, occupational physicians became part of a progressive public health movement that reduced the adverse impact of industrial development. Occupational medicine went on to play a central role in mid-twentieth-century health-care reform, in community health, and in the response to environmental pollution—often far outside its primary mission of care for injured workers and prevention of illness. It has done so within a complicated world of government regulation, labor management conflict, and crosscurrents of political change.

There are four interwoven threads to this story. One is of scientific advances in understanding health problems arising from the workplace, achieved by meticulous scientific research. Another is how protection of workers' health played out as a public issue in American society. The third is how injuries and illnesses that affected workers were managed in practice. The fourth is how environmental medicine played (and is still playing) catch-up.

Occupational and environmental medicine (OEM) has deep roots in both medicine, which is the provision of care to individuals, and in public health, which is protecting health in a population or community. In ancient times, the medical community readily accepted that the environment influenced human health. Hippocrates himself wrote an important treatise on the topic called *Airs, Waters, and Places* that influenced thinking for a thousand years.

Historical Roots

The history of occupational medicine is much, much older than the history of the United States. There are preserved notes from physicians excusing skilled workers on the pyramids of Egypt from work due to medical illness. Protecting the health of workers was less of a priority for ancient civilizations, however, mostly because the workers doing the hardest jobs were usually slaves, whose lives were not valued. Injuries were common and considered a part of life. Workers who were injured or made ill by their work were reduced to begging to survive.

In the Middle Ages, skilled craftsmen (almost all men) and their apprentices lived in towns and cities. Health in the cities was poor and unpredictable, in part because population density and poor sanitation led to frequent outbreaks of communicable disease. Craftsmen were organized into guilds and worked in shops in or near their homes—for example, as weavers, candlemakers, potters, and smiths and fine metalworkers. Although it was a time of technological innovation, the power of machinery was limited to animal or human muscle, and the methods of production were handed down from generation to generation. Working conditions were very poor. Family members, children, apprentices, and hired workers often lived and worked under the same roof as the master or owner, inhaled the same fumes, and drank the same often-contaminated water. Working conditions in the few large enterprises of the day were even worse, especially in the mines and smelters. A disability or death of the father in the family could mean destitution for the family.

Because craftsmen were organized into guilds and trading networks were developing and expanding, the increasingly crowded cities tended to specialize in certain products, such as glass or armor and weapons or tanning hides.

Health hazards from a particular trade could result in injury or disease and were also linked to local environmental hazards, such as water pollution downstream from tanneries. Workers and their families were exposed to both, essentially all the time, a condition often called "the double burden" today.

Toward the late Middle Ages, commercial trade, technology, the use of chemicals, more powerful energy sources (wind- and water-driven mills), trade, the transfer of money (banking), and economic demand, all accelerated. Production was less dominated by cottage industry. Physicians and engineers noticed that certain injuries were common in various occupations but that occupations were often linked to certain illnesses. Miners, for example, had a much greater burden of serious lung disease than other people. Dangerous enterprises often hired physicians with surgical skills to attend to emergencies and sometimes to provide care to workers' families.

The Renaissance in Europe was a tipping point for free expression, technological progress (driven largely by the arts), and the rediscovery of knowledge. The age of exploration brought trade (as well as colonization), the rise of a new type of chattel slavery, and new wealth and demand for more sophisticated products. Soon the Enlightenment, the intellectual movement that favored individualism, freedom, and objectivity, gained ground in Europe and fostered ideas about the rights of all "men" (women were rarely considered) and the possibility of progress, either by reforming existing institutions or by revolution. Forward-looking physicians tried to put medicine on a scientific foundation and attempted (without the benefit of the germ theory of disease or a clear idea of how the body works) to understand how the environment influences health. The stage was being set for the explosion in knowledge, technology, and human rights that was to follow.

By AD 1700, technology and trade had advanced to the point that larger and more sophisticated enterprises were possible and profitable, production became more organized, financial investment became more formal, techniques of instrument-making and fine work were borrowed from the arts, and the sciences began to contribute more practical knowledge of the material world. One of the world centers of large-scale industry was northern Italy; its cities especially were rich, better educated, and technologically advanced. Every trade and craft practiced in the world was found and observed there. A smart physician in Modena by the name of Bernardino Ramazzini, who became a distinguished professor at the ancient University of Modena and later in Padua, took an interest in the health of workers and the communities in which they lived (figure 1.1). Ramazzini wrote two books important to the development of OEM. The first was a treatise on environmental disease, focusing on malaria (as it was understood at the time) and proposed one of the first effective treatments: cinchona bark (a source of quinine). The second, *De Morbis Artificum Diatriba* (On the Diseases of Workers), was hugely influential as the

Figure 1.1. Bernardino Ramazzini, the "Father of Occupational Medicine." Line engraving by J. G. Seiller, 1716. (Wellcome Collection).

first work to bring together knowledge on the hazards and health risks of workers across the economy, drawn from Ramazzini's own observations, and addressed some environmental health risks. Ramazzini is often called the "Father of Occupational Medicine" for his intellectual grasp of the field as a whole and deep understanding of individual trades and occupations. He also demonstrated respect for the worker, unusual in an age when most physicians were part of the privileged and educated class and concern for workers was based on paternalism.

Early Years in the United States

Concepts of human rights and health protection came to the new continent of America with European migration and were incorporated into medical practice by physicians, who, like clergy, were among the better educated in the American colonies. The practical role of physicians in patching up workers after injury was always obvious and initially more important than their role in the prevention of disease. At the time, the new United States had a labor shortage, relatively high income levels, and an average life span longer than in Europe.

Even so, medicine and public health lagged behind Europe. Benjamin Rush was the leading American physician around and after the American Revolution, a signer of the Declaration of Independence. Rush and his followers had a blind spot in assuming that the health situation in the United States was much better than it really was. Harsh reality came with a series of epidemics that broke out in American ports: most famously, an outbreak of yellow fever in Philadelphia in 1793. Because mariners moved around between ports, states could not address the problem individually. The problem had to be managed on a national level. Special hospitals were established in port cities for mariners—one of the earliest organized occupational health interventions in the new country. This was the first federal public health agency, which became the Public Health Service (the research laboratory of which much later became the National Institutes of Health).

By the end of the eighteenth century, in England and Scotland, a combination of mechanization, new business arrangements (more efficient capitalism), and new knowledge powered the Industrial Revolution, which resulted not only in rising wealth but also in hugely increased industrial production, rapid urbanization, global trade, water and local air pollution, and more infectious disease outbreaks in major ports. The new technologies, chemicals, and unguarded mechanical power brought serious health and injury hazards, in addition to worsening sanitation in the crowded cities. New technology was imported into North America piecemeal, but then domestic innovation from the 1790s gradually transformed the United States from an agrarian society to an urban, industrialized, and innovative one, but one with stark dangers and huge inequities, chief among them being dependence on child labor (in workshops) and chattel slavery (for agricultural commodities such as cotton). First, canals and later, railroads became essential for moving commodities and finished products, as well as people after 1830.

During this period, a young English physician named Charles Turner Thackrah was doing for the United Kingdom what Ramazzini had done in Italy, documenting the extent and severity of occupational injuries and illnesses. His 1831 book *The Effects of Arts, Trades and Professions on Health and Longevity* attracted much attention in both the United Kingdom and the United States, where a young American physician, Benjamin McCready, admired and wanted to emulate Thackrah's work. In 1837, McCready wrote a treatise on occupational health in the United States that documented poor working conditions, deteriorating public health standards, and poverty. Aside from winning a prize from the New York State Medical Society, his work was almost completely ignored. People simply believed, against all evidence, as had Rush, that the United States could not have a problem.

Sadly, they were wrong. The Bureau of Labor Statistics was established as early as 1869 to investigate industrial accidents. There were numerous industrial tragedies and accidents involving employees during the 1870s and 1880s reported from U.S. state labor bureaus, such as the collapse of the Pemberton Mill in Massachusetts in 1860, which resulted in the death of 145 workers, and the explosion of the Washburn A Mill in Minnesota in 1878 due to the ignition of flour dust in the factory, which resulted in the deaths of 16 workers. These events were considered unfortunate and tragic but of no great social significance and failed to provoke a national or effective response.

Railroads were especially dangerous in the nineteenth century, with a high risk of derailments and serious and often fatal injuries, among workers, passengers, and people who found themselves in the wrong place (i.e., at a railway crossing) at the wrong time. Large numbers of physicians were employed by railroads. "Railroad surgery," as it was called, was an early large-scale, multistate, nonmilitary organized health-care system and the origin of specialized occupational medicine in the United States. Railroad surgeons soon found a wider role practicing in railroad communities. They eventually developed dedicated hospitals and integrated health-care systems (some of which still exist), medical societies and journals, and innovations in trauma surgery. Some of these hospitals became major medical centers in their cities and unlikely centers of excellence in otherwise isolated communities, such as Clifton Forge, Virginia. The hospitals also trained physicians, including women at a time when they were excluded from other opportunities for postgraduate medical training.

Railroad injuries resulted in a very high number of medicolegal claims and lawsuits. The railroad surgeon was always expected to testify for the employer, which led to the stereotype of the "company physician" taking orders from the company.

As the nineteenth century progressed, occupational injury care and advances in public health served to mitigate the excesses of the Industrial Revolution, which either humanized or enabled capitalism, depending on one's theory of history. After the Civil War and especially during the Gilded Age of the late nineteenth century, working conditions, financial depressions, immigration-fueled crowding in cities, and deteriorating public health, all fed into a rising climate of social unrest and impatience with rampant political corruption and inequities. At the same time, the increasing reliance in the United States on immigrants for its workforce imported new and electrifying ideas about labor and social justice from Europe.

This unstable situation was even more pronounced in Europe, where revolutionary sentiment was taking many political forms, from trade unionism through social democracy (socialization of the means of production), syndicalism (union control of the means of production), and socialism (social or government control of the means of production) to anarchism (characterized by direct action, sometimes violent) and later Marxist-Leninist communism. Cities with large immigrant populations such as New York and Chicago were energized with political and social discussions and study groups, duplicating their European models. However, the United States was different. Although there were a few violent conflicts, the country never approached the same revolutionary crisis as in Europe. The United States also turned a blind eye to racial disparities and the concentration of minorities in precarious, less desirable, and more hazardous work.

Developments in two countries profoundly influenced the development of occupational medicine in the United States. The United Kingdom enacted a series of so-called factory acts that regulated child labor and set minimal workplace protection standards and later the landmark public health acts. Largely to head off brewing revolution, the chancellor of Germany, Otto von

Bismarck, introduced a series of social reforms that included a ban on child labor and workplace safety regulation and also introduced workers' compensation, a no-fault employer-funded insurance system to protect workers' income and pay for medical care after injuries (illnesses came later). These reforms became the cornerstone of occupational health protection and occupational medicine and were widely adopted in the United States during the Progressive Era, the political reform movement that lasted from the 1890s into the 1920s.

The Progressive Era to Midcentury

A hallmark of the Progressive Era was investigative reporting by "muckrakers"—reporters who specialized in uncovering abuses and poor living and working conditions. The most famous such work was *The Jungle* by Upton Sinclair. However, his message about worker health and safety was almost entirely overshadowed by the public reaction over disgusting revelations about food safety and slaughterhouses. The book stimulated the formation of the Food and Drug Administration in 1906 but had no appreciable impact on occupational health. Prevention again took a back seat.

Workers' compensation became the foundation of injury care, rehabilitation, and income replacement for workers who were covered by it, and its payment system supported the practice of occupational medicine by private practitioners outside of corporations. The fundamental principle of "workers' comp" is that workers give up the right to sue their employers, which was difficult and expensive anyway, in exchange for an administrative system that assured rapid and adequate, if not full compensation, for impairment or death. However, it had many exclusions: it dealt almost entirely with injuries at first, and its individual state systems were inconsistent, prone to corruption and political manipulation, often short on benefits, and chronically underfunded. Workers' compensation remains in the aggregate the primary means of funding occupational injury care and lost wages and so constitutes a major but fragmented health-care "system" in the United States, funding care for hundreds of thousands of workers every year.

One of the most active elements of the Progressive Era was the "Settlement Movement," established by Jane Addams, founder of the pioneering Hull House in Chicago, for the benefit of immigrants and impoverished workers. These were community-based centers for health and social education, emphasizing empowerment and education of the poor. Hull House gave rise to many reformers, including Frances Perkins. Perkins was a sociologist and an advocate for workers' rights and health and children. She witnessed and was moved to vocal advocacy by the horror of the Triangle Shirtwaist Fire in New York in 1911, when 146 workers, mostly young women from immigrant families, perished by fire and leaping to their deaths when they were trapped

Figure 1.2. Alice Hamilton, commemorated by a statue at Headwaters Park in Fort Wayne, Indiana, unveiled in 2000. (Photo courtesy of Mark Catlin).

in an unsafe burning building. At the time, workers' health and safety and employment law were the sole responsibility of states. When Perkins became secretary of labor in the Franklin Roosevelt administration, she instituted reforms such as the minimum wage, the time-limited workweek, unemployment insurance, and ending child labor. She established the Bureau of Labor Standards in 1934 to coordinate workplace safety standards and establish a federal role in formulating occupational health and safety standards and to do so based on science.

The Settlement Movement also produced the most extraordinary figure in the history of American occupational medicine. Alice Hamilton was born to a privileged midwestern family in 1869 and became interested early in medicine and public service (figure 1.2). Overcoming the many, and rising, barriers to women pursuing careers at the time, she succeeded in getting a medical education, specialized in pathology, and distinguished herself in public health research. During her time at Hull House, she observed how workers got sick and sometimes died from exposure to lead, carbon monoxide, and "other industrial diseases," which led her to study toxicology and then to teach it as the first woman on the faculty of Harvard Medical School. There, and in subsequent public service in Illinois and Massachusetts, she documented the true dimensions of occupational disease in the United States, made numerous contributions to medical research, and crafted the first proposals for regulation of exposure to toxic chemicals in the workplace. She is considered the founder of modern occupational medicine and the field of industrial (occupational) hygiene, which grew out of it, and a pioneer of sci-ence-based health regulation. She lived to be over a hundred, ironically dying the same year (1970) that Congress passed the landmark Occupational Health and Safety Act. Hamilton, like her predecessors, found the American medical community incurious and disbelieving that occupational health and chemical exposure in general could be a serious health problem, just as ear-lier generations before her had been told that workplaces in Europe were dangerous but things were much better in the United States. She was strongly supported in her work by British colleagues, particularly Thomas Legge and the British tradition he had begun of a competent and professional factory inspectorate. However, it was her own research skills—both in the labora-tory, honed by study in Germany, and in inspection and survey methodology—that allowed her to document the hazards beyond doubt and from one location to another. Throughout the history of occupational medicine, it has been a recurring theme that hazards are denied and their presence must be demonstrated anew in every generation and in every state and country indi-vidually before their presence and importance are accepted and there is political will to control them.

At the same time, models were emerging of committed Progressive physi-cians working with enlightened management. Harry Mock was a surgeon, professor, and medical director of Sears, Roebuck & Company, in Chicago. Mock was a near contemporary to Alice Hamilton. He believed that the workplace could be used for social improvement and that the power of the organization could be harnessed for health gains. He wrote the highly influ-ential textbook *Industrial Medicine and Surgery* (1916) that laid the founda-tions for occupational medicine theory and practice in health care, prevention, health promotion, and education.

Wartime Value and Peacetime Neglect

World War I renewed interest in safe and efficient work to support effi-cient and uninterrupted wartime production. The War Labor Administration within the new Department of Labor mobilized the American workforce and quickly found that massively increasing production brought a high cost in injuries and illnesses and serious industrial accidents that set back produc-tion. The Working Conditions Service was established to regulate civilian work standards based on medical and engineering research and under the supervision of physicians in the U.S. Public Health Service. These mobiliza-tion agencies were dismantled when the war ended.

The Depression was a major setback for occupational medicine as for everything else. Investment in workers' health held little interest for employ-ers when unemployment was high and people were desperate for work. The Depression was an era of frequent occupational health disasters, including the worst in U.S. history at Gauley Bridge in West Virginia in 1930, when 500–1,000 workers, mostly unaccounted poor African Americans, died from a form of silicosis while drilling a tunnel without protection. It was a time when occupational hazards were compounded by worker exploitation and racism directed against Black and immigrant workers and unions were weak. Many state workers' compensation systems were going bankrupt. Still, there were some advances, such as the extension of occupational health protection for federal employees and steady scientific advances, particularly in respiratory protection, building on the technology of wartime gas masks (and leading to invention of the iron lung for polio patients).

During World War II, occupational medicine got new respect, for the same reasons as during World War I: war production was often dangerous; skilled workers were scarce in wartime; and the health, safety, and readiness of soldiers, sailors, and airmen were critical for the war effort. The Preventive Medicine Division of the U.S. Army concerned itself with occupational hazards as well as infectious diseases among troops, and the U.S. Surgeon General conducted surveys and monitored health in critical industries such as armaments manufacturing. To retain skilled workers without violating wartime restrictions on pay raises, employers began offering health insurance as a benefit for employees. Health insurance has been tightly tied to employment in the United States ever since.

After the war, the value of occupational medicine became less obvious. The situation and status of occupational medicine changed radically again, and for the worse.

Setbacks and Gains

In the 1940s and 1950s, most occupational health care was provided either by physicians employed by large companies or by "general practitioners" (GPs, predecessors of today's family physicians), with referral to specialists as needed. The number of physicians practicing "industrial medicine" (as it was then called) as consultants, or as the major part of their practice, was very small. GPs believed that they had the knowledge and skills to take care of almost all workplace problems (largely because the cases they saw were straightforward injuries, not complicated ones) and were concerned about the loss of patients from their practice, loss of income, and competition from new integrated health-care models that were emerging. These models included Kaiser Permanente (which had its origins in providing health care for workers and their dependents), multispecialty practices such as the Mayo Clinic, and the precursors of what later became federally sponsored "community health centers" for low-income families during the "War on Poverty" in the Johnson administration.

At the time, GPs controlled organized medicine. They saw any form of systematically organized or subsidized health care as a threat to one-on-one patient care and payment based on individual charges, separately billed, for every service done ("fee for service"). The GP fee-for-service business model was considered to be the ideal in health care because it was transparent and preserved the traditional "physician-patient relationship" (otherwise known as "continuity of care"), in which every patient or family has one permanent personal physician and services are provided either in a hospital or the physician's private office.

In peacetime, most countries that could do so, moved toward universal, national health-care systems, but the United States moved in the opposite direction. National health insurance had been proposed by President Harry Truman in 1945 but faced a campaign of resistance from organized medicine. The physicians opposing it feared losing their autonomy, compromising the doctor-patient relationship, and having their incomes restricted by fee schedules. Medical practice conducted outside of the traditional fee-for-service model was denounced as unethical, socialist, and anti-American. There were by that time many alternative models of health care, but despite their differences, they were lumped together by the opposition, which called it "the corporate practice of medicine," using the word "corporate" to mean functioning in an integrated way, not necessarily sponsored by a company. The term included medical group practices, insurance based on capitation (fixed payments), physicians salaried by hospitals, government-funded clinics, union-sponsored health plans, early health management organizations (HMOs), and particularly, medical departments of companies. These organized systems were all denounced as "socialized medicine" and demonized as enemies of "good" (ethical and effective) medicine. Occupational medicine was particularly demonized because its practicing physicians worked in companies (and sometimes for unions), and there was great fear that employers would begin offering direct medical care to workers and their families as an employee benefit.

The reputation and prestige of occupational medicine within the medical community did not recover for decades.

Postwar Promise and Scientific Progress

Even so, there was considerable progress in the 1950s in development of the field scientifically. Academic departments sprang up, the professional field of industrial (occupational) hygiene split off from occupational medicine and began to thrive, and a framework of solid and advanced science was created through research in toxicology and the rapidly developing statistical science of epidemiology.

The private sector employed most physicians in the field, and with the new prosperity and corporate support, occupational medicine's forced alienation from the rest of medicine over the health-care issue mattered less. The field started to shed its old name of "industrial medicine" and call itself "occupational medicine" to emphasize that its mission was to protect the health of workers, not the companies. A specialty certification board was established (among the earliest in medicine). A long list of health-protection standards required of contractors for federally funded contracts had already been developed (the Walsh-Healy Public Contracts Act of 1936), and chemical exposure limits (called threshold limit values) were developed after 1941 by a new and influential organization called the American Conference of Governmental Industrial Hygienists (ACGIH). Years later, these became the basis for federal occupational safety and health standards, replacing an incomplete and variably enforced patchwork of state standards.

By the 1940s, a small but growing group of physician-scientists were also becoming concerned about setting limits on exposure or banning chemicals that cause cancer. The field of occupational cancer research had deep roots, going back to the observation of English surgeon Percivall Pott that chimney sweeps developed cancer of the scrotum, because their clothes were grimy with soot containing carcinogenic tars (complicated organic molecules in the polycyclic aromatic hydrocarbon family). These scientists, initially led by German-born Wilhelm Hueper, cataloged many examples (early in the science, they were mainly these same tars, dyes, metals, and asbestos), discovered mechanisms by which chemicals cause cancer, and even advanced the basic science of cancer biology.

The science behind both occupational and environmental health was obviously the same. Occupational and environmental medicine became a logical combination, as had been shown by an incident in Donora, Pennsylvania, in 1948, in which 20 people died and many more became seriously ill due to air pollution. This incident was investigated by the same scientists from the U.S. Public Health Service who did research on occupational health, because they had the right equipment and methods and understanding of the problem. From that time on, environmental problems dealing with air and chemical hazards have been closely related scientifically to occupational health research, often studied in the same laboratories by the same scientists.

Toward the end of this era, in the 1950s, another scientific community was developing methods to study disease in human populations and analyze data, leading to the emergence of "chronic disease" epidemiology. Epidemiologists and biostatisticians studied the incidence of cancer and other disease outcomes in communities, industries, and occupations. This was difficult and tedious work before computers. Patterns emerged that largely confirmed the findings of the laboratory investigators doing toxicological research.

Statistics and laboratory science built on one another until the burden of occupational cancers became undeniable and the case for setting standards unavoidable.

Progress on the ground did not match this forward movement, however. The science behind standards was growing increasingly sophisticated, but occupational medicine and toxicology in practice was a small field dominated by a handful of people. One of them was Robert A. Keogh, a physician toxicologist who ran the Kettering Laboratories, a research institute at the University of Cincinnati, in the 1960s. His special interest was lead, which he unfortunately believed (apparently in all sincerity) was not hazardous at "low" levels. This, and possibly a bias from overly close relationships with the automotive and oil industries (lead was an essential additive in gasoline for that generation of automobiles), caused him to minimize concerns about lead poisoning, as he also did for cancer-causing chemicals. He was a very controlling and persuasive personality and had great influence in Congress and state governments. Although he achieved much that was positive, such as training many fine scientists (many of whom disagreed with him), his legacy today is as an object lesson in conflicted ethics and what not to do.

Scientists such as Hueper pushed back against Keogh and others but found that their conclusions were constantly fought. Regulation of any kind was bitterly opposed by the industry on the grounds that there was not enough data or that two studies did not exactly agree or that the cost of replacement was too great. In the 1940s, manufacturers and distributors of interior lead paint mounted a very effective advertising campaign that kept the product in the market until 1978, despite its known risks to children. How they did this became the working template for resistance to regulation. The same basic strategies were then adapted to the now-infamous campaign to cast doubt on the relationship between cigarette smoking and cancer, with the addition of distorted scientific studies. The same template was used to defer action on occupational hazards, including and especially asbestos. Industry interests, collectively, even managed to provoke a conflict between health advocates: public health professionals focused on cigarette smoking as the greater evil while occupational health scientists such as Hueper thought that preventable occupational cancers were being ignored by the exclusive emphasis on smoking.

The fragmented nature of occupational health regulation and public health responsibility in the United States, together with the tendency of the legal system to favor the defense, made it easy to fight regulation. The legacy of this can be seen today in the tendency to retreat to "scientism" (the attitude that all problems can be resolved by data) and to insist on unequivocal evidence of harm before taking action, rather than accepting that uncertainty is inevitable but workers needed to be protected regardless. One example of this dynamic at play was the decades-long delay in recognizing and compensating workers who developed coal workers' pneumoconiosis ("black lung"), which did not receive federal recognition until 1969.

States then had responsibility for occupational health and safety under the ineffective guidance of the U.S. Department of Labor, and there was little consistency or enforcement, aside from leadership by a few states such as Massachusetts, California, and New York. Working conditions in American workplaces were revealed to be unsatisfactory in a series of surveys and studies after a series of disasters that could not be ignored, especially in mining.

Aggressively applying its existing authority under the Walsh-Healy Act, Congress passed incremental amendments and extensions of existing legislation and leveraged successes in the maritime and (less successfully) mining industries. In the 1960s, the federal government attempted to impose standards mandated for federal contractors and to create new ones through research by the U.S. Public Health Service. However, the federal government lacked the legal authority to do so. That all changed, shortly after another mine tragedy, when a dramatic series of political developments, union advocacy, and partisan maneuvering unexpectedly resulted in a broad consensus-based bill for a single federal agency that covered general industry, construction, and the maritime industry.

The Occupational Health and Safety Act and After

That legislation became the Occupational Health and Safety Act of 1970 (OSH Act), creating the Occupational Safety and Health Administration (OSHA) within the Department of Labor and the National Institute of Occupational Safety and Health (NIOSH) to develop and recommend standards and to conduct research. OSHA began by applying the old Walsh-Healy Act and some ACGIH standards on a provisional basis, but most of the standards were never updated or replaced. Later, in 1978, the Mine Safety and Health Act was passed, creating the Mine Safety and Health Administration (MSHA), with NIOSH also providing research and recommended standards for mining.

This was also a time of rising awareness of environmental health problems. Sweeping legislation, the National Environmental Protection Act of 1970 (NEPA), established the Environmental Protection Agency (EPA), which was given authority for chemical evaluation and registration, regulation of pesticides, and a few other occupational health functions. The new EPA funded much-needed research that soon translated into science-based standards because EPA had both research and regulatory powers combined in one agency.

The OSH Act changed the landscape of occupational safety and health in the United States and gave a huge boost to occupational medicine. For example, NIOSH funded a network of designated educational resource centers (ERCs) around the country, which trained virtually an entire generation of occupational physicians and sponsored high-quality research in addition to NIOSH's in-house laboratories and field-study teams. At about this same time, a new and transformative role model emerged for physicians working in the field and brought occupational and environmental medicine closer together.

Figure 1.3. Irving J. Selikoff, transformational figure in modern occupational and environmental medicine. (Wikimedia, MSOccHealth, CC BY-SA 4.0).

Irving J. Selikoff was a lung specialist and pioneer in tuberculosis treatment in New York and New Jersey who turned his attention to occupational diseases (figure 1.3). His research on asbestos-related disease was groundbreaking and established that the mineral was a serious health risk and cause of cancer. Selikoff was vocal and unsparing in his criticism of physicians who apologized for asbestos manufacturers and managers who tried to ignore or deny the problem. He used his growing fame to advocate for workers' health and reform and to establish institutions and organizations to carry on his work. His influence on occupational medicine was profound and in many ways restored the field to its roots in the Progressive Era.

Selikoff's work on asbestos also provided an object lesson in conflicts of interest and the ethics of occupational medicine. Physicians who worked for asbestos companies and other high-risk industries increasingly came to be viewed in the 1980s as apologists for unethical management. Central to the ethical issue was whether the first duty of the occupational physician was to the company (in his or her fiduciary capacity of advising the employer, with what was best for the company being paramount) or to the worker (seen as patient, with what was best for the individual being paramount). Legally, this was an important distinction because the former was a strictly technical function, not unlike evaluating a person for insurance or military service or taking action in public health emergencies, while the latter implied a sacrosanct physician-patient relationship (echoing concerns of the 1940s) and duty to care. Medical ethics at the time had a blind spot in this area of "dual responsibility," essentially ignoring the issue. In occupational medicine, the quandary was more or less managed, although not resolved, by the widespread acceptance of codes of ethics and by education, which had the net effect of establishing norms of ethical behavior beyond the general ethical obligations of the physician in medicine.

While occupational health protection was being shaped by regulation, the practice of occupational medicine began to change abruptly as part of a widespread reorganization of American business beginning in the 1970s. The change in business practice arose in equal parts from a drive for increased efficiency and profitability, fear of foreign competition (especially from Japan), and disruptive business practices that were part of the new wave of the management theory championed by new CEOs and MBA programs. The previous (idealized) business philosophy was called "corporate social responsibility" and had been dominant since it was formalized in 1953 and called for profit-making companies to emphasize philanthropy, community benefit, and beneficence (the attitude could be paternalistic at times). The new trend was that "shareholder value" (the financial value of the company to its owners) held primacy over "stakeholder values" (obligations to employees, customers, the community, or users of the product). The new belief system was best articulated by economist Milton Friedman's statement that "there is one and only one social responsibility of business: to use its resources and engage in activities designed to increase its profits so long as it stays in the rules of the game, which is to say, engages in open and free competition, without deception or fraud." In other words, employers had only contractual, transactional responsibilities to their employees, the community, and consumers: no obligation to make things better.

Another aspect of the management revolution of the 1970s was that major companies made striking changes in their operations, which included downsizing their workforce, reducing the layers of authority in their management structure ("delayering" or "flattening" management, to remove the middle managers), getting out of activities that did not directly contribute to the profitability of the business, and outsourcing essential services that supported the business but did not directly contribute to profitability. Among the many profound consequences was a reevaluation of corporate medical departments and a nearly universal trend in American business to eliminate corporate occupational health services and with them the midlevel managers that oversaw (and defended) them. Almost overnight, the corporate medical director and plant physician almost disappeared, but it soon became evident that some of the services they provided could not be easily replaced, certainly not by primary-care providers in the community. As a result, companies outsourced occupational health services under contract, often to the same people who had previously operated their in-house services. The result, over three long decades or more, was that occupational medicine came to be provided primarily by physicians in small groups or outpatient clinics who, although not necessarily formally trained or certified as specialists, learned and took over specialized functions and provided injury care on an outpatient basis within the workers' compensation system. This is still the predominant model for delivery of occupational health services, but the corporate medical director is making a comeback (see chapter 6).

After the 1990s, the pendulum seemed to swing back. Larger companies, particularly in manufacturing and those with multinational operations, began building their in-house services back up again. As well, hospitals, which grew much larger, diversified, and networked during this period, have sponsored and aggressively promoted outpatient occupational health services as a revenue-generating opportunity, thereby making them more widely available.

The closure of corporate occupational health departments panicked many occupational medicine practitioners, some of whom even declared the field a dying specialty. However, by the time it was over, the outsourcing trend resulted in much less dependence on corporate management for jobs and proliferation of small clinics across the country in much greater numbers, making occupational health services more accessible to smaller employers. This had the paradoxical and unexpected effect of stabilizing the field of practice over time.

Injury care remained the primary service provided, together with preventive services designed to ensure fitness for work and to prevent disability. Musculoskeletal disorders other than acute injuries, such as low back pain and repetitive strain injuries, rose to prominence and then became the cause of a stinging reversal when a proposed standard for prevention, proposed by NIOSH, in 2000, was struck down by Congress. New chemicals continued to be introduced into the workplace (including entirely new classes of hazards, in the case of nanomaterials), while the old chemical hazards (such as lead, solvents, silica) never went away. Other occupational health professions, such as occupational health nursing, industrial (occupational) hygiene, and safety have often taken on responsibility that in the 1950s would have been within the domain of physicians.

Meanwhile, the leaders of the field, acting through its organizations (primarily, the American College of Occupational and Environmental Medicine, known as ACOEM), built OEM's legitimacy and acceptance as a medical field by formulating a set of competencies that defined, in excruciating detail, what an occupational physician needed to know; this list was effective both as a set of learning objectives for training and also as a riposte to the often-repeated challenge to explain why the field was different from primary care. A few years later, ACOEM developed a set of practice guidelines specifying the proper evaluation and treatment of common occupational injuries and illnesses and establishing the standard of practice. The college was among the first medical societies to do either, and this, together with the passage of time and the healing of old wounds, helped to end the division, disrespect, and isolation that had kept occupational medicine at arm's length from other medical specialties.

Practitioners of occupational medicine continue to be divided into three groups, as they were in 1900: (1) occupational medicine specialists, who since 1953 have a specific board certification to validate their expertise; (2) primary-care providers with an interest in occupational medicine practice, some of whom have obtained advanced training and who make up the great majority of practitioners; and (3) specialists in related fields who have a particular interest in occupational problems in their field of practice, such as occupational lung disease or dermatology. There have never been enough occupational medicine specialists to provide for all the services needed and probably never will be.

Yet another important trend came in the form of renewed interest in the 1960s in what came to be called "population medicine," which involves the management of health issues on a group level for entire communities and working populations. Traditional public health and its sister field of preventive medicine (see chapter 3) relied heavily on education and prevention delivered through medical services. In the 1980s, the field of "health promotion" emerged to emphasize social measures that motivate behavioral change. This gave rise to a synthesis in the form of "wellness programs" that were widely adopted by major employers and involved promoting individual health; providing opportunities to employees for prevention and healthy living; intensive case management of employees with health problems; and health insurance and care policies that favored self-care, good health habits, and identification and management of risk factors. The wellness component of occupational medicine has now been integrated into occupational health services in large organizations and shows demonstrable benefit to employers in terms of productivity and reduced health-care costs as well as enhancing the lives of employees. The key to this development was the recognition that the workplace represents a community and that the combination of simple interventions and consistent motivation yields disproportionately large results.

The field of OEM still has serious structural problems to overcome, including a shortage of trained practitioners (both formally qualified specialists and physicians with sufficient training and experience to function at an advanced level). However, unlike the 1940s, when occupational medicine was the outlier and the rest of medicine was monolithic, the world of medicine has changed around it.

Today, most modern medicine is practiced through large organizations, such as hospital systems, HMOs, or at least group practices, and occupational medicine is no longer an exception. Workers' compensation, while still prone to manipulation and some fraud (which has received high-profile publicity), improved considerably due to state-level reforms in the 1990s, and payments compare favorably now with other health insurance. Academic departments of occupational and environmental medicine, while by no means universal in medical centers, are common and accepted. Due to accreditation requirements, hospitals have employee health services for their employees. Ethical issues that once seemed unique to occupational medicine are now faced by mainstream medical practice and not with any greater success.

The history of occupational medicine may not have been smooth, but it has been relentless.

CHAPTER TWO

Schools of Thought in Occupational and Environmental Medicine

Tee L. Guidotti

This chapter is an introduction to different points of view in occupational and environmental medicine (OEM). Chapter 1 provides a history and gives some insights into how these points of view arose. Chapter 3 is an introduction to the conceptual framework of OEM and prevention science.

Specialties in medicine develop according to their history, not strict logic. There has always been a need for medical care for workers, so occupational medicine became an established field of medical practice early on. Historically, modern occupational medicine developed rapidly in the nineteenth century as a medical specialty concerned with care for injuries until the twentieth century. Most health protection at that time involved prevention of lung diseases and reducing exposure to hazardous chemicals in the workplace, so the emphasis was on air and skin contact with chemicals. Occupational medicine at that time also fit into the traditional medical model of diagnosis and treatment of the individual. The name "occupational medicine" replaced "industrial medicine" when the field established itself as a specialty in the 1950s, after board certification came in.

By comparison, public health as a field was primarily concerned at that time with water, waste, and food and prevention of infectious disease.

Although dating from roots in Hippocrates, environmental medicine was mostly theoretical, with only limited practical application until the public health revolution of the nineteenth century and was dramatically advanced by the germ theory of disease. Modern environmental medicine developed during the time when the physician's role in public health was being taken over by public health professionals called "sanitarians" and the emphasis was on clean water and engineered solutions for populations. The role of the physician was less prominent (except in research), and so development of environmental medicine lagged as a recognized field (see chapter 4 for some of the tortured history).

OEM, Preventive Medicine, and Public Health

In this chapter, the word "specialty" means a recognized medical specialty with its own board certification and professional infrastructure, such as medical societies and journals. In the United States and Canada, the recognized *specialty* has been called "occupational medicine," and in both, the specialty incorporates environmental medicine as a content area. There are three recognized specialties within preventive medicine: occupational and environmental medicine, aerospace medicine, and "public health and general preventive medicine."

Preventive medicine is the branch of medicine that concerns itself with the systematic and scientifically grounded prevention of disease, primarily by providing services to individuals, such as immunization, cancer screening, and individualized interventions, particularly those involving changing health-related behavior. *Public health* is the broad field of health services, medical or otherwise, that concerns itself with the systematic and scientifically grounded prevention of disease, primarily by providing services to populations and communities through collective interventions as a group, to reduce risk from hazards that come from common or shared sources, such as preventing exposure to pathogens or pollutants, government regulation of drugs, and inspection of food products. As a broad generalization, preventive medicine is practiced by or under the direction of physicians, usually as part of primary care, and public health is practiced by trained professionals who are not necessarily physicians, with physicians providing or overseeing certain essential services.

The term "field of practice" means a broad area of medicine in which a provider may practice with or without specific credentials. Many physicians who are not board-certified occupational medicine specialists see injured workers in their practice, know what to look for, and do the basics quite skillfully. The workers' compensation system actually depends on these physicians because there are nowhere near enough specialists in occupational medicine.

Much of preventive medicine (in general) is about one person's health-related behavior and the individual risk of getting a disease or being injured.

At the individual level (particularly, in the subfield known as health promotion), public health acts through health education; immunization (e.g., against childhood diseases or hepatitis or COVID-19); educating people about healthy behavior; motivation; and behavior change to get people to adopt a healthy lifestyle (such as stopping smoking, encouraging fitness, helping obese people lose weight through participation in organized programs, assessing differences in level of health in different communities, and much, much more). However, it is the employer, not the worker, who has control over the workplace, and there is not much an individual can do alone to protect himself or herself or their family against environmental hazards outside the home. Because of this, OEM, more than other preventive medicine fields, relies heavily on control of the hazard and as little as possible on changing the behavior of the individual worker.

Public health practice addresses things that can be done to protect people in *groups* and in whole communities, as collections of people or "populations." Public health practice in the community is about clean water, safe food, tracking down outbreaks of disease to determine the cause, and intervening to stop an epidemic (e.g., COVID-19). In OEM, it is about controlling exposure to toxic chemicals, removing safety hazards, screening for evidence of early disease, ensuring that workers can work safely, and much, much more.

Public health professionals and epidemiologists tend to think of health as an attribute (characteristic) that is distributed in a "population" and can be described statistically, as if the population has a life of its own. Physicians tend to see health as an attribute of individual patients, the sum of which adds up to a pattern in the population, with the statistics serving as a mere summary of what many individuals are experiencing. Both and neither are correct. A population is made up of individual people, but populations exist as a community or society, which is more than a collection of individuals because of relationships. People in groups have structured relationships with one another, whether they live in cities or in isolation. People have families, interact socially, share a common culture or are divided by many subcultures, are divided by class, may engage in conflicts with one another, and have different jobs. These many interactions among individuals in a structured society influence one another's behavior, affect diet and lifestyle, and put them at differing risks for health problems. They may transmit communicable (contagious) diseases or expose people near them to cigarette smoke, for example. A "healthy" population, in this context, is one that has a lower frequency of disease; less disability arising from diseases and injury; less frequent risk factors associated with future disease (such as smoking rates); and less disability, such as incapacity to do a job. The health of a population is much more complicated than the sum of individual health status of all people in the population. The differences from one population to another or within subgroups in the same community lead to differences in health risks or outcomes, which are called *health disparities*.

There is no longer a strict dividing line between preventive medicine and public health, and both approaches are in evidence in OEM. *Health promotion*, which is discussed more fully in chapter 3, is essentially a social engineering approach that prioritizes motivating and supporting changes in health behavior and lifestyle. There is great emphasis on protecting the health of workers and their families through employer-sponsored health promotion and wellness programs. *Community health* is a broad term for a number of approaches that emphasize providing primary care at the community level first and integrating it with the identification of specific needs in the community that require special attention and intervention ("community-oriented primary care"). *Population health* is a school of thought that emphasizes policies and social measures to reduce health disparities that advance public health and access to health care. Population health is about disparities, gains, trends, and distributions. Population health overlaps with traditional public health and is distinguished by its emphasis on what can be done through high-level policy to change social and behavioral factors to promote health. The term *population health management* is often used in occupational medicine to describe the practice of health promotion (see chapter 3), proactive health outreach, and health-promoting insurance policies for employees and often their families.

There has long been a minority of OEM practitioners who advocate that all occupational medicine services should be provided by government public health agencies and integrated into the primary health-care system, as in some countries. This is an attractive model for community service and is approximated in Québec. However, this model tends to sacrifice the specialized expertise of OEM and the clinical medicine component of practice. This was the underlying tension in the 1950s when the specialty of occupational medicine (by that name) was proposed to be an approved medical specialty in the United States. Proponents of a freestanding medical specialty wanted it to emphasize clinical medicine and prevention paid for by employers. Proponents of a predominantly public health approach wanted it to be subordinated within a broader specialty of "public health and preventive medicine." Advocates for this were generally of the position that occupational health services should be managed by government, together with most public health services. In the 1950s, there was a three-way tug of war between the American Medical Association (which wanted occupational medicine to be a part of general practice and primary care), the American Public Health Association (which wanted integration with the public health system), and the then-named Industrial Medical Association (which wanted a freestanding specialty of occupational medicine by that name). In the end, when the board certification was organized, the preventive medicine specialties were given equal status, and occupational medicine emerged as a hybrid of clinical medicine and public health.

Environmental medicine may be the same field conceptually but is very different in history and practice. Most OEM physicians in the community work in occupational medicine exclusively, with only occasional contact with environmental medicine. Within medical schools and at universities, the two are always combined into one department. In the world of large employers, physicians who take care of workers and their health needs usually have some responsibility for environmental health issues as well but spend most of their time on occupational health.

Occupational Medicine: Modes of Practice

OEM is, and should be, guided by scientific empiricism and driven by data. However, unlike a specialty based on an organ system (such as cardiology or pulmonology) or on a technology or procedure (such as radiology or nuclear medicine) or a type of disease (such as oncology or infectious disease), occupational medicine has more in common with "time of life" specialties, such as pediatrics or geriatrics, because it is defined by encounters with the real world for adults of working age.

Occupational medicine is primarily a *field of practice* practiced outside the hospital and involves more than the provision of clinical care of work-related injuries and illnesses, to include prevention, management of the injured workers' recovery of work capacity, management of programs to help the worker stay healthy, and the relationship between work and health generally.

There are four critical dimensions to occupational medicine:

- *Disorders arising out of work and causally linked to the worker-patient's job and working conditions* (table 2.1). These disorders are classified as "occupational injuries" when they are the result of a single event or as "occupational diseases" when they are the result of longer-term exposure or a cumulative effect of a repetitive process. Occupational medicine seeks to prevent them (as part of a team with nurses, industrial hygienists, and safety professionals), to limit the injury and reduce any impairment (functional limitation) that results, and to prevent disability (permanent incapacity) that arises from that impairment when injury does occur. Any medical practitioner may be the "treating physician" taking care of the injured worker. The OEM physician more often acts in a secondary role, often charged with documenting what happened rather than diagnosis and treatment. Frequently, the OEM physician's role is to review the findings of the physicians who took care of the injured worker to advise on causation and compensation for permanent impairment, causation (when the cause is not obvious), and future prevention.
- *Disorders related to work in which there is aggravation (short-term worsening) or exacerbation (long-term decompensation) of an existing condition, due to the*

Table 2.1   List of recognized occupational diseases

1. Occupational diseases caused by exposure to agents arising from work activities
    1.1. Diseases caused by chemical agents (examples—there are many more)
        1.1.1. Diseases caused by beryllium or its compounds
        1.1.2. Diseases caused by cadmium or its compounds
        1.1.3. Diseases caused by phosphorus or its compounds
        1.1.4. Diseases caused by chromium or its compounds
        1.1.5. Diseases caused by manganese or its compounds
        1.1.6. Diseases caused by arsenic or its compounds
        1.1.7. Diseases caused by mercury or its compounds
        1.1.8. Diseases caused by lead or its compounds
        1.1.9. Diseases caused by halogen derivatives of aliphatic or aromatic hydrocarbons
        1.1.10. Diseases caused by benzene or its homologues
        1.1.11. Diseases caused by alcohols, glycols, or ketones
        1.1.12. Diseases caused by asphyxiants like carbon monoxide, hydrogen sulfide, hydrogen cyanide, azide, or its derivatives
        1.1.13. Diseases caused by acrylonitrile
        1.1.14. Diseases caused by oxides of nitrogen
        1.1.15. Diseases caused by *n*-hexane
        1.1.16. Diseases caused by mineral acids
        1.1.17. Diseases caused by pharmaceutical agents
        1.1.18. Diseases caused by nickel or its compounds
        1.1.19. Diseases caused by thallium or its compounds (rare)
        1.1.20. Diseases caused by osmium or its compounds (rare)
        1.1.21. Diseases caused by selenium or its compounds
        1.1.22. Diseases caused by platinum or its compounds
        1.1.23. Diseases caused by organotin compounds
        1.1.24. Diseases caused by zinc or its compounds
        1.1.25. Diseases caused by phosgene
        1.1.26. Diseases caused by corneal irritants like benzoquinone
        1.1.27. Diseases caused by ammonia
        1.1.28. Diseases caused by isocyanates (very common)
        1.1.29. Diseases caused by pesticides (very common)
        1.1.30. Diseases caused by sulfur oxides

Table 2.1 *(continued)*

    1.1.31. Diseases caused by organic solvents (very common)

    1.1.32. Diseases caused by latex or latex-containing products (very common)

    1.1.33. Diseases caused by chlorine

  1.2. Diseases caused by physical agents

    1.2.1. Hearing impairment caused by noise

    1.2.2. Diseases caused by vibration (disorders of muscles, tendons, bones, joints, peripheral blood vessels, or peripheral nerves)

    1.2.3. Diseases caused by compressed or decompressed air (safety hazard)

    1.2.4. Diseases caused by ionizing radiation

    1.2.5. Diseases caused by optical (ultraviolet, visible light, infrared) radiations including laser

    1.2.6. Diseases caused by exposure to extreme temperatures

        1.2.6.1. Extreme cold (hypothermia is rare in the occupational setting)

        1.2.6.2. Extreme heat (of several outcomes, heat stroke is potentially lethal)

2. Biological agents and infectious or parasitic diseases

  2.1. Viral diseases

    2.1.1. Hepatitis viruses

    2.1.2. COVID-19 (novel coronavirus), MERS, and other SARS-related viral diseases

  2.2. Bacterial diseases

    2.2.1. Tuberculosis

    2.2.2. Leptospirosis

  2.3. Zoonoses (animal to human transmission) encountered by animal handlers, herders, hunters, or trappers

3. Occupational diseases by target organ systems

  3.1. Respiratory diseases

    3.1.1. Pneumoconioses caused by fibrogenic mineral dust (silicosis, anthraco-silicosis, asbestosis)

    3.1.2. Asthma caused by recognized sensitizing agents or irritants inherent to the work process

    3.1.3. Hypersensitivity pneumonitis (extrinsic allergic alveolitis) caused by the inhalation of organic dusts or microbially contaminated aerosols, arising from work activities

Table 2.1 *(continued)*

    3.1.4. Chronic obstructive pulmonary diseases caused by inhalation of coal dust, dust from stone quarries, wood dust, dust from cereals and agricultural work, dust in animal stables, dust from textiles, and paper dust, arising from work activities

    3.1.5. Upper-airways disorders caused by recognized sensitizing agents or irritants inherent to the work process

  3.2. Skin diseases

    3.2.1. Allergic contact dermatoses and contact urticaria caused by other recognized allergy-provoking agents arising from work activities not included in other items

    3.2.2. Irritant contact dermatoses caused by other recognized irritant agents arising from work activities not included in other items

  3.3. Musculoskeletal disorders

    3.3.1. Radial styloid tenosynovitis due to repetitive movements, forceful exertions, and extreme postures of the wrist

    3.3.2. Chronic tenosynovitis of hand and wrist due to repetitive movements, forceful exertions, and extreme postures of the wrist

    3.3.3. Olecranon bursitis due to prolonged pressure of the elbow region

    3.3.4. Prepatellar bursitis due to prolonged stay in kneeling position 2.3.5. Epicondylitis due to repetitive forceful work

    3.3.5. Meniscus lesions following extended periods of work in a kneeling or squatting position

    3.3.6. Carpal tunnel syndrome due to extended periods of repetitive forceful work, work involving vibration, extreme postures of the wrist, or a combination of the three

    3.3.7. Other musculoskeletal disorders not mentioned in the preceding items where a direct link is established scientifically or determined by methods appropriate to national conditions and practice between the exposure to risk factors arising from work activities and the musculoskeletal disorder(s) contracted by the worker

  3.4. Mental and behavioral disorders

    3.4.1. Posttraumatic stress disorder

    3.4.2. Other mental or behavioral disorders not mentioned in the preceding items where a direct link is established scientifically or determined by methods appropriate to national conditions and practice between the exposure to risk factors arising from work activities and the mental and behavioral disorder(s) contracted by the worker

Table 2.1   (*continued*)

3.5. Occupational cancer

    3.5.1. Cancer caused by chemical agents

        3.5.1.1. Asbestos (various types)

        3.5.1.2. Benzidine and its salts

        3.5.1.3. Chromium VI compounds

        3.5.1.4. Coal tars, coal tar pitches, or soot

        3.5.1.5. Vinyl chloride

        3.5.1.6. Benzene

        3.5.1.7. Toxic nitro- and amino-derivatives of benzene or its homologues

        3.5.1.8. Ionizing radiations

        3.5.1.9. Tar, pitch, bitumen, mineral oil, anthracene, or the compounds, products, or residues of these substances

        3.5.1.10. Coke oven emissions

        3.5.1.11. Nickel compounds

        3.5.1.12. Wood dust

        3.5.1.13. Arsenic and its compounds

        3.5.1.14. Beryllium and its compounds

        3.5.1.15. Cadmium and its compounds

        3.5.1.16. Ethylene oxide

        3.5.1.17. Hepatitis B virus (HBV) and hepatitis C virus (HCV)

4. Other diseases

    4.1. Eye diseases associated with particular occupations

    4.2. Sleep disorders (especially associated with shift work)

Note: Some disorders that are almost never seen in North America or are of historical interest only have been deleted from this list. No list can be fixed or comprehensive because new occupational disorders are introduced all the time as the workplace changes, as new technology develops, and with scientific research and recognition.

Source: Adapted from International Labour Organization, revised 2010.

worker's job or working conditions (table 2.2). These are called "*work-related* disorders." Occupational medicine seeks to prevent the underlying condition from getting worse because of conditions at work and to limit the additional burden for which work conditions are responsible. Similarly, the OEM physician may be the "treating physician" when the injured worker is seen in a clinic but is often acting in a secondary role as consultant, evaluator for workers' compensation, or examiner to determine what happened.

Table 2.2   Diseases to which occupational factors contribute significantly, by making the disorder more frequent, more severe, more likely to be disabling, or more likely to result in lost productivity at work

1. Diseases caused by chemical agents
    1.1. Conditions associated with smoking
    1.2. Conditions associated with other personal habits
2. Diseases caused by physical agents
    2.1. Musculoskeletal conditions associated with combined burden of occupation and childcare and other responsibilities
3. Diseases caused by chemical agents
    3.1. Conditions associated with smoking
    3.2. Conditions associated with other personal habits
4. Diseases caused by physical agents
    4.1. Musculoskeletal conditions associated with combined burden of occupation and childcare and other responsibilities
5. Diseases caused by infectious agents
    5.1. Infections occurring among health-care workers caring for infected patients and laboratory personnel
    5.2. Emerging infections
        5.2.1. Endemic infectious disease specific to place (e.g., malaria, chikungunya, Zika virus, dengue)
6. Cancer
    6.1. Contribution to total body burden of carcinogenic activity, lifetime risk
    6.2. Cancer risk associated with place
        6.2.1. Radon
        6.2.2. Erionite
7. Mental and behavioral health problems
    7.1. Depression, aggravation
    7.2. Sleep disorders
    7.3. Work-life imbalance
8. Cardiovascular disease
    8.1. Heart disease
    8.2. Stroke
9. Respiratory disease
    9.1. Aggravation of COPD from smoking
    9.2. Work-exacerbated asthma

Table 2.2 (*continued*)

10. Disorders arising from treatment of work-related injuries and illness

    10.1. Side effects of analgesics (used to treat in trauma and musculoskeletal disorders)

        10.1.1. Opioid dependency

    10.2. Second injury after inadequate rehabilitation

    10.3. Side effects of other medications

        10.3.1. Medical side effects and complications

        10.3.2. Inability to return to work because of disqualifying or prohibited medication (for example, law enforcement officers, vehicle operators, and workers in dangerous environments often are prohibited from taking drugs that might affect their performance and decision-making on the job)

- *Work capacity.* Occupational medicine evaluates the worker's fitness level, health conditions, and functional impairment to determine whether the worker can perform a specific job, whatever the cause of the condition. The match between what a worker can do and the requirements of the job determines "fitness for duty" (or "fitness for work"). Loss of function is called an "impairment." Impairment assessment involves the occupational physician evaluating the mismatch between what the worker can do and what is required to do the job, or to do any job, or to perform the activities of daily life and what might be done to overcome the mismatch (called an "accommodation"). The assessment of permanent impairment is essential to determining the level of disability, which determines fair compensation for loss under workers' compensation, Social Security, or private insurance. Medical encounters not related to diagnosis and treatment, such as evaluating work capacity, fitness for the job, and disability, are more common in most OEM physicians' practice than the identification of occupational disease and carry profound consequences for workers' health, financial security, and well-being. These are services in which the worker is not a "patient" in the usual sense and the OEM physician is using medical expertise to manage or prevent a problem rather than deliver clinical care.

- *Population health management.* Again, the physician is applying medical knowledge to protect workers against occupational and environmental hazards (a specialized public health function), promote personal wellness (a health promotion function), prevent avoidable disability, reduce health-care costs, reduce loss from absence and "presenteeism" (being at work but functioning at a reduced capacity due to ill-health), and optimize work productivity. These are services in which the worker is generally not a "patient" in the usual sense and from which the worker gains as much and more as the employer.

These services are critically important, but they are different from the usual, familiar role of a physician because the worker is often not a "patient" in the usual sense and the OEM physician is often not the treating physician. There is a traditional patient-physician relationship when a worker is injured and is being treated by the physician, but just as often, the OEM physician is not making a diagnosis or treating the person. OEM physicians should, and usually do, make it clear when they are acting as a treating physician and when no physician-patient relationship exists.

The OEM physician is applying medical knowledge to make the workers' lives better and to protect the welfare of their families rather than advocating for the worker-patient's idea of his or her own benefit. This has legal implications, because the OEM physician is often called upon to make evaluations or to collect information outside of the usual "doctor-patient" relationship, which by definition implies that the physician always acts for the "benefit" of the patient. What the worker-patient sees as to his or her benefit may or may not be appropriate, truthful, wise, or medically sound. It is common for an OEM physician to work in a situation in which the worker may wish for another outcome, but the physician is obliged to be strictly objective: evaluation for disability that may result in compensation, fitness to perform a particular job, certification of time off work, certification of medical fitness in a safety-sensitive job like an airline pilot, or an independent medical examination to establish the facts of a health problem that may or may not be work related. Not infrequently, the worker may want the disability pension, to qualify for the job, to take additional time off work, to avoid being grounded, or to have a chronic problem classified as work related because of disability benefits. The OEM physician has to stand firm on the basis of the facts and medical certainty. Other medical specialties, such as family medicine, navigate these issues in their own way, but the OEM physician is not expected to be an uncritical advocate for the worker's personal interest. The role is as an objective and dispassionate expert. What the patient thinks would be to his or her own "benefit" is not always actually in the patient's best interest, of course, the extreme example being opioid prescription.

There is a fundamental "creative tension" on the occupational medicine side in OEM with respect to whether the physician is primarily concerned with individual workers as people or with workers collectively as a workforce. Chapter 6 describes how OEM physicians actually practice and defines three levels (primary care, secondary or specialty-level care including "tertiary" care to prevent disability, and high-level services including consultation for problem-solving and medical expert services) for two broad types of service: worker centered and group or population health (see table 2.3). OEM physicians may, in a given job, be providing medical care in a clinic or be called in as consultants or as designated experts or to manage departments. They may be responsible for injured workers in a clinic setting or healthy

Table 2.3 What do OEM physicians do?

	Worker Centered (Individual)	Population Centered (Workforce)	Population Centered (Community)
Tertiary care Expert	Expert services: assess levels of disability, conduct high-level assessments of difficult problems (independent medical evaluation), expert opinions in workers' compensation and other medicolegal services, advise employers on managing health issues	Senior physicians working at this level are sometimes called "chief health officers" and are usually the chief medical officers of companies or heads of agencies	Managing a unit or agency in a department of public health in government, where medical expertise is needed for environmental health and prevention
Secondary care Specialist, consultant	Specialty care: provide specialist services on referral for the management and diagnosis of difficult cases (usually occupational disease) and address particular problems (e.g., difficult rehabilitation problems after injury or exceptional risks as in hazardous chemicals)	Designing and managing programs for population health management that may include health promotion, case management, and insurance issues to enhance health of workers, reduce personal health risk, and support productivity of workers on the job	Broad environmental health responsibilities (unusual for physicians), academia (teaching and research), medicolegal services (such as serving as expert in legal action)
Primary care First encounter, "hands-on"	Primary care: diagnose and treat injured workers and personally give them clinical care (primary care, clinical services)	Primary-care preventive services: fitness for duty (whether the worker can do the job without risk to herself or himself and others), periodic health evaluation (ensuring that prevention is working), and other services that protect workers and those around them	Clinical evaluation of people with suspected medical problems related to environmental problems (rare outside of academic institutions)

workers who need preventive services, or they may encourage health education and promotion or encourage groups of healthy workers who are employees of a particular enterprise with a view toward preventing ill-health. They may also teach, do research, and be engaged in other activities that doctors do. OEM physicians go back and forth with different levels and duties throughout their career.

The provision of care to workers was dominated by surgery in the nineteenth century because of the frequency of injuries to workers during the Industrial Revolution. It reached its zenith during this period in the railroad industry, which was notoriously dangerous. Several national and even international associations of *railroad surgeons* were formed, some of which survived into the twentieth century. The emphasis in this school of thought was on acute care: surgical innovation, access to remote areas (by rail, of course), development of hospital networks sponsored by the railroads, and mass casualty management, because of train derailments.

Industrial medicine and surgery was the first modern school of thought in OEM, popularized in 1919 by Harry Mock (see chapter 1) in a book by that title, which articulated a vision to include treatment of injuries and disease, prevention, and the promotion of health for workers and their families, with attention to environmental health. This vision was largely lost during the Depression but emerged again in the 1950s with the new name "occupational medicine." The reason for the shift in terminology from "industrial" to "occupational" was not arbitrary. It was strongly felt at the time that "industrial" connoted too close a relationship with industry and implied that the worker was a cog in a machine, whereas the term "occupational" placed the worker and the job at the center.

Industrial hygiene (*occupational hygiene* in most of the world) began as a school of thought in occupational medicine that emphasized control of hazards but by the 1940s had become a distinct profession emphasizing chemistry, engineering, and the evaluation of risk. Today few industrial hygienists are physicians.

Health and productivity, workplace wellness, and *worksite health promotion* are interconnected and overlapping schools of thought that the workplace can be a force for advancing the health of workers and their families and in so doing increase the productivity of the workforce. These schools of thought tend to be employer centered and seek to motivate workers to take care of themselves and their families through prevention, exercise and healthy lifestyle, and effective treatment and monitoring of chronic diseases (such as diabetes, heart disease, high blood pressure, and other conditions not related to work). Research in this area emphasizes evaluation, the "effectiveness" of interventions in the real world (as opposed to the "efficacy" of interventions in ideal situations), management at the company level (using incentives, insurance plans, on-site medical services), and the simplest and most efficient management systems possible, avoiding elaborate, sophisticated, high-maintenance, and expensive administration such as might be appropriate in a health-care setting.

A synthesis of the broad area of worker protection and the broader area of health promotion has been undertaken by the National Institute of Occupational Safety and Health (NIOSH, which is a part of the Centers for Disease Control and Prevention) under the name *Total Worker Health*. The core idea is that the health of workers is indivisible whether on or off the job and requires protection and enhancement. Skeptics are concerned that erasing the boundary between personal and occupational health gives employers too much leverage over an employee's personal life, but on the whole, the response of labor unions has been positive because of the benefits to their members.

Environmental Medicine: Schools of Thought

Environmental medicine, the other side of OEM, is closely tied to public health practice. It deals with conditions, exposures, hazards, and risks in the natural and built (human made) environment, not specific to the workplace. Environmental medicine is the medical counterpart to the public health field of "environmental health." The total environment can be divided into the "ambient" environment (outdoors) and the "built" environment (what human beings have created, mostly indoors). The ambient environment can be divided into the natural environment (which itself presents many hazards and health challenges), media (air, water, and land, which for the purposes of this schema includes food grown on it), and ecosystem health (including climate change, stratospheric ozone depletion, and ecosystem destabilization on a smaller scale). The built environment ranges in scale from communities (cities to rural districts) and all their attendant infrastructure to workplaces with and without exceptional risk, schools and other institutions, and homes (whether multiple dwellings or individual houses).

Environmental medicine emphasizes exposures outdoors, in homes, at school, and in other indoor environments and focuses mainly on residents of defined communities (often the country, the state or province, a county or city, or a neighborhood), including individuals living in one place, families, children, people with existing health problems, and people sharing potential exposure to a particular risk factor, such as type of housing, proximity to a hazard, consumption of a product, or a common water supply.

Figure 2.1 is a representation of the scope of environmental health and, therefore, of environmental medicine. There is no sharp division in this schema between the ambient and built environments, because each affects the other. Occupational health is traditionally most concerned with workplaces associated with exceptional risk (factories, workshops,

Total Environment

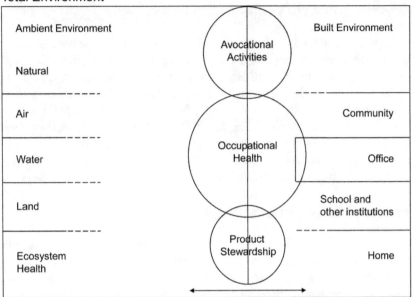

Figure 2.1. Schema for understanding the relationship between occupational health (middle circle) and environmental health (rectangle, representing the totality). Occupational medicine is the medical component of occupational health, together with key related areas (top and bottom smaller circles).

small enterprises) but also deals with workplaces where workers are not at exceptional risk, such as offices. Occupational health overlaps with environmental health concerns in both the ambient and built environments (because some workers work outdoors, and most work indoors), with avocational activities (hobbies and activities that are not remunerative but share many of the same hazards), and with product stewardship (consumer safety and the management of risk).

Environmental medicine shares the same knowledge base, methods of study, medical concerns, and ideas about disease as occupational medicine but differs in where and how it is practiced, in the regulations and legal authority that apply, and in the absence of a specialized payment mechanism for health services in environmental medicine as there is in workers' compensation.

Environmental medicine fits more closely with public health than with clinical medicine. There are a few problems in environmental medicine that are clinical and rely primarily on medical expertise (among them the evaluation of lead toxicity in children). The field has mostly developed to identify and control *exposures*, rather than diseases, and to characterize the *risk* of disease.

Unlike in occupational medicine, very few diseases of environmental origin are specific or unique to environmental conditions. Allergies look like allergies. Cancers from one cause look like the same cancer from another cause. Exacerbation of asthma from air pollution looks like an asthma episode from any trigger. What distinguishes them is the timing and the pattern they show in communities, as reflected in an increased frequency in populations, which can only truly be discerned by epidemiology and public health. For example, there is no specific "air pollution disease," no specific disease that is invariably due to ambient air pollution. To prove that a disease is related to pollution requires demonstrating a statistical relationship through epidemiology, an excessive exposure to a toxic agent, or laboratory testing. Such cases include arsenic poisoning from a water well, lead poisoning in children from indoor lead paint (a hazard of the built environment), poor indoor air quality, water pollution–related outbreaks, food poisoning, and mold-induced allergies. Many of them disproportionately affect children.

Environmental health problems are normally handled by public health professionals trained to deal with the environmental problem, not by physicians. A case of diarrhea, for example, may or may not be due to contaminated water, but the treating physician is not going to be the one to find out. The solution lies in public health management, not medical treatment. The healthcare system is more or less indifferent to cause(s) in the past, and insurance does not usually pay for finding the cause(s) of these illnesses in individuals. A bill for investigating a case of nonspecific illness ascribed to poor indoor air quality is not likely to be accepted by a health insurance carrier. This factor has greatly limited the development of scientific environmental medicine with respect to individual diagnosis and management.

Outside of OEM and public health, the term "environmental medicine" means different things to different people. There are at least five distinct schools of thought on the appropriate definition and content of "environmental medicine." These have arisen out of the unique points of view, professional roles, and histories of five distinct groups of physicians. Each has advocates and organizations, as well as internal divisions, issues, and biases. None of them are comprehensive, although they often claim to be.

The five schools of thought are summarized below.

- **The "medical model," or "mainstream" environmental medicine.** The "medical model" refers to conventional (allopathic) medical practice, in which the patient seeks diagnosis and treatment from a physician expert for a specific condition. Clinical cases are managed one at a time, their numbers are small, and they come from the community. The emphasis is on diagnosis of disease in the individual and the effects of environmental exposures in causing or contributing to the cause of the specific, defined clinical disorder, which is subject to diagnosis and management using mostly conventional clinical methods and approaches of occupational medicine, internal medicine, and pediatrics. The physician gets involved when there are symptoms or signs of disease or when a person has been exposed to a hazardous chemical (or other hazard) and there is concern over whether it has caused harm in that individual. This approach is primarily driven by toxicology and informed by epidemiological research. The organizations that promote this school of thought in the United States have been the Association of Occupational and Environmental Clinics and the American College of Occupational and Environmental Medicine. It is what is taught in medical schools.

- **The public health model.** The public health model of environmental medicine, and environmental health in general, tends to be "hazard driven" in the sense that the line of reasoning starts with recognition of a hazard that is a potential cause of disease. It investigates patterns of exposure and suspect health outcomes in the population rather than the individual and is mostly concerned with prevention. Epidemiology is the principal discipline for physicians in this school of thought. Standards-setting is a major preoccupation as is monitoring and surveillance to assess the adequacy of regulatory standards. The major institutional "homes" for this school of thought in the United States have been schools of public health, the American Public Health Association, and other professional associations (such as the International Society for Environmental Epidemiology and the American Thoracic Society). There is growing participation in this school of thought by major medical organizations as medicine becomes more interested in population health.

- **"Clinical ecology."** This school of thought is not accepted by the mainstream of biomedical science and falls into the domain of unproven theories of medicine, which describe medical systems not supported by scientific evidence or accepted by medicine ("alternative") but are sometimes used by patients together with accepted medical practice ("complementary"). More harshly, this school of thought is often considered "quackery" by mainstream physicians (unconventional, unreliable, or exploitive medicine). This particular school of thought peaked in North America about 20 years ago and has been in decline since, but in its heyday, it was very influential and even persuasive to some health-care professionals. Like mainstream environmental medicine, "clinical ecology" deals with individual cases but is not accepted by mainstream medicine and is seen by its detractors as a distortion of the medical model. It derived from the teachings of the late Dr. William J. Rae of the American Environmental Health Foundation in Dallas, Texas. Proponents attempted to appropriate the name "environmental medicine," by creating their own institutions, such as the American Academy of Environmental Medicine and the "American Environmental Health Foundation." These practitioners are primarily concerned with gaining recognition for their theory of "multiple chemical sensitivity" (often under different names, most recently "idiopathic environmental intolerance").

- **Ecosystem and human health.** Recently, a broad vision of human health and its relationship to ecosystem and planetary sustainability has emerged, driven largely by the concern over climate change and other large-scale changes that affect health and health risk. This school of thought emphasizes the implications of ecosystem change for human health and society. The Medical Society Consortium on Climate Change and Health has brought together 29 organizations, all of them very much in the mainstream of medicine, to advocate and address how climate change affects their members' patients and the practice of medicine. These efforts to come to grips with climate change have also illuminated other broad environmental issues that pertain to individual health, such as ground-level air pollution, the effects of which are much worse with hot weather, and the public health response to climate-related disasters. After a slow start, schools of public health have increasingly taught about the ecosystem and human health as the issues have moved from a theoretical concern into the mainstream of public health theory and practice.

Ideological Schools of Thought

Prevention is not a value for its own sake (no business exists for the primary purpose of preventing its own injuries) nor an employment benefit nor a concession to workers. It is a means to the end of avoiding harm, injury, and loss. "Do no harm" is a religious obligation for people of faith and a categorical imperative for those with a secular worldview. Such high-minded disputation is no more common among OEM physicians in their day-to-day activities than in any other professional group, but it is not less so.

Very few OEM physicians are motivated to enter the field by their beliefs or ideology. Some of them identify with unions, and these often come from working-class families. A small number are motivated by Marxist ideology and adhere to principles of working-class identity and radical justice for workers; they have been particularly important as thought leaders and influential in places where there have been concentrations of like-minded occupational health professionals, such as New York, Chicago, and Seattle. By comparison, the tenets of social democratism and even Marxism have been much more influential on OEM in Europe. In communist countries, where the authoritarian system often rivaled the inflexibility and intransigence of skeptical employers in the United States, occupational medicine was highly esteemed because its value converged with ideology under the Marxist "labor theory of value."

Occupational medicine practice reflects the economy and ideology of the times. As detailed in chapter 1, at various times, occupational medicine has been driven by Progressive Era goals as a reform movement, workers' compensation as a measure for social stability and income security, the emergence (and sometimes the abuse) of scientific medicine, patriotic duty to support the war effort, the battle for National Health Insurance and other health-care reforms, and as a means of improving productivity and prosperity through enhanced worker health. It has been cast as a national priority, an existential threat to solo practitioner ("fee for service") medicine, and an opportunity to use the workplace and the employment relationship to achieving health gains for everyone.

In the 1960s, occupational medicine and, to a lesser extent, environmental medicine got some boost from the philosophy (derived largely from Rockefeller-associated enterprises) of "corporate responsibility," in which major companies acknowledged a responsibility to their community and workers. This mostly took the form of philanthropy and community engagement but also supported a more benevolent attitude in the workplace. The attitude sometimes teetered toward paternalism and control, but this was also an era of high (although declining) union membership, high wages, less income and wealth inequality, and continued gains for organized labor. Unions demanded safer working conditions, and the foundation was laid for the Occupational Safety and Health Act of 1970.

By 1970, this management doctrine was in decline and would be replaced by the idea of "shareholder value," as articulated by economist Milton Friedman: a company has no other purpose or responsibility than to maximize value to its owners, the stock- or shareholders. Attitudes changed abruptly, signified by the ascendancy and election to presidency in 1980 of Ronald Reagan.

Occupational medicine in this era came to be considered by many business leaders as something imposed upon them—required, but a nonproductive cost to be controlled. OEM physicians adapted by demonstrating the value of a healthy workforce and reducing occupational disease and workers' compensation claims, again a utilitarian argument. However, as the power of unions declined, managers became more and more skeptical and began to wonder if they really needed to maintain an expensive medical department.

The role of OEM physicians started to be questioned. The OSH Act came with the enforcement of occupational health standards; prevention fell into the domains of the industrial hygienist and the safety officer, and other health professionals did some of the work at much lower cost. Physicians could not be replaced for medical monitoring when they were required by OSHA standards and for the diagnosis and treatment of occupational disease and injury. This trend constituted a reversion to a clinical model that superficially did not look any different from the role of any other physician and therefore undermined the idea that occupational medicine was a specialty. Finally, an even stronger trend took over.

In the 1980s, companies cut back their in-house medical services in earnest as part of an economy-wide movement toward restructuring to maximize shareholder value, reduce layers of responsibility for greater efficiency, and concentrate on the core business without distraction. Occupational physicians (environmental medicine was still on the margins) were terminated (usually with golden handshakes), and departments were radically reduced or closed by corporate employers in a wave of downsizing. Many of these physicians set up private or networked practices in communities, where, surprisingly, they thrived again because they could now provide services to workers employed by many more employers. In recent years, the private sector has been hiring more OEM physicians, and membership in specialty organizations has been growing again, but the field of practice is still depleted compared to where it was in 1970.

Obviously, such a whipsawed and contradictory history has meant that attitudes toward occupational medicine were subject to the vagaries of politics and ideology. One may fairly ask, why are there such wide swings in the appreciation of OEM? When industry and employers have been in control, OEM was seen as a means to control losses and achieve higher productivity. When unions and a more liberal political administration have been in control, it was seen as a means to achieve labor justice and worker security. With almost cartoonish predictability, employers and political conservatives question the need for occupational health and safety and try to limit the authority of OSHA and unions, and political liberals argue that it is essential and push for more protection but are stopped by allegations of uncontrolled cost, business collapse, and trade disadvantage. Seldom is there a dispassionate analysis of the considerable economic benefits of reducing the externalized costs of injuries, occupational disease, and environmentally related illness and the business efficiency that follows upon attention to these problems, for which there is considerable evidence.

Attitudes toward worker health, environmental protection, and OEM are often projections of partisan ideological views and agendas onto convenient targets: it is easy and simplistic to dump on OSHA, the workers' compensation system, supposedly lazy workers, "tree huggers," and supposedly bloated benefits. But safe, healthy, and decent work takes insight and humane values. Is it not self-evident that protecting the health of workers is essential for a stable, sustainable, and productive society? Apparently, the case needs to be made anew for each generation. In 1970, these objectives were briefly aligned, resulting in passage of the OSH Act at a time when environmental protection also suddenly became a national priority. The country benefited enormously from these "progressive" measures, and the economy surged.

A small, sometimes beleaguered, medical community has carried the weight of a big mission: to protect workers and their families from an often indifferent society. OEM physicians, in their deeply held personal beliefs, are scattered all over the political map, much more than in other medical specialties. Few of them are ideologically motivated. Their reasons for entering the field vary from identifying with management (trending very conservative), through viewing it as a good business opportunity for a practitioner (trending conservative or neutral), to a desire to help workers and their families (trending liberal). The work they do is valuable, supports business, and supports communities and needs to be done, whatever the politics of the moment.

CHAPTER THREE

Theory and Practice of Occupational and Environmental Medicine

Tee L. Guidotti

Most practicing physicians in occupational and environmental medicine (OEM) do not think in terms of theories. They think of themselves first as clinicians, diagnosing and treating individual patients treating specific patients with concrete problems. For them, the clinical side of the field is grounded in mainstream and biomedical sciences, especially toxicology. So it is with the clinical side of OEM, which is predominantly occupational medicine. The prevention side, however, is grounded in public health and population health sciences, especially epidemiology, where theory is profoundly important because it shapes how information is interpreted and used in practice. This chapter takes a broad view of the foundations of OEM practice, rather than research, which is discussed in chapters 11 and 12.

Less than 1 percent of American physicians hold board certification in a preventive medicine specialty (occupational and environmental medicine, aerospace medicine, or public health and preventive medicine). However, many physicians practice occupational medicine without board certification in the specialty. These physicians mostly hold board certification in another specialty or family practice and usually migrate into practice midcareer. They bring with them the values, skills, and insights inculcated by their first specialty experience: a deep understanding of relationships (family medicine), rigor in diagnosis (internal medicine), versatility (emergency medicine), and appreciation for prevention (pediatrics, which is surprisingly common as a background for OEM physicians), as well as the knowledge they have gained in acute injury care, musculoskeletal disorders and rehabilitation, toxicology, mental health, and specialized medical knowledge. As a consequence, OEM is exceptionally rich in theory and concept.

Applied Prevention Science

The theoretical foundation of OEM is grounded in the concept of prevention and how it applies to medicine and in public health. From the time of Hippocrates, the environment has been recognized as a determinant of good or poor health, and management of the environment has been one of the principal ways that society (tribes, cities, empires) has attempted to protect the health of its members collectively. Every occupational disorder, whether a work-related injury or illness, represents a failure of worker protection. Every example of environmental illness, which is generally much harder to identify (see chapter 2), represents shifting the burden of living with the consequences (such as cleanup costs, social disruption, or health risks) of a disturbed environment from the party who created the harm to the public or an unsafe workplace. In both environmental and occupational health, there is identifiable agency (someone responsible) who by intent or neglect "externalizes" (shoves onto others) the harm or cost. This has legal and moral consequences, which are different from a person assuming the risk just for themselves. Prevention in OEM is the investment made up front to keep the harm and costs from being displaced onto others and to avoid it for everybody.

Unsafe work transfers risk from the owner or employer to the worker, the worker's family, and the community, which depends on the economic and social contribution of the worker. It imposes unacceptable risk for the injured worker; for employers who are held responsible, blamed, and likely to incur substantial costs; for the workers who must do their job with a high risk of injury and illness; for families who are left without an income; and for society that has to cope with the externalized cost of disability and injury. There are unavoidably dangerous occupations associated with public safety and national security, but these are exceptions for which protective measures must be stringent and compensation for injury high, to protect workers and their families. All other situations in which a worker is exposed to serious hazard represent a failure of the employer to anticipate and manage risk.

Occupational and environmental health can also be viewed through a moral lens. How much regard people have for their neighbors who live "downstream" and "downwind" and are harmed by environmental hazards and disruption is an indicator of the respect that people have for one another in a society and how much they value life; the respect with which a society treats life, both where people live and on the planet generally, is an indicator of people's responsibility and the maturity of their shared culture and values. Occupational health reflects the value placed on the worker and on income security for the worker's family. Because occupational health and safety also reflect many ethical issues and relations between workers and employers, it is a sensitive indicator of progress in maintaining a civil society in the face of economic change.

Prevention Strategies

Prevention science is fundamentally about maintaining health and avoiding future adverse health outcomes. The scientific basis for preventive services is laid out in detail in textbooks of clinical epidemiology or public health. The two traditional modes of disease prevention, as proposed by the great epidemiologist Geoffrey Rose (1926–1993), can be characterized as follows:

- The "public health" strategy relies on an intervention to change the determinants of risk for the entire population by collective action. The intervention lowers the risk for everyone.

- The "preventive medicine" strategy relies on a selective intervention to identify and control determinants conferring unusually high risk in a subset of individuals by treating or intervening in each susceptible individual and, therefore, requires a screening step to determine who is in fact susceptible, such as taking a screening history or measuring blood pressure. Once an elevated risk is discovered in an individual, there is an intervention to lower it, for that person.

Rose's "public health" strategy is universal, protecting everyone who is covered. As a strategy, public health tries to control the hazard in the community, to protect all people and to reduce risk however a person lives. Public health strategies have the great advantage of reaching everybody; requiring no intermediate step such as screening; and being centrally managed for efficiency, low cost, and reliability. Drinking water disinfection is a good model for the "public health" approach to prevention. Almost all occupational and environmental health measures follow the public health strategy: exposure standards and safety regulations, control of hazards in the workplace, periodic health surveillance to ensure that prevention is working.

Rose's "preventive medicine" strategy, on the other hand, requires identifying people at elevated risk and providing them with an intervention one-on-one. An example of the "preventive medicine" approach is taking blood pressure in an adult or a blood-lead determination in a young child to determine if an intervention is needed to reduce exposure if it is elevated. As a strategy, preventive medicine tries to change what a person does, how they protect themselves, and how they choose to live—for example, by taking drugs such as statins, reducing smoking, and changing diet. (Rose used the example of hypertension in 1985: control to prevent a heart attack requires screening with a blood pressure test and then appropriate treatment to reduce blood pressure if it is elevated.) Preventive medicine services are not easy to initiate and manage on the scale of a population (community or workplace).

The difference between the two strategies has often been compared to the difference between disinfecting drinking water to prevent typhoid (a waterborne disease) and encouraging everyone in a community to boil their water individually to prevent typhoid. Obviously, chlorinating drinking water is much more efficient and ultimately safer because it does not depend on people remembering to boil their water. That is why the public health strategy is always preferred in OEM, both occupational and environmental, if it is feasible. Occupational and environmental health professionals, including OEM physicians, try to control exposure to the hazard above all, because relying on the worker's own actions to avoid exposure to the many and changing hazards in the workplace and on a community resident's personal efforts to avoid risks in the environment does not work well. Controlling hazard at the source is much more effective, more reliable, and less expensive in the real world when it is possible.

Public health measures are designed so that once a system is put in place, the benefits will continue at a lower cost without conscious thought or action on the part of every member of the population. Such measures tend to be cost effective at preventing several problems at the same time. A well-designed ventilation system not only protects workers from one hazard but also reduces the risk from all airborne dusts, chemical vapors, and pathogens (including COVID-19).

Returning to the drinking water model, the entire population and community is protected by collective action to prevent fecal contamination in drinking water, and as long as the system is functioning as designed, everyone in the community is protected. A new water treatment plant is expensive to build, but once it is up and running, it costs very little to protect thousands and even millions of people at once. In the workplace, a hazard such as noise is best controlled by engineering controls to reduce the noise generation at the source, and once that is achieved, all workers in the space are protected, whether they are susceptible to hearing loss or not and whether they remember to use their hearing protection or not. (Audiometric programs to identify workers with hearing loss and to prevent further loss are examples of the preventive medicine approach acting when the public health approach has failed to provide protection.)

Sometimes, screening programs are limited to one point in time, such as tuberculosis or the 2020 COVID-19 population-screening programs or those offered at a health fair. Even one-off screening programs require planning, quality assurance, and a system for referring positive tests for follow-up health care when a problem is found. However, most are ongoing programs.

Once a preventive medicine program is introduced to control a disease or to support health in a community, it must be maintained indefinitely and consistently for long-term benefit. It must be permanent, or nearly so, because new people are constantly entering the population who need the services (children being born or growing up, people who immigrate). It requires stringent quality assurance for every cycle of repetition, because it is hard to repeatedly conduct screening tests without fatigue or occasionally missing something. The cost of the program must be relatively low to ensure that the preventive services are not disrupted by budget shortfalls, and this generally means that the screening test must be simple and one-step. There must be a health-care system ready to intervene when a test is positive. Care must be taken that by error or risk of misadventure (such as complication or being misled in the diagnosis), the medical intervention in cases that screen positive does not cause harm that outweighs the benefit.

Preventive medicine is easy to integrate into health care (although many physicians are lax in offering preventive services, partly because they are compensated poorly for it) and in a limited sense efficient in the sense that it targets only those who need the intervention. However, the preventive medicine strategy is less reliable than the public health strategy.

In practice, public health agencies apply both the public health and the preventive medicine model, depending on the nature of the hazard, and use a third approach called "health promotion," which emphasizes motivating both individual and peer group behavior. Health promotion is foundational to wellness programs in occupational medicine.

Who pays for the service is an issue, since health insurance companies may or may not pay for preventive or screening services. In occupational medicine, the employer is responsible. In environmental medicine, there is no designated payer with only a few exceptions, such as blood-lead screening programs for children that are supported by public health agencies.

Prevention Strategies

The preventive medicine approach, as noted, involves individual-level intervention. This is true even if the objective is universal coverage of the population. For example, immunization is the single most effective prevention intervention yet devised, but it depends on individually vaccinating people one-by-one, requiring a screening step and personal contact with the health-care system.

Preventive interventions are traditionally classified on three levels, a concept introduced in the 1940s by Hugh Rodman Leavell (1903–1976) and E. Gurney Clark (1906–1966), two leading thinkers in prevention (figure 3.1):

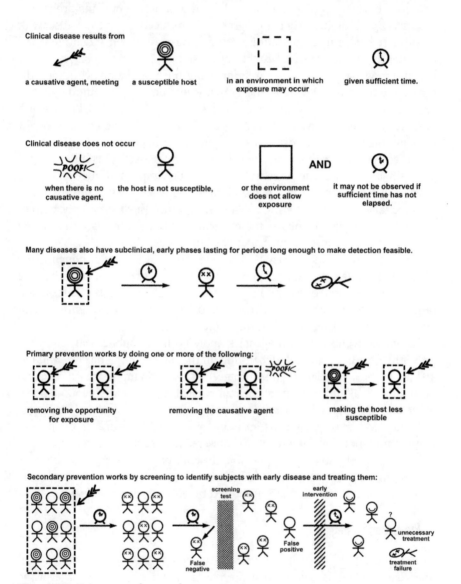

Figure 3.1. Primary and secondary prevention.

- Primary prevention is the strategy of preventing the occurrence of disease in the first place, by reducing exposure to risk or modifying the person so she or he will not be susceptible (e.g., by immunization).

- Secondary prevention is the strategy of detecting early disease or a marker of disease risk early enough for successful intervention, to prevent the risk from eventuating or the early stages of the disease from developing further (e.g., by blood-lead screening).

- Tertiary prevention is the prevention of disease progression and especially disability, by effective treatment and by measures such as disability management, rehabilitation, and avoiding side effects and complications (e.g., by physical therapy).

Primary prevention by prevention of exposure to the hazard is the guiding principle of OEM and the essence of Rose's "public health" approach.

Secondary prevention requires a screening test to identify who is at risk, followed by an effective intervention to reduce that risk. The person undergoing screening does not know that anything is wrong because symptoms have not yet developed. If a person undergoes a series of investigations to find the cause because they have a symptom or an obvious sign that something is wrong, this is diagnosis, not screening: the condition has arrived. An acceptable screening test for prevention must be very safe (because otherwise the harm that could come to normal healthy people may outweigh the good the test would do) and must work well to detect the disease reliably enough to justify an intervention or further testing before symptoms develop. In occupational medicine, there are many examples of periodic surveillance in which workers are tested for evidence of early disease caused by an exposure (e.g., chest x-rays for asbestos or coal workers), mainly to document that primary prevention is working and also as a fallback to identify cases in which primary prevention has failed.

Tertiary prevention is the prevention of disability rather than prevention of the disease itself. The objective is to keep impairment, and therefore disability, to the minimum possible through early intervention, effective treatment, rehabilitation (such as physical therapy), prevention of complications, accurate assessment of fitness for duty (such as fitness for return to work), counseling and social support, retraining if necessary, setting realistic goals, and well-designed accommodation to overcome any residual disability that interferes with personal and family life and the job. Many of these functions are not the primary job of a physician—physical therapists, for example, play a much bigger role in rehabilitation of musculoskeletal disorders. Thus, tertiary prevention is very much a function of quality of and access to responsive health care and support services.

Health promotion is a synthesis of these strategies that emphasizes motivating healthy behaviors by changing individual motivation and practice and by changing group behavior. Health promotion is not limited to health education efforts but involves means of persuasion (such as behavioral psychology, peer pressure, and social marketing), providing healthier choices (such as "heart health" options on menus), public policies that support healthy alternatives, and means of supporting healthy choices once they are made (by encouragement, making participation a group activity, and positive short-term reward to reinforce the behavior). Health promotion is a major strategy worldwide but is particularly embraced by the World Health Organization. Well-designed programs for workers enhance individual worker health, reduce health-care costs, and increase productivity.

Occupational Health Protection

All occupational injuries and diseases are preventable and, therefore, avoidable by removing or reducing exposure to the hazard. Control of disease and injury risk factors at work is achieved by primary prevention, by removing or limiting exposure to the hazard.

Hazards are usually classified by occupational health and safety experts as belonging to four primary categories: physical, chemical, biological, and psychosocial. However, in practice, a more detailed classification is often more useful:

- Physical hazards, which involve forms of energy: noise, heat, cold, nonionizing radiation (such as ultraviolet rays), and ionizing radiation (such as x-rays). Traditionally, occupational health professionals include mechanical hazards in this category, but there are advantages to thinking of the categories separately.

- Mechanical hazards, which involves *kinetic* energy that can cause injury: falls from a height, dangerous machinery, motor vehicle accidents, unsafe working conditions, or unsafe tools. This category is often analyzed using the principles developed by William Haddon (1926–1985), who emphasized the rate of release of kinetic energy and categorized the essential elements of an "accident" or event as "host/personal factors, vehicle, environment," each of which can be examined and controlled.

- Ergonomic hazards, which involves positions or conditions or movements that put a strain on a vulnerable or weak musculoskeletal part of the body. Examples include repeated movements (causing repetitive strain injuries such as carpal tunnel syndrome), posture-related musculoskeletal problems (e.g., positions requiring an arched back or other awkward position causing back pain), poorly designed instruments, and chairs or workstations that are uncomfortable and force the user to reach beyond comfort or efficient movement. (The field of ergonomics also includes human factors in other contexts, such as low illumination causing eye strain and thresholds of perception and response.)

- Chemical hazards, which involve substances that make workers sick in the short term (poisoning) or that cause illnesses in the long term, such as lung disease or cancer. Chemicals may be in the form of gases, liquids, or solids (usually in the form of particles, such as asbestos). Aerosols are small particles of solid or liquid material suspended in air, including dust, smoke, and mists.

- Biological hazards, which may involve living or latent organisms (such as bacteria, fungi, and viruses), organic materials that trigger allergies, or toxic products (venoms and poisons). This category also includes human-to-human transmissible infections (such as tuberculosis or hepatitis) and biological substances that cause allergies (such as asthma or skin rash). Many airborne diseases are transported on aerosols, mostly by inhalation of droplets that spread disease.

- Psychosocial hazards, which involve mental stress in which the stressors include unreasonable demands, traumatizing experiences at work, unsafe conditions in which the worker feels trapped, bullying and victimization, discrimination, overwork, and unfair employment practices. The literature on stress, and workplace stressors, is vast, and there are many schools of thought and theories.

- Location-based hazards, which involve factors that are primarily associated with the location where the work is performed or that arise out of travel, rather than the work itself: violence, dangerous road traffic, endemic diseases such as malaria, epidemic diseases such as dengue, threatening or rabid animals, and the likelihood or frequency of major disasters (such as flooding, earthquake, or monsoons). The category of disaster risk is increasing rapidly because of global climate change and instability. The idea of classifying these hazards attached to location together arose with travel medicine.

Exposure to hazards needs to be controlled to prevent injury and illness. This is usually the job of the occupational hygienist or safety professional. The role of the OEM physician is primarily to ensure that the controls are working through periodic health surveillance (screening for disease that indicates that primary prevention is failing), secondary prevention to prevent the progression of disease in workers who are affected or at risk despite preventive measures, and to support prevention—for example, by evaluating fitness to wear a respirator (to provide a high degree of personal respiratory protection).

The *hierarchy of controls* is a ranking of the effectiveness of control measures:

1. *Elimination, substitution*, or *removal*. If the hazard can be eliminated entirely, this is the preferred measure to remove the worker from exposure. However, it is not always possible.

2. *Isolation, containment*. Separating the worker from the hazard by physical distance or by a barrier that prevents or at least reduces exposure to the hazard.

3. *Engineering controls*. Equipment or designs of the workplace that reduce exposure are effective when the equipment is chosen properly and well maintained. Examples include ventilation and dust control, machine guarding, and locks and tags on power sources.

4. *Behavioral controls*. Measures that change the way people work rank low in priority in the hierarchy of controls because they are much less reliable, depending on changing the behavior of workers, who may or may not understand their purpose, make mistakes, or fail to cooperate. "Administrative controls" (which are now classified under "behavioral controls") includes management tools that focus attention on occupational health and safety, such as written policies, worker and management training, and performance evaluation of supervisors that includes safety performance and audits.

5. *Personal protective equipment* (PPE). PPE is equipment that protects the worker from a hazard at the location where exposure occurs. Examples include respirators (devices to purify the atmosphere the worker is in or to supply clean air), safety glasses (eye protection), hard hats (helmets), protective clothing, steel-toed boots, gloves, and aprons. The effectiveness of the PPE depends on the reliability of the device (most come with safety ratings), proper use by workers, convenience to the worker, and how well adherence is enforced by managers.

6. *Prevention by design* (or *safety by design*). Hazards are best controlled when a new factory or facility is built or renovated or during major maintenance work, because control measures are simpler, cheaper, and more efficient when they can be built in than having to retrofit.

New hazards are introduced into the modern workplace faster than regulations, exposure standards, and control technology can keep up. The scope of occupational health protection is always expanding. At the same time, old hazards do not disappear. They become less visible and affect workers who are least able to protect themselves, who earn the lowest wages, and who are in the most precarious position because of job insecurity. Dangerous conditions, whether from conscious violations of regulations or ignorance, often persist in low-margin industries or industries with a history of abusive practices. They disproportionately harm immigrants and other vulnerable populations who work in these sectors. They may be effectively exported to affect workers in other countries where the work is outsourced. They may be inadvertently perpetuated by ignorance or lack of awareness in small enterprises that lack the means to improve conditions or do not see the point.

Tracking occupational injuries and illnesses is difficult, and statistics are often (even usually) unreliable, except for fatalities. Nonfatal injury rates are easily manipulated, most often by classifying injuries as minor or "no lost time" when in fact the severity of the injury would merit medical care or time off work to recover. Most immediate care for occupational injuries is provided by local practitioners who happen to be nearby or by occupational health clinics that are either on-site or close by in the community. The employer is required by law to post an entry into a log of the injury if it is minor (requiring only first aid) but is required to record all events resulting in time lost at work or hospitalization and report to OSHA. It is not uncommon for employers to underreport injuries or insist that they be recorded as "first aid" events rather than injuries even when they need medical attention. Injuries that would normally involve recuperation at home may be kept off the books as a "lost-time injury" by an employer who has the worker come to the workplace anyway and sit in the corner.

Workers' compensation claims have been shown to vastly underestimate the frequency of occupational disease, in particular, because of long latency and difficulty in diagnosis. The turnover in many low-paying jobs hides disability, especially when employers are uncooperative in bringing the injured worker back to work. Fatalities due to injury, on the other hand, are more difficult to conceal and so are usually counted accurately.

"Monitoring" and "surveillance" are, respectively, general and targeted screening evaluations. They may be required by law or conducted periodically for assurance that workplace hazard controls are protective. The most common monitoring program is "periodic health surveillance," in which the OEM physician performs tests to detect early signs of disease, indicating that preventive measures have failed. More broadly, monitoring programs identify disease that might affect other workers so that the problem can be corrected quickly.

Surveillance (properly considered, a subset of monitoring) is important to individual workers as a form of secondary prevention ("early detection" for treatment) for them, but it is also a measure to identify other workers who are at risk, and in modern occupational medicine, where exposures are not as extreme as in the past, this is its primary role, together with demonstrating that control measures are working.

The most common situation in which surveillance identifies a previously unknown occupational health problem is in hearing conservation. Many workers and employers have no idea how disabling and troublesome even moderate occupational hearing loss can be, or they dismiss it as inevitable with aging. Once lost, it cannot be regained. Regular hearing testing can identify noise-induced hearing loss very early and indicates that measures for noise control and for hearing protection are not working, putting all workers in that area at risk. Once identified, the worker at risk can be warned and encouraged to take measures to preserve her or his own remaining hearing. As important, the employer can be advised that the hearing conservation program has failed.

Productivity and Health

One practical reason for preserving community and worker health has been to maintain economic productivity. The "health of nations" has long been recognized (by no less than Adam Smith in *The Wealth of Nations*, 1776) as a key factor (or "input" in macroeconomic terms) in productivity and wealth creation. Effective leaders know that most workers are more productive over the long term when they are in good health and are incentivized knowing that their families are protected. This unremarkable insight has increasingly found its way into development economics on a global scale and is part of the linkage between health and economic and environmental sustainability. For environmental health (and environmental medicine), this means pollution control, conservation, and sustainable development. Again, this is an unremarkable observation. As a practical matter, the concrete expression of productivity and health is the relationship between productivity and the health of workers, which is where things get complicated.

For occupational health and medicine, productivity and health are even more complicated. It means protecting and, if possible, enhancing the health of workers, reducing the risk of injury and illness, preventing avoidable disability, medical care that is effective and fast, supporting income through compensation, facilitating safe and early return to work for injured workers, supporting the care of family members and dependents that would otherwise require unscheduled time off work, helping workers with chronic illness manage their conditions so they can stay on the job, and giving workers opportunities to improve their own health and fitness through their own initiative. A healthier workforce may be expected to be more productive, incur fewer health care–related costs, and show lower rates of disability at any given age and, therefore, greater workforce participation. Health and productivity have always been prioritized in the practice of occupational medicine, but only in the last two centuries have there been effective means to manage health on a large scale. (The admittedly arbitrary historical benchmark is Robert Owen's experiments in organized welfare and health protection for British workers in his textile factories in the early nineteenth century.)

Maintaining good health and high productivity is a goal that sometimes provokes suspicion. Observers, scholars, and union leaders have often (usually) been skeptical of employer efforts to manage the health of their employees, seeing it as a means of controlling them (which it sometimes has been, as in the case of the exploitive railcar manufacturer Pullman), reducing the employer's costs of health insurance (which it does), and a diversion from the more disruptive task of improving working conditions (which is in no way an acceptable trade-off). The strength of this approach, however, is that done correctly, on the basis of evidence, with worker participation and safeguards for confidentiality and without coercion, the quality of life for participating workers can greatly improve. The behavioral technology of health promotion provided a theory and practice that was well suited to defined populations such as employees. At a time of rising health insurance and indirect costs in the United States in the late 1960s and 1970s, larger employers seized on the idea with alacrity. The approach demonstrated its effectiveness rather slowly, although the idea was always popular, and after some development and methodological improvements (largely a matter of reducing complicated epidemiology to simple management tools), managing health and productivity became an integral part of occupational medicine practice. Harry Mock's 1919 vision of the workplace (see chapter 1) as a setting for health improvement is now very much in the mainstream of occupational medicine.

The measures that management uses to assess loss of productivity are strongly health related. They include the following:

- Absence from work, which is a substantial cost to most enterprises due to lost productivity, unscheduled gaps in scheduling, replacement costs, and administrative expenses. The leading cause is minor illness, and the major management challenge is reducing unscheduled absence without forcing workers to work while they are still ill (which increases presenteeism). This can be partially mitigated by sensible leave policies. Certification of sickness by a physician is an expensive but not very effective means to reduce absence. (The term "absenteeism" is out of favor because it implied habitual absence or abuse.)

- "Presenteeism," a technical term for the reduced productivity that occurs when a worker is on the job but not functioning at full capacity, either physically or mentally; it is a problem of considerable magnitude to employers, estimated 5–10 times the losses due to absence. Elevated levels are often related to inadequate paid sick leave.

- Health-care costs borne by the enterprise through insurance provided to workers. This is an almost uniquely American problem because other countries do not tie health insurance to employment. This situation dates from World War II, when health insurance was provided as an incentive to recruit scarce able-bodied workers during the wartime labor shortage, and it has been a feature of American working life ever since.

These outcome measures are closely related. Attempts to reduce sickness absence beyond a certain level, to an absolute minimum, may increase presenteeism, with greater loss of productivity.

The "health and productivity" (H&P) movement in corporate wellness was partly an outgrowth of efforts to contain rising health-care costs in the 1970s and 1980s, driven by physician fees and hospital costs. Its adoption by management was driven by the promise (not entirely fulfilled) of stabilizing health insurance costs (including the employer contribution to insurance premiums). The language and theoretical basis or business model for "H&P" is therefore entangled in ideas about risk management in insurance, quality of health care, and cost reduction and can become very confusing.

The underlying concepts are actually simpler than they may appear because people use different words for the same ideas. Strategies for protecting the health of individuals, improving the general health of the workforce, and reducing demand for health services may be called "health and productivity" by employers, "loss and liability management" by insurers and risk managers, "demand reduction" by managed care organizations, "health promotion and disease prevention" by public health advocates, and "wellness programs" by occupational health professionals, but from the workers' point of view and that of their families, they amount to the same thing: managed, efficient ways of helping workers to live longer and feel better. However, words have emotional associations and evoke a reaction in many stakeholders. For example, "health and productivity" may sound to a union representative like a ploy to find ways to push workers to work harder. "Demand reduction" sounds like a bloodless way of avoiding paying for insurance costs to someone outside the health-care sector, where it is common jargon. "Case management" may sound like a way to weed out workers who have health problems, when what is meant is a plan to help workers with chronic diseases do better in controlling their condition and staying at work. In talking about these issues, therefore, it is important to be sensitive to how the words sound but also not to overreact to jargon and buzz words.

Ensuring the quality of care provided to injured workers is an important part of all medicine, including OEM, and is a strategy for supporting health and productivity because good clinical outcomes yield earlier, safer, and smoother return to work after an injury with no or the least possible permanent impairment. The best outcomes for both the worker and the employer may involve rehabilitation, retraining, "work hardening" (rehabilitation focused on what the worker actually does in her or his job so as to return to it), accommodation if there is permanent impairment (such as magnifiers for the visually impaired), and case management for workers with chronic disease (such as blood pressure checks for workers with hypertension).

Another way to ensure the quality of care, reduce variability for consistent good outcomes, and reduce overutilization (performing medical treatment or surgery when it is not needed) is to establish guidelines for how common health problems should be treated, based on evidence. Insurance and government payers of health-care costs have adopted such guidelines as a way of controlling costs by reducing what is spent on care that is not proven to work and that, in some cases, may do harm. The specialty of occupational medicine was one of the early leaders in medicine in formulating such guidelines.

Disability

The prevention of disability, and its assessment when it does occur, is a major goal of occupational medicine. It is also a concern for social welfare and stability, mitigated by Social Security, Canada Pension, and health-care insurance for the aged and disabled (such as Medicare in the United States). Disability and chronic illness have placed a rapidly growing burden on the health-care system that will become a progressively greater economic and social problem as fewer productive workers contribute to the economic system that supports them. Some of this burden of dependency is inevitable and is even the result of improved health care and lower mortality.

There are two ways to prevent disability: prevent the cause of impairment so that an injury or illness does not occur; accommodate the impairment so that it is no longer disabling in the sense of impeding a disabled person's earning potential or social role. As the population gets older, more people live to develop disabilities. However, much disability is entirely avoidable, some because they are preventable but many because the workplace or community does not provide accommodation to allow the disabled person to function effectively.

Impairment is a loss of function of the body, such as a shoulder that does not heal properly and remains weak, limited breathing capacity that limits exercise, a change in memory or mental sharpness that reduces cognitive function, or deafness. Impairment can be measured by *functional assessment*, such as measuring strength or limitation of movement or loss of organ function or by an integrated assessment *(functional capacity evaluation)* that tests what the person actually can do *(work capacity)*. While the latter has obvious advantages, not least in predicting which jobs the person can do best, as a practical matter, almost all compensation and employment evaluation systems are based on loss of function. This is measured by documenting the difference in function from either that person's previous capability or the average for people of the same age, such as ability to abduct (raise) the arm at the shoulder or to grip with the thumb. These measures are standardized in a periodically updated book published by the American Medical Association *(Guides to the Evaluation of Permanent Impairment)*.

Disability is a condition of impairment in which the person's capacity to function does not match the environment in which they live and work. Disability is estimated or calculated, usually by vocational specialists, based on what the person can and cannot do, the job market, and the estimated loss in earnings. This distinction is important because, for a wide range of levels of impairment, disability can be limited or eliminated entirely by accommodating the impaired individual. This may involve changing the job, changing the way that work is done, or changing the workplace in ways that allow the disabled worker to do the job she or he is otherwise capable of performing.

Modern concepts of disability evolved from emphasizing the limitations of the disabled compared to those with full function to the idea that disability is a mismatch between the capabilities of the person and the functional capacity required to perform an activity and live in a given environment. This way of looking at the problem has been much more useful because it emphasizes the role of *accommodation*, which is changing the environment or the activity. This is the underlying philosophy behind the Americans with Disabilities Act, for example.

Environmental Health Protection

The theoretical basis for environmental health protection is the same as for occupational health with respect to primary prevention. The fundamental principle is called *the epidemiological triad* in public health (figure 3.2). The epidemiological triad was originally devised (by the pioneering German public health scientist Max von Pettenkofer, 1818–1901) both as a means of understanding infectious disease in the community and of identifying ways to prevent it.

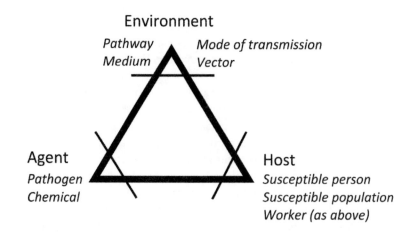

Figure 3.2. The epidemiological triad.

Primary prevention is based on modifying or eliminating one or more of the three essential elements in the causation of disease:

- The *agent* or cause of a disease, such as a pathogen or hazard, which can be removed or controlled; this is the theoretical approach of most occupational health and generally follows the public health approach described earlier.
- The *environment*, meaning what conveys the agent to the host, so that even if the cause cannot be removed, exposure can be interrupted; this is the basic approach in environmental health, control of most infectious disease, and most of the hierarchy of control measures described earlier.
- The *host*, who is the individual susceptible to the disease, so that the host (susceptible person) can be made less susceptible to the disease; this is the basic approach in immunization and follows the preventive medicine approach described earlier.

A triad is something with three elements, and the epidemiologic triad is often drawn as a triangle, as in figure 3.2. Break off any corner of the triangle, and in theory, disease can be prevented. Preventing exposure to causal agents, whether pathogens or toxic chemicals, is primary prevention in occupational and environmental health on a population level. Modifying the environment to reduce the risk of transmitting a disease or exposure to a chemical is primary prevention by removing the pathway of exposure as is immunizing people to prevent transmission of a communicable disease. Cleaning up air and water pollution are obvious examples as are preventing microbial contamination in food and interfering with the reproduction of mosquitoes that carry malaria. Preventing infectious disease (for which the epidemiological triangle was originally developed) may be achieved by modifying the host to make her, him, or a population more resistant to the agent. Examples from infectious disease include immunization and prophylactic antibiotics for the prevention of malaria. The epidemiological triad works well as a conceptual framework for infectious disease and toxic exposure, less well for physical hazards (other than noise and radiation), and poorly for psychogenic stress.

The epidemiological triad also applies to occupational health, although the elements of the hierarchy of control are rarely described this way. Correction of a safety hazard or substitution of a hazardous chemical from production with a less-toxic alternative is removing the agent. Isolation or compartmentalizing hazards is primary prevention by changing the environment—in this case, by interposing a barrier between the host and the "agent," which is the cause. PPE is really creating a barrier at the contact point with the body. Attempts to modify the host in occupational health include immunization for biological hazards such as COVID-19 or hepatitis B for someone who works in health care or against brucellosis for a veterinarian. Efforts to protect workers by treating them in advance to reduce toxic effects have not only been ineffective but sometimes harmful and abusive, and the practice is generally considered unethical today.

The fundamental model of environmental health, and virtually all occupational health, is the concept of "source-effect." In environmental health, and environmental medicine, the standard model for conceptualizing cause and effect is to identify the source of a pollutant, identify its medium and pathways of transport, identify the risk associated with the exposure opportunity, characterize the actual exposure experienced by the "receptor" (in public health, this is people; in ecology, other species), and finally to identify the effect, which is the public health outcome. The source-effect model is often just taken for granted, but it is fundamental in environmental health and, therefore, environmental medicine. For example, a frequent management problem in environmental medicine occurs when multiple cases of a chronic disease, such as cancer, occur in a geographic area or (in occupational medicine) as an outbreak in a plant or office. These situations used to trigger extensive (and expensive) studies using traditional methods of epidemiology and almost invariably (there were very few exceptions), turned up no new and previously unknown diseases and no meaningful associations that could be acted upon. Public health officials stopped doing these studies as a routine and instead learned to look for intact pathways of exposure—if there was no route of exposure, there could be no health effect, and the "cluster" could not represent an exposure-related outbreak. That simplified matters greatly, although big, uninformative community studies have often been undertaken because they were politically irresistible or expedient.

The source-effect model has dominated OEM for over two centuries. However, in part, following the historical influence of von Pettenkofer; in part, from the influence of social sciences; and in part, due to the rise of chronic disease epidemiology (which emphasizes multiple causes and interaction for outcomes such as cardiovascular disease and cancer), more nuanced models have emerged in the environmental health literature that take into account social context, risk perception, and multiple determinants of disease. Such multifactorial and multilevel models have not gained the same acceptance in occupational health, however. This is partly because of the employment relationship and the legal responsibility of the employer, who controls the workplace.

CHAPTER FOUR

Relationships: Interactions with Other Fields and Specialties

Ifeoma Margaret Ama

OEM is rightly considered the most wide-ranging of all medical specialties because it embraces not only disease but prevention and reflects the influence of technology, economics, social trends, and the environment. It is a broad medical specialty that goes beyond the management of occupational and environmental injuries and illnesses. The OEM physician, together with other occupational health professionals, manages the complex factors that determine the health and well-being of workers and community residents. OEM is involved in the identification and mitigation of workplace and community exposures to toxic materials and various hazards such as physical, biological, and chemical hazards, thereby promoting the health of workers and community residents. There is not always a strict separation between the workplace and the home community. For example, with the advancement in internet and technology, more people are self-employed, and some of them spend prolonged amounts of time in front of computer screens. This results in health challenges, including increase in chronic health conditions caused by inactivity such as obesity, hypertension, and diabetes mellitus. OEM physicians are trained to tackle these challenges, as they have a sound understanding of the complex interplay between work productivity and health.

OEM practitioners (in particular, specialists—the specialty is formally called "occupational and environmental medicine") are skilled in evidence-based clinical evaluation and management of acute and chronic conditions, determining fitness for work, and facilitating worker and management communications. The field ranges from preventive medicine activities that are geared toward health promotion, such as organizing flu campaigns and voluntary biometric screenings at worksites, to the emergency interventions and stabilization of individuals in cases of medical emergencies. Also, because the measures used to control exposure to hazards aims at preventing risk to workers without primarily relying on individual behavior change, OEM works with various disciplines to eliminate potential workplace hazards as much as possible. OEM specialists are also involved in management and public health–related activities as well as serving as subject matter experts to help communities navigate through the complex societal issues that accompany industrialization and worldwide technological advancement.

OEM is a field that is relatively insensitive to biomedical technology and largely unaffected by changes in treatment but very sensitive to changes in the economy and social and political contexts. OEM is at the center of health and prevention for workers and productivity in the workplace. It is a broad field of medicine that cuts across prevention of diseases, through health education and research, and treatment and management of diseases including disability management and consultations in medicolegal cases. OEM also has a deep social component because practice also changes with the economy and employment on a local level.

Similarly, OEM cuts across various fields of science and medicine. It involves research using biostatistics and epidemiological methods and research in the toxicology laboratory.

OEM specialists play a huge role in helping affected individuals and their families navigate through the process of getting financial compensation for work-related injuries and diseases, such as mesothelioma, often in collaboration with nurse case managers.

OEM physicians are employed in clinics, hospitals, organizations that range from small companies to multinational companies, academic institutions, government agencies, insurance agencies, the military and public health departments. To be effective, the OEM physician needs to have a working knowledge of the mission of these employers, what constitutes their core business, the associated hazards, and job requirements. This requires an exceptional ability to learn quickly and across many fields unrelated to clinical medicine. It also requires the ability to communicate with managers, workers in these fields, managers and engineers in the technologies involved, and other health professionals who often have no idea what these people do but need guidance to provide the medical services they need.

Once an injury or disease occurs, of course, it must be well managed, through diagnosis, treatment, and rehabilitation. This involves the traditional role of the physician and nurse as clinician. Of paramount importance is recovery of function lost in the injury and the prevention of disability. This can be achieved by providing the best quality of care and, if required, rehabilitation services such as physical therapy. (This is what was meant in chapter 3 by the term "tertiary prevention," the prevention of disability.)

The scope of OEM practice includes workplace health, safety, and productivity:

- Detection, diagnosis, and treatment of injuries and disease
- Occupational health protection
- Productivity and health
- Economic development and health
- Environmental influences on health, both for individuals and communities
- The enterprise and employment relationship
- Disability and work capacity
- Direct connections between the workplace and health, including fitness for duty and other subsidiary services of a medical nature
- Health promotion and wellness in the workplace
- Health-care costs
- Sustainability of human resources and energy

OEM can be seen as operationalizing the agenda and concerns of both corporate and community *sustainable development*, which in its most popular formulation is defined by the widely adopted "triple E" model of environmental, economic, and equitable/ethical sustainability. Environmental sustainability in OEM is defined by both the environmental concerns of OEM and control of workplace exposures: the workplace is a subset of the environment, unregulated exposures have a tendency to spread beyond the "fence line," exposures of workers may be carried into the community, and the effects of occupational exposures are community problems. Economic sustainability in OEM is built into its core mission of protection against injury, disability, and lost productivity and reduction of health-care costs and lost productivity. Equitable and ethical sustainability (sometimes referred to in business management as the "social budget") is reflected in terms of worker protection and equity as part of "occupational justice" (fairness in the workplace), reduction of health disparities, and social sustainability reflected in corporate responsibility or current understanding of the social contract.

OEM balances the interests of the employer, the worker, and the public. The flip side of managing productivity and reducing "presenteeism" (explained in the next section) is a healthier worker with a better quality of life in his or her personal and family life. It is only when wellness strategies are substituted for more urgent priorities (such as worksite health promotion introduced as an alternative to hazard control) or become intrusive (on matters of privacy or lifestyle) that workers' interests are compromised. Proper management of occupational health problems, in turn, protects the health of the public as a whole and strengthens public health services, as demonstrated by the recent experience with COVID-19.

Partners in Worker and Community Protection

OEM physicians handle the medical and some public health functions of occupational health, but they work with and rely on other health and related professionals to do what medical doctors cannot or are not trained to do. This includes the engineering or technical aspects of prevention in the workplace, community aspects of environmental health, rehabilitation and physical therapy, specialized functions such as hearing testing and conservation, and monitoring and measurement of hazards in the workplace and community. There are specialized professions whose members are trained and formally qualified to do these things.

Occupational Health and Safety

OEM is the medical field of practice (and "occupational and environmental medicine," the specialty) in the general field of occupational health and safety (OHS). In the world of safety and loss prevention, OHS is commonly spoken of as the first line of protection against work-related injury and loss, with safety usually being the main emphasis. Although occupational health and occupational safety are functionally separate fields with different qualifications, there is so much overlap that they are often spoken of, like OEM itself, as one field with two divisions. Occupational health and safety is divided along functional lines into recognized professional fields, each with its own credentials and area of responsibility. In contrast, "environmental health" is a public health specialization.

"Occupational safety" deals primarily with injury and physical hazards, which are managed by safety professionals, often called "safety engineers," and implemented in the workplace through safety officers, with variable training. Safety tends to be less of a technical problem because the measures required to control safety hazards are relatively straightforward in comparison to health issues. Most safety practice these days has to do with identifying known safety hazards and correcting them and preventing them through diligent review of work plans and enforcement of safe working practices, and this is what all safety officers do most of the time. At the heart of sound safety practices is behavioral science and methods for motivating safe working practices. How to operationalize behavior-based safety has been the pivotal issue of the safety profession for many years. Safety professionals in the United States vary greatly in the amount of preparation they have for the job and have a network of organizations representing them, led by the American Society of Safety Professionals.

"Occupational health" deals primarily, but by no means exclusively, with toxic hazards and disease risk. It is a broader professional heading than safety. Occupational health professionals include:

- Occupational hygienists (called "industrial hygienists" in the United States), a specialized profession that will be described later
- Physicians practicing in occupational and environmental medicine (including specialists), who will be described in a later subsection
- Occupational health nurses (a specialty field of nursing)
- Expert professions, such as ergonomists, epidemiologists, and toxicologists, which are highly specialized and too numerous to be described to this chapter; these practitioners are usually needed for solving certain problems and tend to practice as consultants.

Occupational health is focused on the identification, recognition, evaluation, and control or regulation of hazards in the workplace, mostly chemical. Occupational health is, by nature, extremely technical, with considerable uncertainty. The degree of complexity tends to paralyze action and lead to endless reviews of the problem. The issues also tend to be much broader.

"Occupational hygienists" (or "industrial hygienists") measure hazard levels (such as chemical exposures) and evaluate the workplace for potential health risks and for violations of current regulations ("standards"). These standards are set by regulatory agencies, such as (in the United States) the Occupational Health and Safety Administration (OSHA). OSHA sets its standards mostly in the form of permissible exposure limits (PELs) for chemicals, noise, and some other exposures, considering the exposure averaged over an eight-hour work shift. However, like most occupational health standards, PELs are not completely or reliably protective. Occupational hygienists, therefore, generally prefer the "threshold limit values" of the American Conference of Governmental Industrial Hygienists and occupational exposure limits established by the European Union, which are lower, more protective, and more current with the scientific literature. The organization representing industrial hygienists in the United States is the American Industrial Hygiene Association.

There has been a general trend in recent years in the form of a slow seesaw between safety and health in interest and support on the part of employers and the government. At intervals, the seesaw tilts rather sharply toward safety, largely as the result of conspicuous accidents, especially involving fatalities. Concern over cancer, hazardous chemicals, and other more subtle effects over time tips the balance slowly the other way, bringing back health as the major management concern.

Biomedical Sciences and Toxicology

OEM, in practice, is closely related to the biomedical sciences, especially toxicology. Toxic chemicals exist all around us; some of them occur naturally, while others are man-made. There are many man-made toxic chemicals that are found in industries and homes, and they can be a significant source of morbidity and mortality. OEM specialists are usually involved in the diagnosis and management of individuals that are suspected to have diseases related to exposure to toxic chemicals.

OEM identifies and collaborates with other professionals to mitigate workplace hazards, which include but are not limited to biological hazards, physical hazards, chemical hazards, and psychological hazards as well as environmental emissions resulting from industrial processes (see chapter 3).

Biological contaminants such as bacteria; viruses; molds; and allergens such as animal dander and cat saliva, house dust, mites, cockroaches, and pollen are a major source of respiratory problems in indoor air pollution, which is not only an issue in homes but also in offices. If these pollutants are not eliminated or reduced, they can be a major source of morbidity and reduced productivity.

OEM, cooperating with hygienists, gets involved in developing strategies to reduce the level of exposure to contaminants in the environment and workplace by working with biological sciences and toxicology to understand the relationship between various toxic chemicals and the adverse health effects they cause, as well as understanding the physical and chemical properties of known and novel toxic chemicals and contaminants.

Chemicals in the workplace pose hazards to workers and can extend to surrounding communities. Some of the diseases caused by chemicals include acute illnesses (usually classified as "injuries") such as burns, skin and eye irritation, and respiratory distress, as well as chronic illnesses (usually classified as "diseases") such as bone marrow suppression; liver injury, with resulting reduction in the function of the liver; and various types of cancers. OEM collaborates with many science disciplines and practitioners in other specialties to understand the properties of various chemicals that occur in the workplace, potential harms that can be caused by them, and preventive measures that can be taken to limit or completely eliminate exposure to such chemicals, as well as understanding the health effects of such chemicals in instances of exposure. This includes elaboration of the symptoms and signs and optimal management of exposures to such chemicals to limit morbidity and mortality. Similarly, OEM works with toxicologists in the evaluation and development of safer chemicals that can be substituted for more hazardous chemicals to reduce mortality and morbidity in industrial processes.

OEM specialists frequently serve as clinical epidemiologists and play important roles in establishing a relationship between various disease-causing agents and their mode of spread. PhD-trained epidemiologists are often called in for special or large-scale studies. This is useful for prevention, diagnosis, and determination of prognosis of chemical-induced diseases. They also help to curb occupational exposures from occurring in homes and public locations.

Environmental Health and Safety Department

The environmental health and safety department (EHSD) in medium to large companies is the management unit in the organization responsible for protecting workers from hazards and ensuring compliance with environmental and public health–specific regulations. These units are usually staffed with safety professionals, hygienists, occupational health professionals (physicians or nurses), and various specialized occupational health professionals such as audiologists (usually on contract). In very large organizations, the EHSD may also oversee and manage environmental regulatory compliance in general, in which case it is often called Health Safety and Environment (HSE). Often, these include product liability issues. HSE is a high-level corporate function and is usually managed at a vice president or senior management level.

OEM physicians work in and with the EHSD in organizations to ensure a safe workplace by providing guidance on the prevention and management of workplace illnesses and injuries as well as preventing or limiting the release of toxic chemicals to the environment. This is achieved by the identification of workplace hazards, regular training of workers on safety standards, regular inspection of equipment and machinery in the workplace to ensure they are functioning as they should, ensuring the timely procurement of all necessary personal protective equipment for workers, designing and redesigning machinery as appropriate to eliminate potential hazards to workers, and ensuring that all waste generated by the organization is disposed of safely. Job evaluations are also done proactively to ensure that safe workplace practices are being adhered to in order to prevent workplace injury.

Another way OEM collaborates with environmental health and safety to promote a healthy workforce is through health promotion, to support worker's health on or off the job. Occupational health protection may overlap with health promotion activities in activities geared toward reducing morbidity and mortality in the workplace (see chapter 3). This is another example of the public health function of OEM.

Environmental sustainability is often a part of the management portfolio in an HSE department. This requires knowledge of large-scale, even planetary, environmental risks and the company's responsibilities. Some sustainability issues are also important occupational health risks as well. Because of the threats posed by global warming, this issue has become particularly important and urgent for workers who work outdoors, such as providing cooling stations and accessible cold water to workers during hot months to prevent or reduce the incidence of heat-related illnesses, training workers on preventive measures to take to avoid heat-related illnesses as well as the warning signs of the onset of heat-related illnesses, advising management on the procurement of appropriate personal protective equipment that are more suitable for warmer months, and early identification and emergency management of workers affected by heat-related illnesses.

OEM works in collaboration with the loss prevention and legal departments of organizations to ensure compliance with various government regulations for the workplace. This includes but is not limited to performing OSHA and company-mandated surveillance exams, establishing and maintaining hearing conservation and respiratory protection programs, conducting periodic interviews and physical surveillance examinations for workers as indicated by their exposures at work, and performing exit interviews for workers when necessary.

In cases of work-related injuries or illnesses that warrant an investigation, OEM specialists often need to visit the worksite and collaborate with the company health and safety department, industrial hygienist, and supervisor of the employee to determine the potential work-relatedness of the injury or illness. Considerable detective work may be involved at times.

OEM physicians collaborate with other professionals in the EHSD to provide management with guidance on preparing policies and procedures for the day-to-day operations of business and ensuring that the guidelines are compatible with maintaining a healthy workforce. OEM practitioners assist in carrying out audits and generating reports that are relevant to workplace safety. In industry, OEM is involved in training individuals involved in medical screening and surveillance, emergency response and first aid, maintenance of accurate records for the proper length of time, record-keeping, and ensuring compliance with regulations, including working with safety personnel to ensure accurate reporting of issues such as workplace injuries to regulatory bodies.

OEM is uniquely positioned to provide guidance to management on judiciously utilizing the hierarchy of controls (see chapter 3) to limit the exposure of workers to hazards at the workplace and on the proper use of personal protective equipment to ensure the safety of workers. They work closely with industrial hygienists and environmental scientists to ensure that adequate workplace safety is maintained. The guidance could range from proper selection of respirators to deciding when an employee's personal illness would preclude them from being able to perform their usual job duties, necessitating transitional duty or even being off work until such a time that they can work safely without posing a threat to themselves or their coworkers. In cases of employees with disabilities, OEM specialists also advise management regarding employee accommodation requests under the Americans with Disabilities Act (ADA).

Ergonomics is another area where OEM collaborates with environmental health and safety. Ergonomics is a field that works to create a healthy and efficient interaction between the worker and the workplace in a way that prevents or reduces adverse health effects that could result from work, while at the same time improving work efficiency. This is done by guiding management on the proper application of ergonomic principles in the workplace based on applicable scientific principles.

OEM specialists play a key role in the pandemic preparedness team in most organizations. They provide valuable guidance to management on maintaining the health and safety of their employees in pandemic situations and in disaster situations. For example, during the recent COVID-19 outbreak, most organizations relied on their OEM specialists to help them develop strategies to reduce the impact of the pandemic on their business operations as much as possible and to keep their workforce safe. In most cases, this was achieved by implementing guidelines geared toward keeping sick employees away from the healthy ones as well as ensuring optimal hygienic practices in workplaces to limit disease transmission.

Other Medical Specialties

OEM collaborates with other medical specialties such as orthopedics, dermatology, family medicine, cardiology, and neurology to ensure the safe and timely return of injured or sick workers to productive work that corroborates with their health status. This also involves disability prevention and management. OEM serves as a bridge between management and other medical disciplines to determine the right timing of return to work based on the health status of the employee. In instances where an individual is not fully recovered but is able to return to work in some capacity, OEM specialists are usually consulted to provide return to transitional duty guidance.

Similarly, OEM specialists help prevent, identify, and manage work-related diseases and illnesses by collaborating with other medical disciplines to ensure the proper management of the worker. They play a major role in managing work restrictions by ensuring that the injured worker gets the necessary rehabilitation and workplace modifications to match their current level of functioning. In most instances, prior to return to work, OEM specialists perform return-to-work evaluations on workers to confirm that they can safely return to work. They also communicate the necessary restriction to management and verify that the work the injured worker would be returning to is within the limits of their restrictions. Upon returning to work, OEM specialists collaborate with the human resources department and the supervisor of the affected worker to tailor the job activities to the changing health status of the worker.

OEM specialists evaluate and manage occupational diseases by thorough history taking, exposure assessment, differential diagnosis, and causation assessment. Furthermore, due to the long latency period (time between exposure to disease-causing agent and onset of disease) of many occupational diseases (e.g., asbestosis), OEM is key to establishing an association between work exposures and certain diseases. This is, in most cases, done by consulting with other providers such as the primary-care providers of the affected individual as well as the specialists who have been involved in the care of the affected individual. This is usually done by collaborating with other consulting clinicians to obtain historical medical records to get a clearer picture of the timeline from the onset of potential occupational or environmental exposures through disease progression to the current manifestations of occupational and environmental illnesses.

Orthopedics and physical medicine and rehabilitation are important specialty partners of OEM. According to the International Labour Organization, there are about 340 million occupational accidents and 160 million work-related illnesses annually, worldwide. Most of the occupational accidents occur in the construction industry. Some occupations are associated with known illnesses and a greater risk of chronic diseases. Musculoskeletal injuries constitute a large proportion of work-related injuries, and orthopedic surgeons are commonly involved in the care of injured workers, especially in instances of fractures, dislocations, ligament tears, or severe joint damage. This necessitates frequent interactions between OEM specialists and orthopedic surgeons involved in the care of the affected workers.

OEM specialists also play a major role in chronic pain management and the implications for safe work. This is done in collaboration with pain management specialists to ensure that workers are well suited to their jobs during treatment for diseases involving chronic pain management. This is especially important in safety-sensitive job positions, as some workers may need to be temporarily reassigned when they are on certain pain medications that could impair their level of cognition. Depending on the level of cognitive impairment, some workers may be unable to safely drive to work and may need to be off work temporarily.

Due to the increasing numbers of females working in industries and manufacturing plants that were previously considered to be high risk when exposure levels were higher, OEM specialists may collaborate with obstetricians and gynecologists to determine the necessary modifications to the workplace and the need for transitional duty for pregnant females if there remains a possible risk. This is done in collaboration with industrial hygienists to determine potential exposures to hazardous agents in the workplace and to device means for reducing such exposures, which could range from workplace modification to transitional duties away from hazardous areas up to excused leave to prevent potential teratogenicity to the developing fetus.

Certain medical problems, such as a progressive nerve condition in the pattern of peripheral neuropathy, require collaboration between the neurologist and the OEM physician to identify or rule out possible occupational causes. More commonly, allergists and pulmonary physicians may work with OEM practitioners to identify asthma triggers or aggravating exposures in people with respiratory disease.

Government and Policy

OEM specialists serve as subject matter experts, but the creation of policy and laws that ensure the safety of the workplace and the environment require experts in law, government, and policy. International expertise may be required for important issues in the international practice of OEM as when companies have operations in different countries.

The OEM physician has a major role in risk communication. The OEM practitioner at an advanced level has the skills to explain the problem in enough technical detail that rules can be formulated, either as regulations or as internal company guidelines. There are several ways by which this is achieved, including presenting science and research in an articulate manner to lawmakers in order to back up the need for the creation of certain policies to ensure the safety of workers, the workplace, the environment, and community residents. An occupational example of an intervention that helped to curb human exposure to a serious carcinogen was the stepwise, often ragged progress made in limiting exposure to benzene, which was characterized by extensive justification of rules, legal challenges, and even a Supreme Court decision. Worker protection would not have been achieved without OEM physicians who were able to do the right studies, explain their implications, and design the medical surveillance programs that protected workers. An environmental example of such an intervention that helped to curb human exposure to pollutants was the Clean Air Act of 1963, which helped to cut pollution and protect the health of American families and workers. Since its inception, the Clean Air Act has also inspired innovation in cleaner technologies and has made the United States a global market leader in this area.

Similarly, another policy that has benefited society is passing a law requiring drivers to have a commercial driver license in order to drive a commercial motor vehicle. This process involves completing a medical examination to verify that the health status of the driver is compatible with safely operating a commercial motor vehicle and obtaining a medical examiner's certificate as proof of completing the medical examination. OEM specialists are usually involved in the process of conducting medical examinations on commercial vehicle drivers to ensure their ability to safely operate commercial motor vehicles.

OEM specialists work in collaboration with government agencies like OSHA and NIOSH during investigations into work-related injuries as well as in instances of environmental releases of toxic substances. They play a major role in collaborating with the government to enact laws to curb the generation of and human contact with various environmental and occupational hazards that are dangerous to people's health and well-being.

OEM specialists serve as a useful resource to community residents and their leaders to advise them on ways to limit adverse health outcomes that result from exposure to gases/chemicals that may be released into their environment from manufacturing plants and other industries that are near the communities as well as those that are generated by the community residents in the course of their day-to-day activities. In fact, many OEM physicians work or advise on environmental as well as occupational health issues in the course of their careers.

Legal

In some cases of work-related injuries and illnesses, OEM specialists serve as expert witnesses in legal proceedings. There are often legitimate questions about whether an illness (more often than injury) arose from a work- or community-related environmental exposure, from another cause, or more or less at random. Due to the increase in the financial burden of personal insurance on individuals, some workers may be tempted to transfer the financial burden of their chronic medical problems to their employers by claiming that their symptoms started at work or was aggravated by work. On the other hand, in a bid to lower the number of OSHA reportable events, employers might be tempted to attribute injuries that occurred at the workplace to personal injuries that occurred outside work. This often becomes a delicate situation where the expertise of OEM specialists becomes critical to determining the work-relatedness of such injuries or illnesses. In some cases where a resolution is not achieved outside court, some of such cases are brought before a judge in court, and OEM specialists often serve as expert witnesses to assist with the legal proceedings.

OEM specialists are involved in the process of determining impairment ratings, which is the process of conducting a medical evaluation and then attributing a percentage between 0% and 100% to the level of an individual's impairment. Impairment ratings are especially useful in work injuries that result in permanent partial disability where a worker may have permanently lost the full use of a specific body part and it is deemed that the worker has reached maximum medical improvement. The impairment rating helps to justify the receipt of partial permanent disability benefits by the affected individual.

Insurance

OEM specialists work with insurers to determine the validity of workers' compensation claims and, therefore, financial compensability for work-related injuries and illnesses. Their expertise is also useful in determining the need of certain interventions during the care of work injuries and illnesses to ensure that resources are used prudently to achieve the best level of care for the worker. This may result in approval or disapproval of certain imaging, specialist consultations and procedures based on sound medical and scientific evidence.

Environmental Engineers

OEM specialists work with environmental engineers to develop technology or improve on existing technology to reduce or eliminate exposures of workers and community residents to hazardous agents emanating from human activity or that occur naturally. Engineering controls is the second level of the hierarchy of controls after elimination. In instances where elimination of potential hazards is not feasible, engineering controls are used to reduce potential hazards in the workplace. An example of an engineering control is HVAC technology.

Military

The military is a major employer of OEM physicians and often trains physicians in OEM to serve as preventive medicine officers. These OEM specialists serve as medical experts to advise the military on measures to take to ensure the health and safety of military personnel on active duty, both during training and in combat. Some OEM specialists work in the military to ensure compliance with standards in the military workplace, which includes many industrial settings as well as specialized hazards, and help to develop protocols geared to respond to and mitigate public health disasters.

Agriculture

Agriculture is a vital economic sector with many occupational and environmental hazards. OEM physicians are highly underutilized in agriculture. There are over a billion workers in the agricultural industry worldwide. Agricultural workers face unique health issues such as animal-acquired infections and related hazards, hazardous equipment and machinery, heat-related illness, falls, musculoskeletal injuries, noise exposure, exposure to pesticides and other chemicals, unsanitary conditions, and issues related to child labor. OEM specialists are crucial in maintaining the health and safety of agricultural workers. Their skill set places them at a vantage position to provide guidance to policymakers, employers, and workers in the agricultural sector.

Furthermore, due to the increase in the use of pesticides and the potential for chemical contamination of agricultural produce, OEM specialists provide guidance to relevant authorities to ensure that the agricultural produce being sent out to the public is either free from chemical residue or has levels safe for human consumption. This is very important because chemical residue on farm produce, including grains, fruits, and vegetables, could lead to adverse health effects in humans. OEM plays a critical role in documenting associations between toxic exposures and disease processes as well as advising authorities on measures to take to reduce exposures and their resulting adverse health effects.

Travel Medicine

Travel medicine is another area that is within the scope of practice of OEM specialists. There are a number of complex issues that are faced by travelers such as health risks due to acute or chronic illnesses; environmental risks including air safety concerns, security concerns, and automobile accidents; risk of major disease including infectious diseases, epidemics, and pandemics; immunization needs, including mandatory immunizations prior to entering certain countries; risks of prolonged immobilization such as long air travels; and safety issues related to jet lag. On location, there is often a high risk of serious hazardous conditions that need to be anticipated, such as malaria prophylaxis, traffic accidents or major trauma (and transfusion safety), rabies (from dog bites), and medical emergencies that may require medical management in a location with limited resources or facilities or even medical evacuation. OEM specialists often provide travel consultations to individuals, often with the assistance of infectious disease specialists, prior to the worker-traveler's departure to the destination, during the travel and upon their return. In many organizations, OEM specialists work in collaboration with the security department to ensure the well-being of workers who travel for job assignments.

Public Health

OEM plays a key role in public health. OEM specialists typically play both administrative and clinical roles in public health departments. They are a useful resource in the development and implementation of public health policies. They serve as subject matter experts to community leaders and other members of the community. They advise the government on the steps to take in situations of natural and man-made disasters and are well trained to provide guidance to local clinicians on various health issues. They also oversee the administration of certain vaccinations to community members and champion various health promotion campaigns for the communities that they serve. They oversee the public health officials that do routine inspection and certification of certain businesses like restaurants, and they respond to and investigate reports of issues that could potentially pose threats to the health of the community.

Research and Epidemiology

OEM plays an integral role in research and epidemiology. An example of the role of OEM in research and epidemiology is in cases of suspected occupational or environmental illnesses. OEM specialists conduct research to determine the relationship of such illnesses with exposures to toxic substances in the environment or the workplace. This is largely done by utilizing epidemiological methods to scientifically establish the association between the said exposures and the resulting illnesses. They also collaborate with epidemiologists to define the patterns of spread of known and emerging diseases, which is crucial to controlling the impact of the diseases on the lives and well-being of community residents.

Social and Behavioral Sciences

Over the past couple of years, the relationship between mental health and work productivity has become more obvious, and occupational mental health has taken a front seat in many organizations. OEM works closely with behavioral health specialists to mitigate loss in productivity that results from mental health disorders among workers. This has become organized in bigger organizations with the establishment of employee assistance programs (EAP) that are sometimes housed under the company's occupational health department. EAPs are usually run by behavioral health specialists who work in collaboration with OEM specialists to promote total worker health.

In the workplace, OEM professionals play a role in overseeing government and company-mandated drug and alcohol screening of employees. They also oversee the counseling of employees with substance-use disorders and addiction issues.

Prevention of workplace violence is another area that occupational mental health weighs in. They offer expert guidance to management in developing policies that promote safe workplaces. OEM specialists collaborate with psychologists and psychiatrists in the mental rehabilitation of employees as needed.

CHAPTER FIVE

Profiles: Practitioners in Action

This chapter features profiles of occupational and environmental medicine (OEM) physicians who are currently or were recently practicing and who represent the diversity of practice in the field. They are not typical—they are successful, leaders, and well known in the field, and sometimes outside of it. The chapter leads with Dr. Paula Lantsberger because her story describes in detail the establishment and management of an exemplary occupational health service, which may make the other profiles more easily understood by example.

The profiles were not chosen at random. As illustrated in chapter 7, the practice of OEM (which is systematized mainly for occupational medicine) can be viewed as a pyramid with two sides visible to the viewer, one representing care for the individual worker, and the other representing population health management and prevention, built on three levels: primary care, secondary (consultation) care, and tertiary care (high-level or program management, research, and planning). The selection of practitioners is intended to feature physicians working each of the six possible pigeonholes at least once, to showcase the many practice patterns (see chapter 7) and to show the diversity of problems and challenges in OEM.

Paula A. Lantsberger, MD, MPH, FACOEM

Dr. Lantsberger is currently in consulting practice in Spokane, Washington. She was president of Occupational Medicine Associates for 26 years, serving clients in eastern Washington. She trained in internal medicine and occupational medicine at the University of Pennsylvania.

Early in my practice of occupational medicine, I found myself standing in the cramped space of a tunnel at the bottom of a hydroelectric dam on the Columbia River, watching a welder repair the turbine. I could hear the sound of rocks clicking as they rushed past the outside of the seawall of the dam holding back the Columbia River. The turbines are located at the river bottom, at a depth of 185 feet. The seawall was the only protection from hundreds of thousands of acre-feet of water holding back the entire Columbia River.

This precarious location represented all the aspects of occupational medicine, from safety programs for lockout (or tag out) ensuring that the seawall wouldn't accidently be opened with workers and visitors inside the turbine chamber to the complicated means of keeping workers' lungs safe in a very confined workspace. I reveled in the wonder of OEM as a physician in the private practice of occupational medicine. I realized how lucky I was to practice in such a varied and interesting field of medicine.

I have had the privilege of practicing occupational medicine for 33 years in Spokane, Washington. Most of that time was in a privately owned clinic together with two other physicians. We provided the full scope of occupational medicine services to our community. The physicians in our clinic were primary-care specialists, two from internal medicine backgrounds, including myself, and one from emergency medicine.

We began practicing together in 1988 in a hospital-based occupational medicine practice. After five years of working under the hospital administration, we came to realize that we did not agree with the financial practices and recruitment policies of the hospital-based system. We particularly objected to remaining independent contractors while the hospital hired new physicians at nearly double what we were paid and required onerous non-compete agreements. After unfruitful negotiations, we concluded that we simply needed to own the practice ourselves to provide the best service for our patients and client companies. So, reluctantly, the three original physicians chose to start their own clinic.

We formed Occupational Medicine Associates in 1993. Looking back at that time, starting a practice was quite simple. We found shared office space with a company that specialized in independent medical examinations (see chapter 3).

I am a person who considers shopping for bargains a competitive sport. I was able to find office furniture at minimal cost. We bought used office furniture from a large department store that went out of business. We found chart storage shelves that were removed from a library remodeling project. The hearing booth was free from the widow of a physician just for the cost of shipping. We used our landlord's x-ray machine for radiology services. A local software company provided a free program for medical billing. Advertising was limited to one large ad in the Yellow Pages. Most of our promotion was word of mouth.

We had fostered good relationships with our client companies, and most of the companies moved over to our new practice. To ensure that this was seamless, we hired a marketing person for two years to transition clients to our new practice. We acquired 80–90 percent of the companies from the former hospital practice within two years.

The philosophy of our practice was to provide outstanding, ethical, science-based occupational medicine services to our patients and client companies. We had a strong commitment to furthering the field of OEM, teaching and serving in leadership positions. I set the record for the most pregnant person ever to deliver a lecture at the Governor's Safety conference in Washington state. I was two weeks overdue with my first son and went straight to the hospital after the lecture to deliver my son the next day.

The practice of occupational medicine has always been appealing for me as a mother. The practice is usually 8–5; it was rare to take a phone call after regular hours, and there were no night or weekend hours. Owning the practice ourselves, each of us could adjust our schedule to do the type of examinations that we liked the best. One of our doctors had a long-term relationship with a local fire department, and he continued to remain their primary contact for 20 years. Personally, I liked complicated cases that required much research on causation and that were challenging to treat.

As a group, we decided to go all in with the specialty practice of OEM, and all three of us physicians continued our training to become board certified in occupational medicine. This was possible because, at the time, there were nonresident, flexible programs through which one could obtain the MPH (Medical College of Wisconsin) and a structured, supervised practicum training in clinical and applied management in occupational medicine (University of Pennsylvania). Those programs made it possible for me to train as a specialist over an extended period (it took five years!). I was able to master the core MPH content in biostatistics, epidemiology, social and behavioral sciences, and health services administration and environmental health sciences despite working full time, raising two children (I enrolled in the program in 1993, six months after the birth of my second son!), and caring for my elderly parents. I graduated in the top 20 percent of my class, in 1999! Once he himself was board certified, our senior physician was able to be the site supervisor for my own year of occupational medicine residency with the University of Pennsylvania External Residency Program.

I began the University of Pennsylvania External Residency Program in 2002. The director at the time was Dr. Ted Emmett, who had developed the original program in 1997. The National Academy of Medicine had encouraged the development of the external track program to help fill the need for physicians trained in OEM. The program required monthly attendance for four days in Philadelphia on campus and multiple site visits from the faculty to our clinic locations. The program emphasized the core competencies of the American Board of Preventive Medicine that were covered in two-month segments directed by an expert in the specific competency. Each segment required a project presentation based on each resident's unique practice situation. The requirements have now expanded to a two-year residency requirement. The director at that time was Dr. Judith McKenzie (see chapter 8), who was outstanding at teaching biostatistics and analytical thinking. The residency program was one of the best educational experiences I have had in all my years of training. The faculty and training were exemplary. I completed the program in 2003 and passed the board examination in the fall of that year. The board requires recertification every 10 years with a new exam, and I am board certified through 2024.

Our office was designed to be a full-service OEM clinic. Many clinical activities that are essential to the practice of occupational medicine require additional training and have their own certification examinations. These include certification to become a medical review officer (MRO) to review drug screens under 49 Code of Federal Regulations (CFR Part 40). The training requires an initial 15–18 hours of instruction and has a requirement to take a recertification examination every five years. MRO work was a large part of our practice. We performed drug-screening services for up to 1,500 different companies around the nation. Certification for performing commercial driving examinations is required by the FMCSA (Federal Motor Carrier Safety Administration) as of May 2014. Certification as an examiner required a training course and a passing score on the certification exam. The exam is required to be repeated when the recertification examination is developed by the FMCSA. This work, too, was a major part of our clinic's practice.

This was not all. Our staff required additional certification to perform the screening services in the office: audiometric testing and hearing conservation programs (Council for Accreditation in Occupational Hearing Conservation, CAOHC), screening pulmonary function testing (National Institute for Occupational Safety and Health, NIOSH), and drug and alcohol screen collection (Drug and Alcohol Testing Industry Association, DATIA). Our staff were registered as assistants for the drug and alcohol testing programs and for reporting exams to the FMCSA.

After our first year in practice, we rapidly outgrew the shared space with the other clinic. We undertook a building project to build a new office building. We had to design the layout of the examination rooms; the location of the testing areas for drug screens, pulmonary function testing, cardiac treadmill testing, x-ray; a triage room for suturing and casting; offices for the staff and assistants; hearing booth; space for medical records; and reception space. We were able to partner with a local builder who provided funding and a process for acquiring ownership of the building. The building process took about a year from groundbreaking (with explosives to break up the basalt rock!) to the final move in. My younger son took his first steps across the waiting room on his first birthday on move-in-day in 1994.

We specifically designed the physician's office space to be one large open room in order to encourage collaboration and communication. We relied extensively on each other's shared experiences and clinical knowledge. I read compulsively and followed an invaluable online list (Occ-Env-Med-L) to stay on top of developments. We obtained all the books and subscribed to all the newsletters that we needed for our own specialty library.

The doctors in our office frequently made the observation that maybe we should have gone to law school in addition to medical school. The practice of occupational medicine requires a thorough knowledge of dozens of federal regulations, state regulations, and local laws. Many of the examinations in the office were performed to meet the criteria for different safety regulations to keep workers healthy in the work environment. The DOT (Department of Transportation) driver's examination ensured a commercial truck driver could safely drive vehicles without sudden medical incapacitation. The FAA examination process was to ensure the health of pilots flying private and commercial planes. The pulmonary health of workers is covered by a myriad of regulations depending on the inhaled substance, whether it is coal dust, silica dust, cotton fibers, asbestos fibers, or many other dusts that can harm the lungs of workers. We had to be aware of the regulations regarding ADA accommodations, HIPAA rules regarding communications with workers and employers, state rules regarding the treatment of injured workers, and the paperwork necessary to communicate these findings to the employers and workers. We created dozens of forms for reporting the results of the exams that had to meet the criteria for the specific rule governing that exam. Over the years, we developed 1,800 different protocols for evaluations, reflecting the specific needs of each company and each type of work for that employer.

In addition, we had to be familiar with the workplaces. That required going out to the plants—the work sites of our client companies. That was my favorite part of the practice. Getting to put on my jeans and work boots to tramp through a lumber mill to operate a machine to remove bark from a log, visiting the aluminum smelter and rolling mill to watch huge crucibles of molten aluminum swinging on cranes down the aisleways, gearing up for active fire training with the fire department, and visiting a railroad yard to climb onto train engines was part of the excitement of the practice. When we saw workers in our office, we knew their working conditions and hazards, and they had confidence that we knew what their work entailed.

The most interesting and toughest work site visit I had was visiting a magnesium smelter in a small town north of Spokane. The plant was trying to identify the source of an unusual odor that was bothering the workers. The fascinating part was seeing the melted ore at 1202 degrees Fahrenheit in large crucibles and watching the sparks flying as the metal was poured into ingots. The color of the molten metal was like looking at the sun with a glowing orange radiance. The hardest part was the request to climb to the top of the smokestack to smell the unusual odor. I am terrified of heights. I was the only woman on the team, and I was not about to chicken out in front of the men. The ladder was a vertical metal ladder, with a small cage around it. I clung to the rungs with an intense focus on only the rung in front of me, all the way up to a small platform at the top of the tower. Buffeted by local winds, I clung tightly to the railing as the inspection party sniffed and sampled the fumes from the top of the stack, while I grimly avoided looking down, knowing that I would soon have to descend back down the ladder. One of the crew wryly mentioned my white-knuckle grip on the rungs but only after we had arrived back on the ground.

The physicians of our office had a commitment to provide the best medical care to our patients, provide the best advice to the employers, and follow best practices in OEM. We held the welfare of our patients/workers foremost. We occasionally produced what we referred to as "The report guaranteed to make everyone unhappy." Everyone included the employer, the worker, and the insurer. It had to be honest, unsparing, transparent, and proactive. In this, we were guided by the ACOEM Code of Ethics.

We realized that we were providing an irreplaceable service for our local community of 300,000. At the same time, the physicians in our office were aging. Being a small practice, it was nearly impossible to recruit new physicians to join the practice. Because it was our firm policy to compensate our employees well, with competitive salaries, vacation time, medical plan, dental plan, vision plan, simple IRA, uniform allowance twice a year, and a membership card to a large discount warehouse, our expenses were high. This limited the income of the physicians to slightly under the national average. The positive trade-off was we had very loyal and long-term employees, some of whom had 10–21 years of service with us.

We would have to sell the practice. That is not so easy in a small city. We interviewed several potential buyers including large chain corporations, local hospital organizations, and health plans. Our requirement for selling the practice was that the new entity employ all our employees for at least a year after the transition, at their same salary and seniority status. In a meeting shortly before the transition, the negotiators were astonished that we had such long-term employees. We did not realize how unusual the longevity of our staff was for a private office. We sold our practice to a nonprofit hospital organization in 2019. I agreed to stay through the transition and retire in January 2020.

Most doctors have difficulty with fully retiring, and I had a plan for a very part-time practice of performing independent medical examinations, disability insurance examinations, expert witness work, and causation analysis research. I began transitioning to this practice by performing most of the rating examinations in the office and performing expert witness work for multiple years prior to the sale. I thrive on doing extensive research of the literature for relevant articles regarding causation and treatment. I started the new solo practice in January 2020. I only see two patients a day on two days a week. Part of this decision was my desire to spend as much time as possible with my retired husband and family. I was also trained with the Social Security Disability system to review cases. In our state, doctors reviewing cases are issued a laptop computer and can work from home. With the combination of these activities, I can earn nearly as much as I did in full-time practice. It is delightful to sit on the deck at our lake cabin with a laptop reviewing charts as compared to spending a full week in the office seeing patients.

It was quite different starting a new practice in 2020 compared to the start-up in 1993. I had to set up a website, change the contact information on dozens of websites for licensing and registrations, develop an online presence and fax service, and set up billing and accounting and my own protocols and procedures. Unlike 1993, I do not have a Yellow Pages ad. My only advertising was sending letters to about 20 doctors in Spokane to offer my services for performing rating examinations. The word-of-mouth advertising and our long-standing reputation make for a highly effective means of marketing. The one thing that did not change was my bargain hunting for office equipment. I was able to outfit the office with a desk, office chair, two patient chairs, an exam table, and two side tables for under $500. My new office is just a single room, no reception area, no waiting room, just space for me and the patient.

In retirement, I have noticed the main thing I miss is interacting with patients and hearing their stories. Some of my favorite stories included the railroad conductor being stalked by a mountain lion walking along the tracks in the mountains at night, the stories of commercial divers working on deconstructing a grounded cruise ship, the firefighter stories of controlling raging infernos, the secret marijuana growing operation beneath the manufacturing floor of a local company, and the stories of the working lives of thousands of workers over the years.

It was a long journey from being a new doctor in practice in 1988 to my "semi-retirement" in 2020, and I am grateful for the practice and the time that I was able to spend in the three different aspects of OEM: hospital based, private ownership, and now a consulting practice. The collegiality of OEM physicians is a definite bonus for choosing this specialty, and I will remain forever grateful to all the mentors and colleagues in OEM for sharing their knowledge and support.

Chang Rim Na, MD, MPH

Chang Na is chief of service, Kaiser Permanente Occupational and Environmental Health. She trained in internal medicine and in occupational medicine at Yale University (see figure 7.5).

I am a "frontline clinician" in Bakersfield, California. I practice OEM in the Central Valley, which is the stretch of land between the Coast Range and the Sierras, extending from southeast to northwest in the middle of California. Bakersfield is in Kern County, at the southern end of the valley. It is a stark but beautiful area, close to mountains and deserts. Much of it looks more like the Old West than what you might think of in California.

The Central Valley in general, and Kern County in particular, has an economy primarily based on agriculture but also features big industry, such as oil production, alternative energy (wind and solar), and warehouses for large corporations like Amazon. Due to its location inland in an arid valley with limited local water supplies, and air emissions from industry and from the many trucks that drive through, we have unique challenges in environmental quality. There are also unusual health risks for residents such as Valley Fever (coccidioidomycosis), pesticide toxicity, and nitrate contamination of drinking water. It is a region of big health disparities, pockets of poverty, cultural diversity (more than you might think), and spotty health care.

My journey to OEM began during residency. I was fortunate to complete my internal medicine residency at Yale University, where there is a thriving OEM department with fellowship opportunities. OEM seemed to me to be a very exciting and diverse field that is often overlooked by medical students and residents as a career option. During residency, I was given a chance to do a clinical rotation in the OEM department, and I was hooked. The attendings were wonderful and had interesting research projects. My own graduate thesis during fellowship was on snake bites in the Southwest, and I was able to gather the data and do fieldwork with the National Park Service.

After finishing my fellowship, I moved to Central Valley with my spouse, who is a women's imaging radiologist. We wanted to forge our own path in a medically underserved community, where both women's health and OEM were priorities. We had much to learn about the culture and needs of the community, and our dedication and love for the area grew over time. Through the county and state medical society, we are active in legislative advocacy to use our voices as physicians to push for improved health for our community. (And yes, this is a not-so-subtle plug for folks to get engaged through organizations like ACOEM, so we can join our voices together for advocacy work!) I have been able to participate in community discussions about environmental pollution and its impact on health in unincorporated communities in the area with state legislators and serve as a medical expert on community boards that serve to improve air quality and community health. I have also been given the privilege of serving as president of the Kern County Medical Society, even though I was a relative newcomer.

All to say, my day-to-day as an OEM specialist in Central Valley is always interesting with a wide range of issues from musculoskeletal injuries in warehouse workers to pesticide poisoning in agricultural workers and Valley

Fever in oilfield workers drilling in coccidioidomycosis-studded soil. If I ever had any doubt about whether OEM was the right field for me, my experience living here has shown me that this was definitely the right career for me and that we need more OEM experts in the world.

Tanisha Taylor, MD, MPH, FACOEM

Dr. Taylor is chief medical officer of Robert Wood Johnson Barnabas Health's Corporate Care with clinical duties out of the Monmouth Medical Center–Southern campus in Lakewood, New Jersey. She trained in internal medicine and occupational medicine at Yale University.

I was drawn to the field of occupational and environmental medicine (OEM) due to the diversity of interests in the field, including the safety of workplaces and the impact of the environment on the health of communities and individuals. Unlike many specialties and fields of practice in medicine, OEM is unique in its focus on the workplace, the home, the larger environment, and the community, in people and potential exposure sources. OEM physicians have specialized training in population health and management in addition to patient care and have various roles in their organizations. Additional master's level studies are required in public health for specialty certification.

Practice settings in OEM are also very diverse including hospitals, industry, academic institutions, health departments, clinics, and the government, among others. I found hospital environments and health care–related exposures of particular interest and chose to work in a hospital system. I was asked to join the team with the express purpose of increasing the efficiency of managing work injuries, both from the perspective of safety and reducing cost. My team was successful at managing work injuries and controlling costs with a necessary focus evolving to case management, safety, injury prevention, and wellness. Open communication among previously siloed departments followed rapidly, especially within the Department of Employee Health, Safety, and Wellness and between our department and other services in the hospital system.

On a day-to-day basis, I manage acute as well as chronic work injuries, manage cases through to return to work, and participate in various committee meetings. Committees that require my regular participation include infection control, safety, safe patient handling, workplace violence, and special pathogens. The COVID-19 pandemic thrust the field of OEM front and center as the nation and the world struggled with lockdowns and how to reopen, including how to go about returning to work safely. Hospitals were at the forefront of managing employee safety, masking, exposures, testing, acute and long-haul COVID-19 illness, return-to-work challenges, and vaccination (figure 5.1).

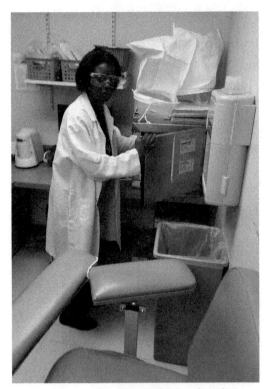

Figure 5.1. Dr. Tanisha Taylor in the clinic at Corporate Care, which provides occupational health services to area employers as well as employee health services for workers and staff in the RWJBarnabas health-care system. She is shown preparing doses of vaccine to immunize health-care employees against COVID-19. (Courtesy Dr. Tanisha Taylor).

During the COVID-19 pandemic, my responsibilities expanded to participation on the newly developed vaccine task force for the logistical planning of vaccinating employees and subsequently the public. I was also managing acute COVID-19 illness in employees as well as the Post COVID Syndrome that later emerged and causation analyses to determine the work-relatedness of COVID-19 cases. COVID vaccinations were ultimately made mandatory in our system, affecting components of our postoffer onboarding process. Like other OEM physicians who work in medical center occupational health (a well-developed area of emphasis within OEM), I was instrumental in adjusting policies surrounding COVID-19 exposure, testing, and return-to work-procedures, as well as vaccination. Other policies requiring review and adjustment surrounded COVID-19, include travel and return-to-work policies.

OEM physicians are often asked to determine an employee's capacity to work safely, such as during a postoffer physical as well as during fitness-for-duty determinations (see chapter 3). OEM physicians must evaluate workers within the constraint of various laws including the Americans with Disabilities Act, the Equal Employment Opportunities Commission, the Genetic Information Nondiscrimination Act and HIPAA, the law dealing with disclosure of health-related information by providers.

One credential unique to the field is that of medical officer review (MRO) certification, where the physician reviews drug screens to determine whether an employee has a legitimate prescription and whether or not there is a potential safety risk. Recent laws regarding medical marijuana and legalization of recreational marijuana have moved across the states, creating challenges for employers and MROs in how safety is addressed in the workplace surrounding marijuana use. I review drug screens with employees during the postoffer process and during fitness-for-duty determinations, as well as in cases where an employee's ability to work safely is called into question. This is particularly important in safety-sensitive positions where an impaired employee could cause serious harm to themselves and others, and in our case, to patients.

OEM, as you can see, touches on many aspects of working life, community health, social concerns, controversial issues, and emerging problems. One of the rapidly emerging issues we are trying to deal with is the response of hospitals and health-care institutions to climate change.

OEM physicians have an important role in educating their respective organizations of the importance of employers' roles in mitigating climate change. Hospitals consume a significant amount of energy and nonrecyclable resources. They have an obligation toward energy conservation and educating their employees. At the same time, their primary mission is the care of individuals who need these resources. As an OEM physician, I have a role in helping to mitigating the coming climate change crisis by educating employees as well as organizational leadership to do better while still providing excellent care.

Ernest C. Levister Jr. MD FACP, FACPM

Dr. Levister retired from a referral-based consultant practice in San Bernardino, California (serving the Inland Empire region), specializing in cardiopulmonary and other physiologically based evaluations. He started as a chemical engineer and was attracted to OEM because of its close connection with science and technology and the physiological basis of fitness for duty, exercise/exertional tolerance, and the diagnosis of many occupational diseases. He is also an advocate and philanthropist who has supported opportunities for minority and underserved communities, especially by encouraging students and health professionals to take an interest in OEM as a means of strengthening communities.

I grew up in a low-rent housing project in Harlem. A fascination with how things work and a flair for science led me to Lincoln University, in Pennsylvania, where I graduated with a degree in chemistry and then to Lafayette College, where I became the second Black student since 1826 to graduate with an engineering degree. After graduation, I was an instructor at the School of Engineering at Tuskegee Institute in Alabama. I later worked in solid-state physics, developing processes and quality assurance for manufacturing the germanium crystal, which was the forerunner of the silicon chip, for the Radio Corporation of America (RCA).

After serving in the U.S. Army Medical Corps in Europe, I practiced medicine in Virginia and then served in the U.S. Foreign Service as a medical attaché in West Africa. In Europe, I cared for active-duty and retired military and their families. In West Africa, I cared for Americans who were in the country on official duty and Peace Corps volunteers. I became interested in medical diplomacy, the assessment of impairment and disability, and how to set priorities in complicated logistics.

I decided to move to California in 1981 because environmental concerns, the progressive attitude toward occupational and environmental health, and personal injury litigation provided me with fertile ground to apply my three areas of greatest interest: engineering, medicine, and, as I was learning, the law.

Early on, I had realized that environmental and workplace injuries that impacted humans causing disease, superimposed on underlying susceptibility and comorbidities. These issues presented challenging diagnostic and therapeutic problems. It seemed to me that the underlying pathophysiological mechanism of disease was the key to assessing causation and treatment for optimal outcomes. It seemed to me that this problem lent itself to an engineering system–analysis approach to problems and that I could use my background in technology to build a clinical platform to develop solutions.

Although I was a solo practitioner, I started and rapidly grew a referral-based practice that was ultimately capable of performing comprehensive pulmonary function testing, treadmill stress testing, echocardiogram, and the full range of ultrasound diagnostic imaging. The practice ran its own office and approved (CLIA) laboratory. Our one-stop, comprehensive approach for physiological evaluation provided the accurate, scientific information we needed to file a comprehensive report that addressed causation, treatment, and impairment of work-related and environmental health issues. Our evaluations were frequently the subject of depositions and expert-witness court appearances.

I have a rich academic life with two University of California affiliations. As a clinical professor of internal and occupational Medicine at UC Irvine, occupational medicine residents rotated through my office. As vice-chair of the Council of Advisors to the Bourns College of Engineering at UC Riverside, I have input into some of the same issues of technology and policy on the engineering side. I am a sort of living link.

I also served as a commissioner for the City of Riverside's Environmental Protection Commission. Much of my time recently has been devoted to advocating for the establishment of a medical school on the campus of UC Riverside. I believe it should be responsive to community needs above all and should place as much emphasis on population health as clinical medicine. The Inland Empire has serious environmental issues with water, air quality, and environmental justice in its fragmented minority and underserved communities. I am particularly concerned about the future in the face of climate change and how it may make health problems worse.

Philip Harber, MD, MPH, FACOEM

Dr. Harber is currently professor at the Mel and Enid Zuckerman College of Public Health at the University of Arizona and professor emeritus at UCLA, where he led occupational and environmental medicine for many years. He trained in occupational and pulmonary medicine at Johns Hopkins.

While a pulmonary fellow at Hopkins, I was waiting impatiently to do a bronchoscopy procedure that had been delayed, and so, to use the time productively, I attended a lecture about welders' lung diseases. This topic seemed to me more interesting than my anticipated research project, which was to study a dog model of asthma. Accordingly, I decided to change direction and arranged to enter an integrated training opportunity at Hopkins that combined an MPH, occupational medicine, and pulmonary medicine.

Looking back over the intervening forty-some years, I ask myself, was this career an unanticipated destination or a lifelong journey? Four stories from my career will explain what I mean.

Story #1: Clinical anecdotes lead to laboratory research and systems approaches: respirators.

In the clinic, I saw three patients from a steel mill who declared that they could not wear respirators. We did extensive physiological testing (we could do it then because utilization review was not a thing), but the results didn't explain their complaints about ability to use respirators in their working conditions. At the time, I was living in the hot, humid Washington, DC, area, and so, to replicate the experience, I mowed my lawn while wearing a borrowed respirator. It certainly was intolerable for me.

Back then, respirator intolerance was assumed to be due to the worker's inability to overcome the device's airflow resistance, so respirator users, who were nearly all from heavy industry, were evaluated when they were tested by a hands-on examination and a maximum ventilatory volume (MVV test—basically a test of huffing and puffing). Later in Cincinnati, where I had my first academic appointment, and then in Los Angeles, my laboratory used surrogate airflow resisters and dead space loads to characterize effort under realistic conditions. We found that even subjects with moderate obstructive airway diseases (COPD, asthma) are able to overcome the very low resistance of modern respirators, so I reframed the question: "What determines *respirator tolerance*?" rather than just "How much added resistance is too much?"

As a practicing physician, I recognized the obvious—a systems approach must supplant the previous narrow focus on the respirator resistance and filtration media efficiency. Protecting workers requires that the right device must be available exactly when needed for a worker who is adequately trained, motivated, and fit tested. So, we quantitatively assessed the trade-offs between more complex devices compared to wider availability through decision modeling and did a multiyear randomized trial of three practical worker-training approaches (a brochure, computer-based training, and a video). This was eye-opening, not only for the results but also because of the window it opened on the workplace!

This project taught me that occupational medicine is not just about worker exposure and performance but also about work organization and the "real world" of practical work. Most workers, particularly those facing the least well-controlled hazards, do not work in large corporations with extensive in-house occupational medicine and industrial hygiene expertise, we found. We need to think through flexible solutions that would help workers where they actually do their jobs.

Story #2: What is the answer to your identity: "Which are you: (a) pulmonologist with special expertise in occupational lung disease or (b) an occupational medicine specialist with particular knowledge of pulmonology?"

For me, the answer is both. Although I still see some general pulmonary patients, my clinical practice evolved to emphasize occupational lung disease and then expanded to assessment of work ability, ADA (Americans with Disabilities Act, see chapter 3) compliance, toxic exposures, and practical ergonomics.

The cultures of the internal medicine specialists and the OEM physician are different. At lunch with my pulmonary colleagues, we typically talk about the "unusual patient" we just saw. Among OEM physicians, we share stories. These stories come from our patients' work histories or from our own experience, such as driving freight trains, visiting underground mines, working atop hammerhead cranes in the largest U.S. ports, visiting chemical plants, and spending time in prisons and detention facilities (figure 5.2). I attend both the American Thoracic Society (ATS) and ACOEM meetings, where a topic such as "occupational asthma" is seen from very different perspectives: the pulmonologists want to diagnose and treat, and the OEM physicians want to explain and prevent. Together, if you master both, these are complementary points of view that lead to a fuller appreciation of what is going on. Without understanding the big picture, however, specialty thinking can narrow your vision down to "when you are a hammer, everything you see is a nail" or "let's just prescribe a bronchodilator." I've written much about how to overcome the blinders put on us by the clinic experience.

Figure 5.2. Dr. Phil Harber doing a worksite tour of a mine. "Walk-throughs," as they are called, are important for identifying and anticipating hazards but also give the OEM physician valuable insight into working conditions, safety equipment and practices, the layout of particular workplaces, and an opportunity to learn from workers. (Courtesy Dr. Philip Harber).

Story # 3: What we do in academic life is an "industry" and a "workplace" too.

I only recently started to think about higher education and research as a high-risk hazard industry. I had always thought of the campus as fundamentally different from "industry." However, after I was asked to chair a working group to improve the employee health and safety at the University of Arizona, the experience forced me to rethink our own health and safety hazards. I came to realize that "higher education and research" constitutes a major industry with many hazards and unique and often difficult organizational structures. Some, but certainly not all, overlap with medical center occupational health. Leveraging the diverse expertise within ACOEM facilitated our newly published comprehensive book, *Occupational Health in Higher Education and Research.*

Story #4: Service and leadership roles: Well-grounded OEM specialists—whether in clinic, research, or public service—all need a foundation of understanding across many disciplines.

Like many senior OEM physicians in academia, I have worn many hats: teacher, consultant physician, principal investigator or research collaborator, clinical service chief, residency director, department vice-chair, university occupational health director, grant reviewer, adviser to government agencies, and thought leader. As I progressed in my career through teaching, research initiatives, administrative duties, and national leadership positions, I realized my limitations more than my strengths. I came to appreciate the unusual breadth of knowledge we need to be effective in OEM: molecular biology, laboratory toxicology, epidemiology, behavioral science, public policy. No other field of medicine is so deeply grounded in the real world and lived experience.

Returning to the original question, was this career an unanticipated destination or a lifelong journey? I can say that OEM gives me an exciting journey rather than a final destination.

Zeke J. McKinney, MD, MHI, MPH, FACOEM

Dr. McKinney is program director of the HealthPartners Occupational and Environmental Medicine Residency at the University of Minnesota School of Public Health and affiliate assistant professor in the Division of Environmental Health Sciences.

I grew up in an underserved, primarily Black area in Minneapolis. All around me I could see how health outcomes are affected by much more than what happens in the examination room: individuals' living situation, financial stability (or the lack thereof), access to health care, availability of good nutrition, and employment opportunities. My family strongly encouraged education and achievement, and my mother worked as a nurse in both clinical and public health settings. So it was a natural for me to pursue a career as a physician. This was all the more true because rates of chronic disease, hazardous community exposures, and apprehension to engage in health care are higher in Black communities, and generally for obvious reasons.

Black Americans (and particularly men) are highly underrepresented in medicine, particularly in academic or research settings. In a practical context, that means Black patients and children are very unlikely to see doctors who look like themselves. So, for me, here was a chance to serve my community differently than most of my contemporaries could. It has been extremely important for me to serve as a role model for young people in my community so that they can see what is possible for them to achieve and how we can use education to have an impact on those around us. In particular, there must be some representation of underrepresented communities to try to build or rebuild trust in the health-care system.

Well-established evidence documents undertreatment of communities of color in clinical settings and even instances of research atrocities in which these same communities were victimized. These issues of trust and representation became all the more apparent with the COVID-19 pandemic, wherein

Black, Indigenous, and People of Color (BIPOC) were more profoundly affected in terms of exposure, severity of disease, death, and limited access to vaccines. The evidence of these systemic issues rose more to the forefront of society's awareness following George Floyd's murder at the hands of law enforcement in Minneapolis in the first months of the pandemic, and the local relevance of this event made my role as a community physician much more significant.

I was initially most interested in family medicine as a means to bridge this gap. However, as I got a better look, I was deterred by the health-care system that forced clinicians to see more patients in less time. It seemed like a recipe for failure in my goals of addressing some of the root causes of disease outside of the clinic, including environmental and behavioral determinants of illness. So I began thinking that work is a social determinant of health. The importance of work became more apparent during my surgical internship, when I saw a staggering number of work-related traumatic injuries, from severe electrical burns to disfiguring degloving upper-extremity injuries.

Occupational medicine as a medical specialty and OEM as an inclusive field attracted me on many levels. Much like primary care, you get to do a little bit of everything, so you're a generalist. However, because of the specialized knowledge of the hazards of workers and the environment, you're also a specialist. There is plenty of clinical work, but at the same time, there are population health and policy issues, the medicolegal complexities of the workers' compensation system, the evaluation of environmental hazards, and the use of public health techniques to characterize individual and system-level hazards and develop solutions to address them.

Most importantly to me, as a preventive medicine specialty, we focus on the upstream causes of illnesses and injuries and, above all, how to avoid them. This differs so much from much of allopathic medicine, which focuses on treating acute disease and then seeing someone again when the next problem happens. In particular, I have really liked learning more about toxicologic exposures, which happen both in the workplace and in the community and about which the medical community still has an immense amount to learn. This type of work is critically important because environmental exposures have continually increased with the industrialization of human societies.

The need for a medical specialty to address environmental hazards, whether inside or outside the workplace, is all the more necessary because these hazards are inequitably distributed. An extreme example of such a hazard is the COVID-19 global pandemic, during which "essential workers," performing tasks that cannot be done remotely, are having greater exposures to the disease, and BIPOC communities have more of these jobs. Unfortunately, there is a shortage of OEM physicians, in alignment with other areas of medicine, but the shortage is even greater due to limited allocations of consistent training funding.

I would describe myself as an academic occupational and environmental medicine physician. So my time is split between clinic, research, and teaching. In a teaching context, I have worked as faculty and program director in the residency where I trained. I am the director of clerkships in OEM for our medical school, to increase awareness about our field and its importance to other medical specialties and the community.

In a clinical context, my growing practice primarily involves complex workers' compensation cases and environmental exposure cases. The complex cases are often years old and may lack a clear diagnosis. They may not have benefited from comprehensive management of multiple injuries that occurred at the same time, whether work related or not. My practice also involves the evaluation of exposures to dusts, chemicals, or molds. My practice is unique in our area and unusual in the midwest as a whole for its focus on exposures. This type of practice is difficult because there is not much clear pathophysiologic understanding on some of these complex clinical conditions that are historically not well understood. They are syndromic in nature, more clusters of symptoms than defined diseases, that go by various names such as "multiple chemical sensitivity syndrome," "idiopathic environmental intolerance," or "sick building syndrome." Because of the uncertainties, patients have not been able to get as much help as they would like, so there is a huge need in this area for understanding and knowledge.

In terms of research, I have been focusing on first responders, particularly firefighters, who have significant occupational hazards, including hazardous exposures, and severe outcomes such as cardiac disease, cancer, and PTSD. In addition, my colleagues and I have been working to identify and address occupational health disparities.

The field of OEM is best described as involving environmental hazards. Some people have joked that if clinical care for adult health problems is "internal medicine," we should be called "external medicine." Because OEM physicians cannot be specialists in every clinical domain, we have to rely on partnerships with other specialists, including primary care, to deliver optimal care to patients and communities.

The important delineation between "occupational" and "environmental" exposures often is simply the degree of exposure, to the extent that workers may often have exposures to a greater degree, in terms of dose or duration, than the community. In addition, the workers' compensation system and regulatory agencies, such as OSHA, are important factors in how occupational exposures are addressed, but there is nothing like that for environmental medicine.

The difficult and interesting part of our specialized expertise is that there are innumerable workplace and community settings in which exposures and hazards exist. So it requires systems-based thinking to understand the myriad factors contributing to risk, such as duration, dose, and hazard control, and then a broad understanding of clinical conditions that can be caused or impacted by these different types of exposures.

As a physician with a public health and prevention focus, I have been using various advocacy platforms to address health inequities, in the spirit of the fourth principle of medical ethics: justice. Justice is not only achieved in the examination room with fair and adequate health care but as fairness in social determinants of health, which account for more than half, and probably a majority, of health outcomes that our patients experience.

I serve in a leadership position in local, state, regional, and national medical organizations. In my community, I raise awareness about workplace and environmental hazards and how the workplace can be a good place to implement preventive services.

I try hard to integrate my OEM training not only in environmental hazards but also in public health, prevention, risk communication, and environmental hazard control. Most recently, I have been working as an investigator on the Astra Zeneca COVID-19 vaccine trial, for which my institution is a local site. In this work, I have been using my role as a well-known local Black physician to build trust in communities of color regarding engagement in research as well as a trusted source of factual information about the pandemic and vaccinations. This has led to some exciting community-based partnerships, such as with my barber. His shop has been featured in COVID-19 social marketing from the Minnesota Department of Health. Together, we have implemented a vaccine clinic right in the barbershop to reach people where they are, in the community (figure 5.3).

Figure 5.3. Dr. Zeke J. McKinney engaged in community education and outreach for COVID-19 immunization outside a barbershop in Minneapolis. Barbershops are important centers of communication and social interaction in the Black community. (Courtesy Dr. Zeke J. McKinney).

Raúl Alexander Mirza, DO, MPH, MS, former army major

Dr. Mirza is director of clinical public health and epidemiology at the U.S. Army Public Health Center.

I entered the military through the Health Professions Scholarship Program, which the Department of Defense created to offer prospective military physicians and other clinicians a paid medical education in exchange for service as a commissioned medical department officer. The length of my scholarship was two years due to a late application start—I'd only become aware of the scholarship program at the end of my first year of medical school. The scholarship ideally covers the length of the doctoral or professional education. My service obligation was three years following my two years of paid medical school. I graduated from the Edward Via Virginia College of Osteopathic Medicine, and the army promptly commissioned me as a captain in the Medical Corps. I completed a transitional internship at the Walter Reed Army Medical Center in Washington, DC, and earned a master's in public health from the Uniformed Services University of the Health Sciences and then completed sequential residencies in general public health and preventive medicine and occupational medicine.

The training was exceptional. The military amply funds its public health residency programs. My residency training included unparalleled experiences ranging from practical public health missions in remote tropical and subtropical locations notable for endemic vector-borne diseases of military importance to occupational health experiences in the most safety-sensitive and military-unique industrialized work environments containing bio-select agents and toxins, chemical warfare agents, explosives, and nuclear hazards. For me, these experiences led to an instant professional love affair—the marriage of medicine, public health, service to country, and unprecedented challenges. I ultimately declared occupational medicine as my primary medical specialty in the army.

The Clinical Public Health and Epidemiology Directorate, which I direct, is home to the Occupational Medicine Division. I had the honor of serving as the division chief for five years as a military officer first and later as a federal civilian employee. An occupational medicine specialist (officer or civilian) manages the Occupational Medicine Division and supervises a multidisciplinary professional team of physicians, nurses, physician assistants, epidemiologists, health system specialists, and administrative staff officers. The activities of the Occupational Medicine Division are described in the section on military medicine in chapter 7.

In my experience as the division chief of occupational medicine, the most significant responsibility under my charge was to manage an operation capable of assuring army leaders that the overall army occupational health program performed at ideal standards to protect and preserve workers' health. As chief, I had to remain current with the Department of Defense, army, and the Department of Labor occupational health and safety requirements and adapt these to internal mission objectives and tasks. I managed and delegated a portfolio of baseline projects that addressed long-standing and routine occupational health program requirements affirmed in federal and military regulations. Additionally, army and medical leadership expected our team to routinely consider historical program assessments and novel and emerging occupational health issues to inform our mission's planning and development of new requirements. I communicated new requirements by preparing annual action plans with objectives focused on program quality improvement, data system and program innovation, compliance, and emerging and evolving health threats and hazards. The plans also described tactics for hosting continuing education opportunities and disseminating practical guidance about unique military occupational hazards, program administration, and clinical practice to the army's occupational health program staff.

In my capacity as a division chief, I completed an annual budget plan for the division's critical financial requirements: staff salary, travel, training, and equipment. Resource managers and I worked with the U.S. Army Public Health Center leadership to obtain approval for proceeding with our division plan as intended, backed with resources. I was accountable to the leadership to provide them with regular briefings on the progress made on the annual plan, including resourcing.

I was honored to supervise a fantastic staff as division chief. We had a successful mission, in part, because I recognized the utmost importance of the staff's knowledge currency and productivity by ensuring that they had the necessary technical tools, resources, logistics, and training to meet the challenges of our demanding mission. I emphasized and respected work-life balance and encouraged my team members to work to the full scope of their position and skill set. In my experience, instilling confidence in the staff's abilities, trusting them to plan and make decisions to overcome challenging issues, and encouraging their creative thought were the secret ingredients for success. In earnest, the mission was exciting, but taking care of my staff with dignity and respect had been most professionally gratifying.

In chapter 7, there is a case study of one of the high-level, high-visibility initiatives that came under my responsibility. To achieve our goals, we made full use of our division's resources. I am proud of what we achieved.

In 2014, I left my position as division chief to deploy to Afghanistan. At the time, my objective was to support and lead the overall public health mission underway, while the theater transitioned from combat operations (Operation Enduring Freedom) to a train, advise, and assist mission (Operation Resolute Support). The U.S.-led mission enabled the Afghan National Security Forces to protect the Afghan people, neutralize insurgent networks

Figure 5.4. Dr. Raúl Mirza, while deployed to Afghanistan. (Courtesy Dr. Raúl Mirza).

(including their safe havens), and support the government of the Islamic Republic of Afghanistan (figure 5.4).

I served as the only preventive medicine and occupational medicine officer for most of my deployment in Afghanistan. I provided my expertise to joint entities such as the U.S. Forces-Afghanistan and the North Atlantic Treaty Organization International Security Assistance Force headquartered in Kabul. The scope of the population I supported included 38,000 U.S. and coalition troops throughout the Combined Joint Operations Area. I coordinated and collaborated with other medical experts, theater commands, and coalition partners to mitigate public health threats; maximize the health protection of U.S. Armed Forces; and oversee, enforce, and improve operational public health and occupational health policies.

I managed in-theater epidemiological investigations, analyzed reportable diseases and injuries, and conducted syndromic illness surveillance to inform operational missions and senior leaders' decisions. A quarter of the way through my tour, I was the only senior public health official in Afghanistan who recommended policies, procedures, and training to mitigate the risk of infectious and endemic diseases with significant potential to impact the health and capabilities of the U.S. and allied forces. I led initiatives to mentor other public health staff and centrally coordinated all in-country public health assets. I served as the sexual assault forensic medical examiner and the medical review officer, and codeveloped the first-in-theater health and wellness medical program. I also had the honor of working in distinctive medical programs. These programs included the medical emergency response detail during President Barack Obama's visit to Afghanistan, medical and casualty evacuation planning for Afghanistan's first democratic presidential election, and assistance to the Patient Evacuation Coordination Cell, which managed hundreds of medical evacuation missions.

After my deployment to Afghanistan, I returned to my position as the chief of the Occupational Medicine Division at the U.S. Army Public Health Center. I continued to hone my leadership and technical skills while taking an interest in the other nine clinician-led divisions under the Directorate of Clinical Public Health and Epidemiology. As my leadership skills, knowledge base, and overall potential grew, I volunteered to lead directorate-wide initiatives; the U.S. Army Public Health Center director eventually chose me to be the director of clinical public health and epidemiology, making me accountable for a more complex mission with many more professionals under my charge.

In summary, serving as an occupational medicine specialist in the military has brought extraordinary opportunities to explore unique occupational and environmental health issues. In practice, I have been able to engage in a spectrum of activities that influence and support clinical practice, program administration, personnel supervision and management, policy development, corporate oversight, specialty advocacy, professional training, public health research, and program development.

Occupational medicine in the army is an exciting specialty with boundless potential for leadership opportunities and professional variety in industrial and operational environments culminating in a challenging and gratifying career. There is no other occupational and environmental health program on the planet like that in the U.S. military.

Clarion E. Johnson, MD, MPH, FACOEM

Dr. Johnson retired as global medical director of ExxonMobil. He trained in cardiology and occupational medicine at Yale. He is now a highly influential national thought leader in medicine and health care, health services, global health, and research priorities.

My experience in OEM as a corporate medical director has been a truly rewarding experience. It has provided me with the opportunity to work across a diverse playing field that includes governments, academia, NGOs, the military, and other corporations.

I had parents who cared passionately about education, and my father owned a small business. This exposed me very early to business principles and was invaluable in shaping my interests. They believed in and stressed education, which made me an excellent student during my parochial elementary years. Later, in college, at Sarah Lawrence, my great teachers opened my eyes to the beauty of science and the concept of lifelong learning. Yale Medical School challenged me to think and in addition fostered a critical eye for "sound science." So this was the foundation with which I entered medicine: education, ambition for a purpose, an appreciation for business, and scientific rigor.

In the military, I began to think in terms of populations. My research thesis adviser was Dr. Curtis L. Patton, the first Black to do a postdoctorate at Rockefeller University. He once stated that Africa should be the breadbasket for the world; however, disease prevented farming in large areas. While I trained in internal medicine and cardiology, I always looked beyond the individual patient to what my training meant for population health. OEM has allowed me to think not just about employees but the communities in which they live. The opportunity to work with diverse groups has taught me about communities and communication across cultures. My work on the level of population health stimulated me to develop metrics for the occupational and community groups for which I had responsibility (because you cannot manage what you cannot measure). My work with colleagues has taught me the value of cooperation and that everyone—medical colleagues, other health professionals, workers, or just fine people living their lives in the community—have something to say and insights worth listening to. The depth and ability of my colleagues in this field to share and teach have been incredibly rewarding.

J. Brent Pawlecki, MD, MMM, FACOEM

Dr. Pawlecki is the chief health officer at Wells Fargo and previously held corporate medical director positions at other major corporations, including Goodyear Tire and Rubber. He trained in occupational medicine, internal medicine, and pediatrics at Yale and Bridgeport Hospital and obtained a master's in medical management degree at the University of Southern California.

Early in my career in the Emergency Department in Bridgeport, Connecticut, I would frequently get called to care for the workers who came into the Industrial Medicine Department down the hall, which was my first introduction to worker health. Later, while working in a practice of urgent and primary care on Long Island, I cared for workers in the surrounding community from large and small businesses. These included manufacturing, package handling, and workers on cargo ships and from numerous other work sites. Seeing these workers in their role and learning about the unique challenges they faced in their work environments, along with the unique health concerns of the workplace, piqued my interest and led me to learn more about the field and practice of occupational medicine.

The role of the corporate physician is to manage a broad spectrum of potential health, social, and environmental challenges to help support the business needs for a healthy, engaged, and high-performing workforce. No matter what the focus of the business, the corporate physician supports the production of goods and services of the company by maintaining one of the most valuable assets of the corporation—their workers in all capacities, including knowledge workers, laborers, and experts in a field.

The corporate environment requires a different skill set from the ones developed in a hospital or practice setting. The motivation and language of business is different and requires a differing approach, which for many physicians involves a need for additional training, perhaps by attaining a formal business degree or coursework from a leadership program.

The corporate physician manages a broad spectrum of potential and actual health, social, and environmental challenges, while strategically navigating the health needs of the workforce and identifying best-in-class programs and providers. This may include critical issues related to employee health, product protection/stewardship, public relations, and legal and regulatory compliance. This demands a rare combination of business and health insight, technical proficiency, and agility for rapid situational assessment and response on a daily basis. It is essential for this subject matter expert to have an in-depth understanding of the business, its strategy, and its challenges in order to create and deliver high-quality health and wellness offerings that target opportunities and provide a healthy and productive workforce.

Pouné Saberi, MD, MPH

Dr. Saberi trained in occupational and environmental medicine and in family medicine at the Hospital of the University of Pennsylvania. She practices OEM at the VA Medical Center in Philadelphia. She has served as national president of Physicians for Social Responsibility.

For me, it all began during my MPH program, which was integrated with my medical school curriculum at Tufts. I did a project with the Department of Health in Boston, in which I accompanied a health inspector who visited the homes of asthmatic children in lower-income communities. We evaluated the home environment and indoor air quality in detail. I remember thinking it was so much better to see people in their home or work environments. Knowledge about the environment in which someone may live or work was a novel dimension to me, and I found it as fascinating as knowledge about the human body. I liked the objectivity of measuring something so ephemeral as the atmosphere our patients were breathing in, in the same way as in medicine we objectively measure something inside their bodies.

OEM has been my second medical specialty since 2012, after 10 years as a family medicine physician. I wanted to do OEM as a specialty, mainly to learn the environmental topics. Once I started the residency, I realized how much I liked the occupational topics as well. After completing my OEM residency, I took on the role of section chief at Employee Occupational Health at the Veterans Health Administration (VHA) in Philadelphia.

In my primary VHA role, in Philadelphia, I apply national mandates and federal guidance to direct local programs such as medical surveillance; employee immunizations; emergency management; voluntary deployment; and since March 2020, implement federal guidance on COVID-19. This role is very much like being the medical director of any large organization with many employees, either a corporation or a large public agency (see chapters 6 and 7).

This past year I took on two additional roles.

My second professional role, and the first new role, is clinical lead in OEM for Veteran Integrated Services Network in our region (VISN 4), which covers all VA facilities in all or parts of four states. The VISN system is dedicated to making patient care more responsive and the management more efficient and integrated to provide needed services to veterans. The other side of my role is to assist senior VISN leadership in implementing federal directives for local facilities. This position is like serving as corporate medical director for a network of health-care employers. I like interpreting federal directives and memoranda and putting them into practice. I think of my role as a translator between the clinical and administrative branches of the medical centers. I take pride in removing barriers so that VHA staff can provide top-notch clinical care while adhering to regulatory requirements for accountability and quality assurance.

My third professional role is conducting exposure assessments for War-Related Illness and Injury Study Center (WRIISC), in order to determine what hazards veterans were exposed to during deployment. As the clinical consultant for WRIISC, I conduct extensive interviews with veterans to explore the environmental exposures they experienced during their military career. This is pure OEM: I document the occupational and environmental hazards for their medical histories. I conduct structured, templated interviews; the exposures are somewhat defined, and in the VHA, payment for the consultations is not an issue. I have a group of colleagues with experience on whom I can rely.

My experience with the VHA, and especially WRIISC, has given me a unique point of view. The exposure assessments for the VHA I currently conduct could be a model for clinical environmental medicine. They are an opportunity to chart a path forward in addressing the difficult nature of this specialty. There are so many obstacles to getting accurate information on occupational exposure in the workplace and environmental exposures in the community. We need to know this to determine how our patients are affected and when compensation is justified. Often, we can only obtain this information when there is a legal action, which introduces huge distortions and court battles.

My first love remains environmental medicine (see chapter 2). My training in OEM helped me see the amorphous nature of environmental medicine compared to occupational medicine. I don't find that environmental medicine has been nearly as developed as other fields of practice, but it also has not been overly codified or overstructured, so there is room to grow and innovate. I don't think there is an established curriculum, an accepted mechanism to conduct clinical visits related to exposures, nor are there tests that can be easily obtained, like laboratory or imaging. There is certainly no mechanism for financial reimbursements.

In general, in the United States, the dominance of business necessity trumps public health. Business has been touted as the catalyst for innovation, but it also impedes correction of problems and health disparities due to nondisclosures.

Many physicians and providers cannot see their roles extending beyond the clinical visit. I appreciate the population-based approach of OEM and the goal of making people healthier. In my own practice, this is done by applying regulatory protections and by providing guidance to employers. Our job is to articulate what needs to be done and how. This, by definition, makes OEM providers advocates as well as practitioners.

Outside of my work, I use my OEM skills to address other environmental problems. In particular, I have been speaking and teaching recently about the health impacts of climate change, which is having adverse effects on workers in the workplace as well as on community residents. I insist that much can be done, even now, to prevent the worst. But I am deeply worried.

Wayne N. Burton, MD, FACOEM

After a career of more than 30 years in corporate occupational medicine, Dr. Burton is now a consultant on health and productivity and broader issues in health care. He trained in internal medicine at Northwestern Memorial Hospital, in Chicago.

My career in corporate occupational medicine, and especially the banking sector, has taught me the wisdom of the classic teachings of Ramazzini (see chapter 1), who was writing about the clerks and administrative workers he observed in the late 1600s:

> The maladies that afflict the clerks afore said arise from three causes; First, constant sitting, secondly the incessant movement of the hand and always in the same direction, thirdly the strain on the mind from the effort not to disfigure the books by errors or cause loss of their employers when they add, subtract or do other sums of arithmetic. . . . In a word, they lack the benefits of moderate exercise.
> (Bernardino Ramazzini, *On the Diseases of Workers*, 1700)

I arrived in Chicago in 1974 to begin my internal medicine residency at Northwestern University Medical Center. I had come from Oregon and planned on returning following completion to join my uncle's practice in

Pendleton, the original home of Pendleton Blankets. At the time, occupational medicine was not even a blip on my career radar screen.

Early in my residency, I met the medical director of International Harvester Company (IH) (now Navistar) who was in private practice of internal medicine along with other corporate medical directors. The headquarters for IH was just a short walk from the medical center and provided me an exposure to the world of occupational medicine. In it, I could envision a career in which my training in internal medicine could be complemented by my interests in research, population health, and well-being. I completed an additional year at Northwestern as chief medical resident and then joined IH in 1978. My practice of internal medicine at Northwestern continued and provided an opportunity to serve as the internist for the medical center's chemical dependency program.

Essentially, my four years at IH served as a fellowship in occupational medicine at a global company with 100,000 employees that manufactured tractors, engines, and a variety of products including the Scout—a precursor to today's SUVs that was durable, heavy, and delivered single-digit gas mileage. My experience in the identification and treatment of chemical dependency resulted in being asked to lead the IH occupational health nurses in U.S. plants who had completed a course in workplace alcoholism and drug abuse as well as the company's Employee Assistance Program (EAP). Those partnerships provided the material and learning experience for the publication of two papers on the value of treating alcoholic employees as a means of retaining productive workers while reducing their overall health-care costs. My interest in research had been fully ignited.

Leaving behind the manufacture of farm equipment, trucks, and engines, I was recruited in 1982 to become the first medical director for the First National Bank of Chicago (FNBC), which, through mergers and acquisitions, would eventually become part of JPMorgan Chase. So began my 35-year career as chief medical officer (CMO) of a global financial services company. At FNBC, I managed the on-site clinics, an in-house executive physical program, the EAP, and was specifically tasked with helping the head of benefits, Don Hoy, to address the double-digit annual increase in health-care costs and the 20–30 percent annual increase in short-term disability costs. At that time, there was little information as to what was driving these costs.

After organizing and analyzing reams of medical and short-term disability claims, I found two conditions driving both types of claims: pregnancy and mental health. In collaboration with my colleagues in benefits, we took several bold steps. For pregnancy, we developed an incentivized work-site prenatal education program that led to lower medical costs for the participants, fewer low birth–weight babies and a lower cesarean section rate. With regard to mental health, a consulting psychiatrist was hired and high-cost mental health medical claims were managed in-house. The EAP changed from a traditional focus on chemical dependency to general behavioral health, with particular attention to parent and family issues. Dan Conti, a clinical psychologist, was hired to manage the EAP and the behavioral health strategy. A wellness program was launched that included a health risk appraisal (HRA) in partnership with Dee Edington at the University of Michigan. Perhaps most important, we saw the need for an integrated health data management system. In 1986, after two years of studying options and establishing the return on investment (ROI), Don Hoy and I met with the bank's chief financial officer (CFO). We requested a $100,000 investment in our proposed computer system.

Two minutes into the meeting with the CFO, we had our approval. The system would provide an electronic medical record for our clinics and integrate medical and disability claims, health reimbursement data, wellness program participation, and personnel data; a powerful report generator was also included. The system became a national standard and provided analytics for the direction and evaluation of health and wellness interventions. Over the next two decades, the system grew in scope through additional investments in hardware and software while the company grew through acquisitions and mergers. In 2005, Bank One was acquired by JPMorgan Chase, and I became the CMO.

In 2009, I was recruited by American Express (AMEX) to deliver a global health and wellness framework similar to my work at JPMorgan Chase.

Figure 5.5. Dr. Wayne Burton being presented an award for fighting for population health management at a team meeting in Fort Lauderdale, Florida. (Courtesy Dr. Wayne N. Burton).

Consequently, an integrated health data management system was installed that included an electronic health record for the on-site clinics, the EAP was reorganized with a single vendor for the over 50,000 global employees, a clinical psychologist was recruited to head the program, well-being programs were expanded to global coverage, and the U.S. safety team was integrated into our occupational medicine department. The number of work-site clinics was expanded from 10 to 30 globally, and in many of the clinics, the staff were enhanced with a part-time EAP counselor and a health coach. AMEX received the ACOEM Corporate Health Achievement Award, the C. Everett Koop Award, and several others.

After almost 40 years in corporate occupational medicine and the publication of over 100 peer-reviewed papers, some critical success factors stand out: (1) integrated data are essential to manage the health and productivity of the workforce; (2) comprehensive medical service must include behavioral health; (3) culture of health programs (e.g., well-being and disease management interventions) must be data driven and continually evaluated; (4) leadership support (i.e., C-suite) [an informal term for the suite of offices at corporate headquarters where all the "chief" officers are located] is essential; (5) success is not possible without attention to diversity; (6) occupational health unceasingly evolves and develops—follow the data and continually innovate, adopt new technology, communicate, and market the interventions you lead.

CHAPTER SIX

Corporate Sector and Private Practice

J. Brent Pawlecki and Paula A. Lantsberger

Occupational and environmental medicine (OEM) is practiced by physicians in many diverse settings and with much greater variety than most other medical specialties or fields of medical practice. This chapter examines patterns of practice in the private sector, either in corporate medical departments and facilities sponsored by the employer or in the community in clinics serving the needs of workers from many employers. Both have long traditions in the history of medicine, each with its own advantages for the physician in practice and its own challenges.

This chapter begins with the corporate sector because it explains in a more straightforward way the various functions that the OEM physician must manage and that employers expect and pay for. Within a large organization like a big company, a large facility, or a hospital, there is an organizational framework, budget, strategy, and common set of goals to be met. The corporate medical department is managed within this structure and is part of the strategy and goals of the company. Community-based providers perform most of the same medical functions, but as contract or external or outsourced providers and are usually not as deeply involved in other health-related, insurance, or policy issues for the employer. OEM practice in the community functions entirely outside the organization and like a more traditional medical office but must still meet these same goals and conform to the policies of the company (as well as all applicable laws and medical standards). Community-based providers are reimbursed for their services by insurance (mostly workers' compensation) or by employers (for functions of a preventive nature or surveillance) (see chapter 3).

The Corporate Sector

J. Brent Pawlecki

The corporate practice of medicine is an unusual setting that most physicians do not consider a career path until they happen to come across it. It is rarely taught in medical school or mentioned during postgraduate training.

Corporate medicine is like working in a small community where everyone knows you, yet it is often spread across cities, countries, and continents. Corporate medicine is a unique opportunity to practice medicine on the public health level, working to make a community healthier, and on the individual level, helping an individual worker with a work-related acute or chronic personal health issue. Ultimately, the role of the corporate physician is to promote a healthy, engaged, and high-performing workforce. Table 6.1 is a matrix of occupational health service responsibilities in large organizations, to serve as a point of departure.

Table 6.1 Matrix of occupational health service responsibilities in large organizations

Medical Level→	Individual Level: Worker	Group Level: Workers	Community
Management Level↓			
Operational	Clinical care, case management	Health hazard identification	Environmental/ product hazard management and control
Tactical	Prevention-oriented health services, preplacement evaluation	Comprehensive occupational health services	Regulatory affairs
Strategic	Health promotion	Health policy, cost containment	Risk/liability, loss prevention, product stewardship

Source: Modified after Walsh by John W. F. Cowell.

Today's corporate physician needs to know the enterprise's business thoroughly, not just the major business lines but the processes, materials handling, sourcing, and supply chain. The corporate physician is responsible for ensuring that health, safety, and environmental programs comply not only with regulations but also with best practices, in order to protect the reputation and integrity of the employer.

The corporate environment requires a different skill set from those developed in a hospital or practice setting. The motivation and language of business is distinct and requires a different approach, which for many physicians requires additional training, perhaps by obtaining a formal business degree or coursework in a leadership program.

The focus in corporate medicine is not health for health's sake but to support the business's needs for a healthy, engaged, and high-performing workforce. The value that work brings in supporting a person's purpose in life is a core focus for corporate physicians to assist the company in producing its goods and services. No matter what the product or service of the business, the corporate physician is hired to support its production by caring for one of the most valuable assets of the corporation: their workers in all capacities including knowledge workers, laborers, and experts in a field.

There is no single framework for the role of a corporate physician, as it depends on the company and the industry. At the level of the "chief medical officer" or corporate medical department, which the corporate physician leads or staffs, the role ceases to be primarily medical and becomes one of oversight and management. Usually, the scope of management responsibility starts with overseeing injury care and health services, workers' compensation, occupational health protection, health promotion, medical leave policy, travel medicine, and insurance and the general health portfolio of the organization. The role of the corporate physician invariably includes environmental health, product stewardship, global health and security, and disaster and emergency management. Within these broad areas fall critical incident response (and continuity of operations), disability management and policies, health-care benefits design, and interface with human resources. The more integration and less fragmentation of these individual functions, the smoother the corporate medical function tends to operate. Some organizations integrate their other health-related professional staff with the medical function, such as industrial hygiene and ergonomics. This prevents fragmentation of effort and ensures smooth coordination and alignment of goals with the medical staff and the corporate physician. Duties may also include health and well-being strategy, operations and oversight, sustainability goals, and working with company leadership to provide a perspective on the health of the workforce.

Today's corporate physician, particularly at the highest level (chief health officer, chief medical officer, corporate medical director), must certainly have a strong knowledge of the field of medicine but must also be able to navigate relationships from the chief executive officer to the workers on the plant floor, the call center, or the sales force. The corporate physician has to know the organization as or more deeply than he or she knows medicine.

The corporate physician must also have strong ties to the communities where the company operates. This includes working relationships with the local hospitals, emergency response, public health department, local social support networks, and local government officials.

Serving as the subject matter expert but rarely the decision-maker, the corporate physician must be comfortable in the position of *not* being the most important person in the room, until he or she actually is, such as occurred during the COVID-19 pandemic. The expertise brought by the corporate physician helps inform the corporate leaders in their decisions on how to lead the company, but health knowledge is not the sole driving factor. And the corporate medical leader must be comfortable navigating that.

There is no single path to becoming part of the corporate world. Some physicians follow a direct path from an occupational medicine practice, but others stumble into the field later, after practicing as emergency physicians, general practitioners, internists, and even pediatricians. Others have been in specialty practice (e.g., pulmonary medicine, infectious disease, physical medicine) or surgical fields. But all are or become intrigued with the unique practice environment and its opportunities and challenges.

Growing into the roles of management generally involves years of experience or accomplishment in doing the job. Increasingly important is an additional advanced master's level degree, generally in business administration, environmental health, law, health care or hospital administration or public health. The skills so obtained focus on biostatistics, population health management, business management, and regulatory aspects of employee health.

Structure

As a support to the business, the medical function fits into the corporate structure in the manner consistent with its place in the organization that best allows it to meet that need. In some companies, the medical team supports mainly the occupational health function, managing workplace injuries, return to work, safety, and ergonomics. Other companies utilize the medical expertise primarily in supporting overall health and well-being, with a heavy emphasis on benefit and wellness design. In others, the role serves more as a consultative expert providing input and guidance in the product and services and in the welfare of the overall workforce. Most commonly, though, the role includes portions of each of these functions and relatively limited opportunities for hands-on clinical care.

Where the medical team fits into the corporate structure depends on the company, the management team, and where the strategic fit seems greatest. In some, it is within the human resources function. In others, it is best aligned with the environmental health and safety activities. The security, research and development, finance, or legal functions may be the most appropriate in some cases. No matter where in the organizational hierarchy the corporate physician and medical department reside, it is essential to work throughout the organization to meet the strategic needs.

All organizations benefit from an explicit occupational health and safety policy that specifies their responsibilities to their employees and their employees' responsibility for safe work practices. A good occupational and environmental health policy should confirm the company's commitment to protect the health and safety of its employees and of persons living or working near company operations and should assign responsibility and track accountability for the actions and decisions required to maintain this commitment.

The corporate medical department and the occupational health and safety department strive to create a fair balance between employee rights and obligations and those of the company, fostering a very positive influence on labor/management relations while producing a healthy, safe, and high-performing workforce. The responsibility of a corporate physician is to provide an accurate and objective evaluation. In the world of occupational medicine and workers' compensation, in particular, the physician is not expected to be an uncritical advocate for the "patient." The treating physicians (whether they are specialists or primary-care physicians) in the community, on the other hand, may not have knowledge of the work site or the employee's job tasks, and they are not necessarily objective experts in the occupational needs of their patients.

The nature of the role and responsibilities of the corporate physician vary by the unique needs of the company, but there are frequent components that may exist. Table 6.1 shows how these roles and responsibilities fit into the medical and management dimensions of the corporation's operations.

Health Strategy, Benefits, and Design

The corporation, along with its employees and dependents, is a prime opportunity for population health management through health-care benefits design and delivery, leveraging the structure of the company for health promotion (see chapter 2). In the role as subject matter expert for the company, the corporate physician my play an important role in analyzing, understanding, and managing the health and well-being of the workforce through benefits design. In many countries, health-care costs are a significant concern for the company in managing its costs and talent. Keeping healthy people healthy and managing health conditions earlier can prevent medical conditions and complications and thus help to control costs. Understanding the disease processes, particularly as the incidences present themselves, is an opportunity for use of the unique skill set.

The collaboration between benefits plan designers and the corporate physician may not happen organically. The connection needs to be actively cultivated around a health strategy to contain health-care costs while maintaining a healthy workforce. Maintaining a population health perspective to address health-care costs and to design financial instruments (benefits plans) is important for an organization seeking a healthy and high-performing workforce.

The design ideally incorporates an integrated approach to cover both work-related and underlying health conditions. The U.S. National Institutes for Occupational Safety and Health (NIOSH) has developed the unifying concept of *total worker health* as a road map for managing health in organizations (see chapter 2).

The creation of a culture of health and safety is much discussed in corporate circles. This requires a supportive environment and strategically designed programs but also a sense of commitment by management and visible inclusion in corporate policies. A comprehensive well-being program should involve the corporate medical department, human resources, benefits, safety, public affairs and communications, legal, and finance, along with leadership alignment and visible support.

Disability and Absence Management

Reductions in worker productivity are a loss to corporations and hard to track because they are indirect costs. The major health-related causes are absence (formerly called "absenteeism"), disability time off work, and "presenteeism" (impaired on-the-job productivity so that the worker is present at work but not functioning at normal capacity and so being inefficient and ineffective on the job). The costs of presenteeism are significant and often higher than absence.

Lost productivity due to absence is driven by sick days and incidental absences for health reasons. Lost productivity due to presenteeism is driven by poor health and low-grade symptoms due to various chronic medical conditions, such as asthma, diabetes, depression, migraine headache, and arthritis. Engaging with, supporting, and accommodating employees with chronic medical conditions in simple but well-designed disease management programs has been shown to improve on-the-job productivity and reduce the likelihood of chronic absence.

Short-term disability (STD) benefits are salary continuation income for workers. STD benefits generally begin after a defined number of consecutive workdays off for illness or injury. It ends when the employee returns to work or transitions to long-term disability or separation from the company. These transitions are bound up with workers' compensation policies (at the state level) and the provisions of long-term insurance (private) that may be carried on behalf of the employee.

Losses from disability can be reduced through prevention by identification and control of workplace hazards, early provision of appropriate and effective medical services to prevent disabling outcomes or complications, rehabilitation services, and flexible policies on return to work from a work-related illness or injury, including accommodation that permits safe and effective return to work.

When addressing injuries and illnesses that happen at or away from the work site, the involvement of the corporate physician provides great value in understanding the health condition and ability of the employee to safely return to work responsibilities. Knowledge of the work site helps the OEM physician know what the job actually requires and determine whether an accommodation is needed in order to prevent further injury.

This function sometimes occurs within an on-site clinic, but it may be a part of the disability management process. Some companies operate a full disability and absence management function for their workforce, while others utilize external services to perform the operations. The corporate physician can play a valuable role in serving as a knowledgeable "bridge" for the worker and the company. Work provides a valuable sense of purpose for individuals, but it is important to return the worker when well enough to do so, but not excessively, as the longer a worker is out, the harder it is to get them back to the workplace.

Executive Health

Executives within a corporation frequently have intense schedules with long hours and demanding business travel schedules. Many companies offer executive health programs to identify and address medical issues, while improving the health and well-being of these key corporate assets. The examinations may be performed by in-house medical personnel or by an external vendor or health system, frequently supplementing and coordinating with the care of the executive's primary physician. These are strictly confidential examinations, which are efficient means of identifying problems early, to promote a healthier lifestyle with encouragement by the most senior company leadership and recognition of the importance of their own health.

There are some companies that oppose the executive exam function for financial or philosophical reasons (as it can be seen as providing special treatment that is not offered to nonexecutive workers) as well as concerns about the overuse of testing in these programs that may have questionable value or even potential harm from the additional testing.

Rather than these examinations being considered a perk, the interaction can foster close access of the corporate physician to senior leaders who can help support the many programs that are a part of the health strategy. The examination process can serve as an opportunity to update travel immunizations and to identify behavioral health or personal issues that could interfere with the overall health or performance of the executive.

Clinic Operations

On-site clinics are common responsibilities for the corporate physician by providing oversight of operations and, frequently, direct clinical care for employees. Commonly, they provide occupational health and urgent care. Depending on the company's needs, the scope of services may be limited to the treatment of workplace injuries and illness. This may include compliance with health monitoring and protective equipment, such as drug testing, vision and hearing testing, and respirator fit testing.

Additionally, companies may expand the services to include physical therapy, employee assistance programs, wellness and prevention programs, and return-to-work evaluation and disability management. They may also provide primary care when it fits into the company's strategic objectives.

Provision of clinical care is often outsourced, not only in international or remote locations but in places where the local medical establishment can provide routine care more cost-effectively. Depending on the country where the clinic is located, such clinics may be operated by an internal medical department or outsourced to an external national vendor, hospital system, or local occupational medicine physician practice. No matter the means of staffing, auditing occupational health programs for quality and effectiveness is essential to their overall success.

For international operations and traveling personnel, the corporate physician must oversee the needed care for injured and ill travelers and will play a central role in the navigation of an unfamiliar health system, including decisions about the need to evacuate should the local health system be unable to provide the proper care. Corporate physicians work closely with the security and human resources teams to address the health needs of these employees and their families.

Emotional and Mental Health

Mental health disorders represent one of the most common health problems of workers globally and comprise an area that the corporate physician can play a vital, unique role in navigating the health condition with the workplace. The COVID-19 pandemic has increased awareness of the toll faced by workers with mental health issues, such as anxiety, isolation, substance abuse, and depression. Mental health and substance abuse conditions are often underdiagnosed and undertreated, resulting in avoidable medical costs, absenteeism, disability, and lost on-the-job productivity (presenteeism). Research has demonstrated that depression and stress account for major economic losses in the workplace, including lost productivity and performance.

The corporate physician may play a valuable leadership role integrating workplace tools, such as employee assistance programs (EAP) along with on-site clinic providers, health benefits, and absence management services when appropriate. They can play a particularly important role in promoting mental awareness and helping navigate the company and community resources to minimize the widespread effects and influence of these disorders on worker performance/productivity. The workplace can serve as an important location for mental health and substance abuse interventions.

Emergency Preparedness, Business Continuity, and Crisis and Incident Management

The importance of the corporate physician to the success of the business was highlighted during the COVID-19 pandemic, when business decisions were made with the guidance of their medical expertise. As the subject matter expert regarding health and medicine, the physician is able to address the business continuity planning and response, which is a core activity for all corporations. The incidents include natural disasters and weather events (i.e., hurricanes, tornados), power disruption, fires, infectious diseases (anthrax, coronavirus, norovirus), and earthquakes. These incidents can adversely affect the facilities, the systems, or the people. Health threats such as global pandemics or localized large outbreaks of infectious disease do have the potential to disrupt business on a global scale, and as such, detailed planning is required.

The corporate physician needs to be prepared to deal with periodic communicable disease outbreaks such as tuberculosis (TB) or measles as well as other health threats. Even with appropriate planning, critical events seldom play out exactly as predicted; planning and frameworks for response and leadership actions must be flexible if they are to be successful.

External Connectedness

The corporate physician's network is the most valuable asset because almost every situation encountered will have been seen before by someone among their colleagues. It is important to foster those relationships carefully.

Some ways in which this might be accomplished include attending key national and international conferences, subscribing to updates and notifications from the Centers for Disease Control and Prevention (CDC) and the World Health Organization (WHO), and getting to know the key players in the field. The relationships maintained in this network provide incredible support when needed.

In addition, familiarity with the local health resources in the community, including the local ministries of health and health departments in locations important to the business, is important to success. Participation in external organizations such as local and global business groups on health and business coalitions allows benchmarking and sharing of innovative strategies.

It is also important for the corporate physician to develop expertise and recognition that brings credibility to the business and facilitates professional interaction. Through research, publishing, and presenting, the physician leader gains credibility and contacts outside of the business, which can lead to new and innovative ideas to bring back to the corporation. This is also done by strategic hiring of strong and insightful people into the medical department of the corporation to remain clinically and strategically updated.

Core Skill Set

Being an expert clinician and good physician does not automatically translate into being a good corporate physician or leader in corporate health affairs. Physicians often assume the role of corporate physician or medical director without prior business experience or training. However, medical training alone is not enough to play this critical role. In order to be effective in the corporate setting, key skills in leadership, strategic planning, finance, communication, and networking are essential and must be learned.

A strong executive presence while maintaining a high degree of professionalism and integrity is essential for success. At the same time, the physician must be recognized as a trusted professional and should seek to maintain enthusiasm, self-motivation, and high energy with a passion for quality health care.

The ability to be a powerful communicator with outstanding written, verbal, and creative presentation skills to both clinical and nonclinical groups is another essential skill. The corporate physician leader will have to cultivate and "sell" initiatives to the organization and its decision-makers. As one of the few people in an organization with knowledge of the health of its employees, this position is well suited to influence with intimate knowledge of the products or services produced, the organizational culture, key influencers, processes, risks, and its customers. Corporate physicians of large organizations with global reach must be particularly sensitive to cross-cultural communication. Messaging must be consistent, culturally appropriate, at a suitable level of literacy in the language of the recipient, and tied to local conditions and experience. Global communication is not just a matter of translation but requires cultural sensitivity, local references, and the ability to express ideas in the vernacular of the workers, managers, or stakeholders who are the intended recipient.

A challenge to remember is that the corporate physician is there to support the operations of the business. Business leaders must synthesize health input along with other business conditions and priorities in order to successfully meet the business's needs. When it comes to the operations of the business, the corporate physician is not the most important person in the room, unless a specific health issue is impacting the business. It is important to remain credible, trustworthy, and pragmatic as the needs of the business are the reason the physician, an expensive resource, is part of the operations.

Private Practice

Paula A. Lantsberger

The private practice of occupational medicine can involve being part of a nationwide network of clinics, or it can be as small as a stand-alone office with a single doctor. Occupational medicine has traditionally been practiced in a variety of clinical environments (see chapter 7 for a discussion of practice settings). As was noted by Dr. Pawlecki earlier in this chapter, the traditional approach to occupational medicine was to provide services to an employee in a corporate setting, providing services exclusively to that company. This changed a few decades ago when corporate medical departments downsized or were outsourced and medical services external to the companies they served proliferated to fill the gap. This put OEM services within reach of smaller and less well-funded employers.

The specialty of occupational medicine has often struggled to provide occupational medicine services to the whole of the working sector, from tiny single-owner/employee businesses to large corporate and governmental agencies. Most companies in the United States, over 98 percent, have fewer than 100 employees, based on U.S. Census data. Companies this small cannot afford even a part-time medical director. These employers must find a doctor who is well versed in occupational medicine practices and who can provide the services necessary for the company to comply with local, state, and federal regulations.

Community-based services serving multiple employers now predominate in the occupational health-care system, especially since the management trend to outsourcing that occurred in the 1980s and 1990s. These include individual physicians, group practices, hospital clinics, and freestanding occupational health centers, all of which accept patients from several local employers on a contract or fee-for-service basis. This is probably the only practical model for providing services to small enterprises, however, given the high overhead costs of maintaining internal services for small numbers of employees. There are disadvantages to occupational health services serving many employers. They are in a relatively poor position to influence management and usually lack the capability to advise on the control of hazards. On the other hand, they are easy to integrate with larger health-care systems and bring occupational health services within reach of smaller employers at a reasonable cost and level of quality.

The private practice of occupational medicine can be in a variety of settings. Some occupational medicine providers work within a network of clinics that are either nationwide or regional. These clinics generally provide the whole scope of services necessary to allow the client companies to comply with regulations and to promote healthy workplace practices. There are hospital-based clinic organizations that structure part of their service line to provide occupational health services to employers in their region as part of the overall marketing of the hospital services. Even with the trend toward corporations buying small practices, there are still a large number of privately owned occupational medicine clinics around the country that provide services to employers for the care of their workers. In some cases, larger companies will have a small health department, often staffed by a nurse, with space for a physician to visit periodically to provide occupational medical services to the workers at their plant.

Several models exist for the provision of occupational health care to many employers from an external facility. The most common are the following:

- Occupational medicine in primary-care practice (office-based or urgent care centers)
- Consultation practice in occupational medicine
- Multispecialty group practice
- Hospital-based clinic
- Occupational health center (successor to the "industrial medicine" clinic)

The delivery of occupational health services at a high standard requires support from staff with administrative skills beyond office management. To communicate successfully with all parties, including workers' compensation boards, employers, workers, regulatory agencies, and insurance carriers, requires special skills and the ability to appreciate a problem from many points of view. This is why a dedicated office staff familiar with workers' compensation procedures, terminology, and reporting requirements is essential to efficient and responsive occupational health services.

The scope of work for each of these practices can vary widely depending on the local businesses. The basic focus of some clinics can be as limited as only providing commercial driver license (CDL) exams to companies that have CDL drivers. Some clinics provide a scope of services that can evaluate and treat workplace injuries, which are primarily orthopedic injuries. These clinics are frequently paired with a general urgent care clinic that treats other medical conditions besides workplace-related injuries. A more specialized occupational medicine clinic with physicians trained and board certified in occupational medicine can provide complex evaluations for the occupational diseases, toxicology, traveler examinations, health promotion programs, and other services in the scope of occupational medicine. There are also clinics that specialize solely in performing independent medical evaluations and medicolegal evaluations for workers and employers.

Whatever the format and structure of the community-based occupational health service, the providers need to demonstrate essential competencies but go beyond routine care for minor injuries, as might be provided in urgent care centers or primary-care practices without OEM training and expertise. The American College of Occupational and Environmental Medicine (ACOEM) has provided a list of 10 core competencies that physicians practicing occupational medicine should have knowledge and mastery of. These competencies encompass three broad areas of practice. The first is the clinical care of the worker on a primary level providing injury care and work-related examinations. The second level is consultative services for more complex cases involving causation, toxicology, environmental management, work fitness, and legal casework. The third broad area of practice involves management of corporate health, pandemic preparedness and exposure management, and research-oriented practices.

The 10 core competencies include the following skills and knowledge of these segments of clinical practice:

- Clinical occupational and environmental medicine (OEM)
- OEM-related law and regulations
- Environmental health
- Fitness for duty and disability management
- Toxicology
- Hazard recognition, evaluation, and control
- Disaster preparedness and emergency management
- Health and human performance
- Public health, surveillance, and disease prevention

Clinical OEM involves decision-making regarding the diagnosis and treatment of injuries, medical monitoring of workers in the workplace, and determination of fitness of the worker for the job tasks essential to the work. This is the area of occupational medicine that most physicians start with for their entry into the specialty of occupational medicine. Many urgent care clinics include this service for their patient populations. The physician should be familiar with the requirements for medical monitoring for different workplace settings. The physician should be well versed in clinical care as well as having extensive knowledge of regulations that apply for special work requirements such as hazardous materials exposures, respirator use, and commercial driving regulations. With increasing trust and confidence, the OEM physician may become both the employer's principal adviser for occupational and environmental management and administration and the workers' best advocate for effective health protection and safe work practices.

OEM-related law and regulations include state and federal laws and regulations regarding the safety and health of the worker in the workplace, including occupational exposure standards, OSHA procedures, workers' compensation law, and the Americans with Disabilities Act. The physician will need to have the skills to collaborate with other professionals including industrial hygienists, human resources, safety specialists, and others to provide compliance with the programs to keep workers safe. Community-based occupational health services often lack this connection with hygiene and other specialists.

Environmental health refers to the workplace environment and a working knowledge of the community environment. Although OEM physicians in community-based clinics rarely have the opportunity to investigate environmental disease from a public health perspective, the workers and their families who are evaluated in the practice live in an environment that also has an influence on their health. (This is sometimes referred to as the "double burden": residents in the community may be exposed both at work and at home.) The physician should be able to recognize the environmental exposures that can affect the health and safety of the worker. Good communication skills are essential for the physician to evaluate the exposures and to effectively communicate the information to all the involved groups in an exposure in the community or workplace. The physician should have a good knowledge base for evaluating exposures involving toxicology and exposure assessment. Occasionally, there are questions about the family' or children's exposure that the OEM physician should be able to answer, especially as they pertain to pesticides, household exposures (such as mold), and environmental lead. This is particularly critical for hazards (such as lead) that can be brought home on a worker's clothes.

Work fitness and disability management are critical to tertiary prevention (see chapter 3) and make up a major part of OEM practice in community settings. The occupational physician has to make a fitness-for-duty assessment with every patient seen in the office, explicitly or implicitly (by letting the worker go back to work). Determining the ability of the worker safely to perform the job tasks of the individual job is an essential duty for the physician.

The physician should be aware of the job requirements, preferably having visited the job site or other similar job sites, or having an adequate job analysis to determine the essential criteria for the worker to be able to safely perform the job. When treating an injured worker, the physician must be able to work with the employer or vocational counselor to coordinate a plan for the worker to return to work or to recover sufficiently to be retrained to a new position or to apply for disability benefits.

Although routine acute care practice at occupational health services is heavily weighted toward injuries and musculoskeletal conditions, occupational disease and the effects of chemical agents are a major and serious part of routine practice and underlie the rationale for regulations, screening services, and preventive services. The OEM physician should have a deep understanding of toxicology and how to perform a risk analysis of the different environmental sources of hazards to the worker, the worker's family, and the local community. (Ideally, the physician would have a close working relationship with an industrial hygienist.) The physician should know where to find essential information on toxic hazards, how to utilize and interpret safety data sheets (commonly abbreviated SDSs), and how to establish and manage surveillance programs for workers. This requires that the physician have a thorough knowledge of regulation regarding medical monitoring, exposure assessment, and treatment of toxic exposures.

The physician should be able to evaluate the risk of exposure, determine control measures, and help to coordinate with other occupational health professionals to devise programs to protect the health of the workers and the public from the hazard. Industrial hygienists ("occupational hygienists" in many countries) are experts in anticipation, recognition, evaluation, control, and confirmation of protection from workplace hazards. The OEM physician usually has a working knowledge of the principles of industrial hygiene. The physician must know enough to incorporate questions about hazards in the workplace, protective measures used, and their effectiveness into the medical and occupational history and know how to interpret the answers.

Disaster preparedness and emergency management have always been part of the services provided by OEM physicians and in fact were among the major reasons why high-risk employers retained physicians when the field began to take shape in its modern form 200 years ago. OEM physicians are concerned primarily with protecting workers and the workforce during a disaster or major disruptive event, resiliency during an emergency so that workers can work safely, continuity of operations so that the enterprise can perform essential functions for the community (especially for critical infrastructure such as utilities, transportation, health-care services, and food distribution), community recovery so that the economic life of the community is minimally disrupted, occupational health services for emergency responders (such as firefighters, police, and first-receiving hospital staff), and identification and management of specific hazards (such as infectious agents or unusual hazardous materials). OEM physicians have played a major role in the COVID-19 pandemic by designing programs for exposure control, worker health, community health, and travel recommendations (see chapter 5 for some examples). The physician should be part of the management team for workplace exposure control of infectious diseases as well as disaster planning for natural disasters that can affect the workplace. The workers providing services in disasters must be protected with adequate planning for their needs for exposure control, shelter, clean water, and nutrition.

Health, productivity, and human performance are closely bound up with workforce health promotion, case management for workers with chronic conditions, insurance coverage, exposure to occupational and environmental hazards, and preventing avoidable absence and "presenteeism" (see chapter 3). The physician can advise on programs designed to enhance the health of the worker and find ways to support healthy practices in the workplace. This is more difficult to do when the physician is outside the enterprise in a community setting, but it is not uncommon for employers to rely on a community-based physician as their medical adviser and health consultant once a strong and trusting relationship has been established.

Public health, surveillance, and disease prevention have emerged as even more important in recent years. In addition to the obvious role of workplaces as places where people congregate and interact, health risks prevalent in the community as a whole may be seen early in the workplace (such as COVID-19) and may be concentrated in the workplace (such as health-care institutions) or present management issues that require a public health approach (as in the early days of HIV/AIDS, when employers often did not know what to do and sought guidance). The OEM physician should be able to evaluate individual and population risks in coordination with local agencies and employers to develop programs for exposures to public health, occupational exposures, and community exposures. The events of the COVID-19 pandemic have underscored the need for public health guidance that is science based and properly communicated to the workers and the public.

The effective OEM physician in private practice must be well versed in both the skills of occupational health management and clinical medicine. The practice of occupational medicine involves both broad knowledge of medicine from clinical case management of workers' injuries and primary prevention to ensure the safety of the worker. The private practice of occupational medicine allows the physician to choose from simply providing care with a single focus on one aspect of worker evaluations to a very complex clinical structure providing all the essential elements of occupational medicine.

CHAPTER SEVEN

Practice Settings

Tee L. Guidotti and Raúl Alexander Mirza

OEM physicians are employed in clinics, hospitals, organizations that range from small companies to multinational companies, academic and research institutions, government agencies, insurance agencies, the military, and public health departments. The duties of OEM physicians in civilian enterprises are almost exclusively in occupational medicine because for environmental health there is no health-care payment system as there is for workers' compensation. On the other hand, OEM physicians serve in relatively large numbers (given their few numbers) in regulatory agencies, in government-sponsored research, and as advisers to federal and state agencies. This is partly because of content expertise but also because OEM physicians are accustomed to working in large, complicated organizations and thinking in terms of policy.

This chapter will describe civilian practice settings for OEM in general and specific practice settings other than corporate and private community-based practice, which are discussed at length in chapter 6. It will then conclude with a detailed look at occupational health in the military.

At the end of this chapter, a section is devoted to OEM in the military. OEM physicians in all branches of service have many challenges in environmental medicine, particularly during deployment, and often confront novel hazards and technology.

Practice in or for government agencies is similar to corporate practice (see chapter 6) but generally restricted by the mission of the government agency. Below the level of federal and state government, occupational health services are usually outsourced to local providers, but some large counties support occupational health services for their employees and for critical occupations such as firefighting and law enforcement. Of course, there are also many OEM physicians who serve in an advisory or expert capacity in government, most of whom do not have patient contact as part of their duties.

Occupational Health Services

The occupational health-care system is built on different assumptions than the general or personal health-care system. In a traditional fee-for-service setting, the primary relationship is that between physician and patient (the traditional "physician-patient relationship"), supplemented in modern times with the managed care organization, insurance carrier, or other third-party payers influencing that traditional role to an increasing degree through managed care, prior approval and utilization review, and payment restrictions (figure 7.1).

In occupational health services, the number of parties involved includes, at a minimum, the physician, the patient, the employer, a government regulatory agency (such as the Occupational Safety and Health Administration), and the workers' compensation carrier or disability insurer (figure 7.2). Information must be shared among these parties as a legal obligation. (This obligation exists separate and apart from HIPAA, which formally does not apply in workers' compensation although confidentiality is maintained outside the parties.) The physician often acts outside the physician-patient relationship, reporting to the employer or to the carrier rather than exclusively to the

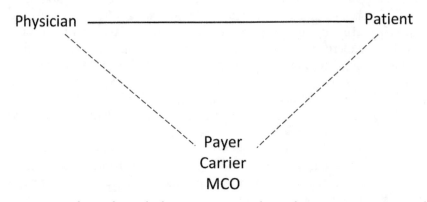

Figure 7.1. The traditional physician-patient relationship was one-on-one and assumed "fee for service" payment for medical services, with the role of insurance limited to compensation for services rendered. This model is mostly long gone and replaced with managed care. Direct payment by patients continues mostly in boutique medical practices and nonessential care, such as cosmetic surgery.

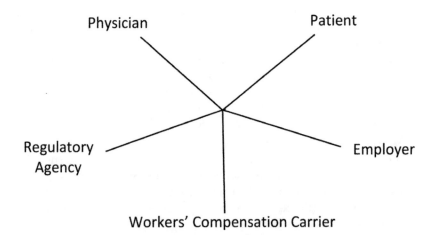

Figure 7.2. The occupational health system includes several players with a legitimate role in the process and need to access information.

individual worker-patient. This means that occupational medicine is practiced in a fishbowl, with many parties observing and monitoring and having a legitimate interest in the causation of the injury or illness, the diagnosis, and the progress of the case.

The occupational health-care system functions somewhat in isolation from the mainstream, personal health-care system and according to its own mission and logic. Physicians outside this system, who may see the occasional occupational injury or perform a routine periodic health surveillance, often have an incomplete grasp of the total system and think that what they see is all there is. Simple acute injury care can be done equally well by primary-care practitioners. Workers' compensation reporting and fitness for duty require a higher skill level and understanding of occupational issues. Complicated case management is a more specialized function requiring training and experience. The population health management functions in occupational medicine are qualitatively different from patient care and require knowledge of prevention science and program management. Occupational medicine practice at the higher levels is less clinical, more concerned with causation and prevention, and more oriented to population health and program management.

Like medical care in general, occupational medicine is practiced on three levels:

- *Primary care.* Primary-care OEM services deal with acute problems on a more basic level of medical complexity, such as most injuries in the workplace. Most of this basic care is provided by clinics, family physicians, emergency rooms, urgent care centers, and other primary-care providers without specialized occupational medicine support. Occupational health services that specialize in this level of care add value because they are organized for efficiency in dealing with workers' compensation, and their business model is to be preferred providers for work-related injuries in a high-volume, low-margin operation in which reimbursement for services is constrained by a set fee schedule and to offer routine surveillance (such as OSHA-mandated evaluations) at competitive prices.

- *Secondary care (referral and consultation).* Specialized occupational health services receive referrals for more complicated cases or that are engaged in managing complicated problems on behalf of an employer. This specialized level of care is geared to problem-solving and is not readily standardized for efficiency. It usually involves a mix of diagnoses for patient problems or consulting services for population-level program management issues. Such practices are usually part of a primary-care system, thereby generating referrals internally, or are hospital based. Some larger occupational health services and most university-affiliated clinics operate this way.

- *Tertiary care.* Individual expert practitioners, small specialized groups (usually in a field such as toxicology), and university-based services typically deal with complicated cases, are called in to solve special problems, design and manage population health programs, and conduct independent medical evaluations. In addition to medical expertise, tertiary practice often involves consulting on the management of operations, quality assurance, and designing or managing programs for clinical screening, as opposed to the day-to-day operation of such programs.

Occupational medicine services (and, to a limited extent, environmental medicine), like general health services, can be seen as a pyramid with three well-defined levels and with two sides visible: individual care of workers and population health management. Pyramids, of course, are three-dimensional, and in this analogy, there are other sides, but they are not visible to the viewer. (The literal-minded reader might imagine a side facing away from the viewer that deals with environmental medicine, for example, which because it is much less well developed as a system than occupational health care can be turned facing away from the reader for simplicity of presentation.) This is illustrated in figure 7.3.

Business management at the top of the pyramid is not usually a problem. However, practicing primary-care occupational medicine requires an infrastructure and a team approach that requires coordination, knowledgeable support staff, and experience dealing with employers. The delivery of occupational health services at a high standard requires support from staff with administrative skills beyond office management. Communicating successfully with all parties, including workers' compensation carriers, employers,

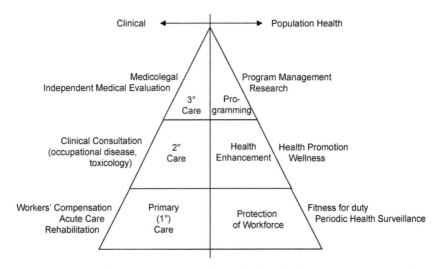

Figure 7.3. OEM physicians may practice at the levels of primary care, secondary care (referral and specialized care), or tertiary care (case management, medicolegal, or high-level specialty services) and either for individual worker-patients or for groups and populations (such as programming for the workforce). It is not usual for an OEM physician to serve more than one function and to migrate among the various "boxes" over the course of a career.

workers, regulatory agencies, and insurance carriers requires special skills and the ability to appreciate a problem from many points of view. This is why a dedicated office staff familiar with workers' compensation procedures, terminology, and reporting requirements is essential to efficient and responsive occupational health services.

Community-Based Practice Settings

Several models exist for the provision of occupational health care to many employers from a facility based in the community. They share many common features and are managed in a similar manner, as outlined in chapter 6. The most common are the following:

- Occupational medicine in primary-care practice (office-based or urgent care centers)
- Multispecialty group practice
- Hospital-based clinic (not to be confused with hospital employee health service)

- Occupational health center
- Consultation practice in occupational medicine

These various models of occupational health-care facilities have their own strengths and weaknesses.

Existing primary-care practices (doctor's offices, urgent care centers, small clinics) are important providers of OEM care, especially in communities where dedicated occupational health services are unavailable or underdeveloped. It may seem logical simply to provide occupational health services with a primary-care practice—just see injured workers along with everyone else. When primary care is the only alternative in the community or the goal is to expand in this direction, it may work acceptably well, but it tends to break down with higher volume. Most small practices are at a disadvantage in managing workers' compensation, since the reporting requirements and detail are not the same as for Medicare, Medicaid, and commercial health insurance. Combining occupational health services with general primary care invites problems with long waiting times and delay in return to work (a major complaint of employers).

Occupational health services that are owned, operated, or embedded in health-care institutions, such as multispecialty group practices and hospitals, face a common set of problems. They are sponsored services, and although they may be not for profit, they are business-driven entrepreneurial activities in which the service is expected to fit in with a broader business plan to expand into a new "market" for health care. The model is expected to achieve economies of scale for overhead, lab work, and physical therapy services and to feed the specialty referral system. Too often, the overhead is unrealistic, and development and marketing are not allowed to develop according to their own medical and business logic, which requires an emphasis on prevention, rehabilitation and early and safe return to work, and responsiveness to the workers' compensation system. Clinical occupational medicine practice often requires the screening of large groups of well persons, in situations in which the price for services such as chest films and pulmonary function testing is a determining factor. This puts hospital-affiliated services, in particular, at a disadvantage because they are expected to conform to the institution's overhead cost structure.

Hospital-based occupational health services, which are not to be confused with occupational health services for the hospital's own employees, have become the dominant format for providing occupational health in the United States. Most hospitals have promoted their services through selective business contacts rather than media advertising. Like group practices, one incentive for hospitals is to cultivate a patient base likely to enroll in their health maintenance organizations and to use the hospital and its outpatient clinics for their personnel's health care.

Hospital "employee health services" are occupational health services that manage the occupational health needs of the medical center's employees and staff and function much as they might in other enterprises and institutions. However, they usually report to and are closer to the medical staff in their institution than to the corporate management of the health-care system or the hospital administration. This is because medical centers have a large number of highly specialized hazards, strict regulatory and accreditation requirements, and a high standard to maintain patient safety, which can easily be compromised with poor occupational health management. Such departments are resources for occupational medicine within the health-care institution and sometimes are open to provide occupational health services to other local employers. Because of the medical, regulatory, and organizational complexity of medical center occupational health, such units are often quite large and sophisticated (see figure 7.4 and profile in chapter 8).

An "occupational health center" is current terminology for what was once called an "industrial medical center" (see chapters 6 and 8 for one example described in detail). These are freestanding, largely self-contained health-care facilities, sometimes loosely affiliated with hospitals but functioning as autonomous business units. They are often located in industrial parks, near airports, and close to concentrations of commercial or manufacturing activity. Most of them serve workers at a wide range of local employers and are particularly heavily utilized by nearby industries with a relatively high injury rate. Others

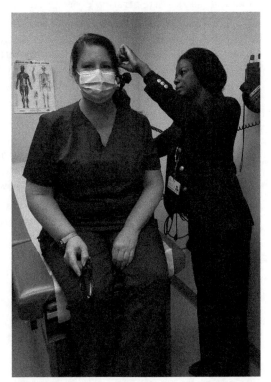

Figure 7.4. Dr. Tanisha Taylor's medical practice is a hospital system–based. She is chief medical officer of Robert Wood Johnson Barnabas Health's Corporate Care, where her duties include care of medical center employees. She is profiled in chapter 5. (Courtesy Dr. Tanisha Taylor).

specialize in a particular industry (aviation, the offshore oil industry, semi-conductors) and have deep expertise in that sector. Occupational health centers focus on cost-effective management of minor trauma and preplacement evaluations. The primary advantage to injured workers and employers is rapid access to care, early return to work, one-stop provision of all essential services, and correct and timely reporting and filing of paperwork, especially that required by workers' compensation and commercial drivers' medical evaluations (which is very time sensitive). The business model emphasizes high-volume care, triage for cases that are complicated, high efficiency of operations to keep overhead under control, a relatively small nursing and support staff, and importantly, adequate parking. An occupational health center can be operated with efficiency and effectiveness as a viable health-care enterprise when the support systems (patient flow, medical records, laboratory access, referral) are designed for the purpose of primary-care occupational medicine. In practice, this means that some services (such as MRI, CT scanning and all invasive procedures), less common clinical consultations (e.g., in neurology), and most long-term care and follow-up are not offered on-site but obtained from partners or local health-care institutions. On the other hand, rehabilitation (physical therapy), screening tests for periodic health surveillance (such as audiology and routine pulmonary function testing), and a limited range of prevention services are almost always kept in-house (figure 7.5).

The occupational health center model came to be dominated by a few large national networks in most states by about 2000. However, in response to the massive increase in people covered by health insurance in recent years because of Medicaid expansion and the Affordable Care Act, those networks often used their infrastructure to move into general primary care, turning their facilities into urgent and primary-care centers. It is not clear that occupational health services were as well served by this model, and it may have created an opportunity for medical entrepreneurs in OEM at the local level.

A small number of full-time private practitioners in OEM, who are usually located in major cities, practice primarily as consultants. Their practices may be independent or associated with academic institutions. In the setting of academic institutions and teaching hospitals, occupational health consultation clinics combine clinical practice with teaching and research. They mostly serve as independent medical examiners in workers' compensation cases; as expert witnesses in disputed cases; and as high-level consultants in toxicology, epidemiology, and often, aerospace medicine. Most patients are referred to such clinics from other physicians or are well known to local employers, in a particular industry, or by reputation. This tertiary level of practice requires formal credentials, experience, and a willingness to serve as an expert witness in a court case.

Figure 7.5. Occupational health centers provide all essential services in one location with a trained support staff, physicians knowledgeable about OEM, and expedited referral for problems outside their scope. Here, Dr. Chang Na (profiled in chapter 5) conducts an audiometric screening test. (Courtesy Dr. Chang Na).

Military Occupational and Environmental Medicine

Raúl Alexander Mirza

OEM is particularly well developed, diverse, and challenging in the military. Each service manages its own program, to meet the specific needs of the army, navy, and air force. Aviation medicine is common to all the service branches, and they all have significant environmental medicine and public health responsibilities that are reflected in operations, training, responsibility for overseeing contractors and civilian employees, and the degree to which "preventive medicine officers" (as they are usually known) are involved in health protection during deployment.

In a high-technology environment, military OEM offers constantly changing occupational health challenges. Military residency training includes unparalleled experiences ranging from practical public health missions in remote tropical and subtropical locations notable for endemic vector-borne diseases of military importance to occupational health experiences in the most safety-sensitive and military-unique industrialized work environments containing bio-select agents and toxins, chemical warfare agents, explosives, and nuclear hazards.

Military occupational health is unique and may have the most extensive occupational health programs in existence. The programs protect the health and safety of a varied workforce and assure military leaders and supervisors that their workforce is medically qualified to perform their essential job functions safely, fit for service if deployed, and that the potential for work-related adverse health effects is eliminated or appropriately mitigated and monitored. The military workforce that benefits from occupational health services includes approximately 1.36 million active-duty service members and 826,000 Department of Defense civilians. The military occupational health program also covers foreign national civilian employees who work to support U.S. military operations at installations outside the United States and its territories, non-appropriated fund civilian employees (including over 120,000 Department of Defense employees who are paid from funds that are not appropriated by Congress, who work across the globe in military exchanges and morale, welfare, and recreation programs, and who are paid from funds generated by these activities), and contractors under certain circumstances. In all, the total military workforce represents over 550 exclusive occupations. To ensure that there are sufficient numbers of OEM physicians to meet operational needs, the military even funds its own public health residency programs.

The armed service's branches (i.e., army, navy, and air force) operate their separate occupational health programs through a medical command structure or, under particular circumstances, by an operational commander; each service program constitutes a global enterprise. The services operate fixed occupational health clinics in three continents and can mobilize critical occupational health clinical functions during wartime operations. Military occupational health programs support the entirety of the Department of Defense and sometimes provide support to other U.S. government agencies and organizations and host nations and allied partners. Ultimately, occupational health practices support the sustainment of the military's essential resource: its workforce.

The scope of occupational and environmental hazards subject to primary and secondary prevention and surveillance by military public health and occupational health programs includes chemical, biological, explosive, radiological, physical, and psychological hazards that inherently arise from military-industrial processes and environments. All service branches and components generally record identified and assessed hazards for individuals and similar exposure groups in the Defense Occupational and Environmental Health Readiness System. In all, the Department of Defense monitors and responds to the potential presence or occurrence of more than 100 occupational and environmental hazards that could potentially cause medical injury or disease.

The army has the largest program. The secretary of the army delegates the responsibility for the army occupational health program to the army surgeon general. The army surgeon general serves as the commander of the U.S. Army Medical Command. Under a simplified description, the medical command divides its activities into four regional health commands whose commanders have direct oversight of the military treatment facilities in their respective regions. The military treatment facility commanders are directly responsible for the totality of their facility's health-care mission, including occupational health and the occupational medicine clinic. The Office of the Army Surgeon General establishes policy, official procedures, and requirements for the army's occupational health program.

Further, the Surgeon General's Office relies on a field operating activity, the U.S. Army Public Health Center, to deal with public health issues of strategic importance. Specifically, the U.S. Army Public Health Center responds to public health matters with the potential to degrade individual medical readiness, army mission capabilities, and the quality of garrison environments. The U.S. Army Public Health Center contains two core elements dedicated to occupational health: the Occupational Health Sciences Directorate and the Clinical Public Health and Epidemiology Directorate. These organizational elements represent the overall occupational health mission, including clinical (e.g., occupational and environmental medicine, occupational health nursing, and vision and hearing conservation) and nonclinical elements (e.g., industrial hygiene).

The Clinical Public Health and Epidemiology Directorate is home to the Occupational Medicine Division. The Occupational Medicine Division executes a mission that anticipates and is responsive to the needs of a war-fighting organization whose industrial, operational, and tactical activities are as diverse as they are widespread. The division's core mission sets have evolved to meet the challenge of supporting an ever-adapting army and emerging public health issues. The division supports the totality of army occupational health activities strategically positioned across the globe, comprising more than 70 clinics and 350 professional staff.

The division's core initiatives are the following:

- Advance the quality of the army occupational health program.
- Standardize the delivery of army occupational health-care services.
- Monitor and promote occupational health program compliance.
- Modernize the army occupational health program through policy and advocacy.
- Investigate and respond to occupational and environmental health threats.

An occupational medicine specialist (officer or civilian) manages the Occupational Medicine Division and supervises a multidisciplinary professional team of physicians, nurses, physician assistants, epidemiologists, health system specialists, and administrative staff officers.

The Occupational Medicine Division develops occupational health practice guidelines; prepares and interprets policies and procedures; conducts clinical consultations, training, and on-site field assistance; and provides continuing education to occupational health program staff. The division staff guide new occupational health-care professionals from outside the military into the unique military structure and mission. Further, the division monitors corporate-level occupational health program performance, evaluates the compliance of occupational health services with regulations and directives, guides exposure investigations, responds to occupational health outbreaks and novel occupational hazards, augments official program inspections, and coordinates and collaborates with partners from the other service branches and federal agencies. The division prepares responses to news media and congressional inquiries on a wide range of topics such as heavy metals, polyfluoroalkyl substances, airborne hazards, mold concerns within indoor environments, and potential exposures to chemical warfare agents. To keep the pipeline of OEM physicians open, the division supports the Uniformed Services University Occupational Medicine Residency Program with funding, leadership, and a residency rotation at the U.S. Army Public Health Center.

The range of issues in OEM in the military covers most of the same issues that might be faced with the corporate practice of medicine in the private sector, including fitness for duty, the evaluation of disability, and periodic health surveillance with a strong emphasis on prevention, probably even more so than in the civilian sector, but there are also a wide array of highly specialized and challenging problems. In addition, there are specific issues seldom seen outside the military, such as the respiratory effects of smoke from burn pits or evaluating exposure to JP-8 (the high-performance jet fuel). The rapidly changing technology of weapons, communications, and support in the military results in many novel military hazards. This is well illustrated by the following case study.

In the early 2000s, the army began manufacturing insensitive munitions explosives (e.g., insensitive munitions explosives (IMX)-101), a high-performance explosive composite mixture intended to eventually replace 2,4,6-trinitrotoluene (TNT). The army requested the development of an agent such as IMX-101 to yield an explosive force equivalent at least to TNT but more stable. Therefore, the army desired a novel insensitive munition explosive that was less sensitive to shock, fire, shrapnel, and improvised explosive devices. The army planned for several weapons systems with IMX-filled projectiles. The novel IMX-101 comprises 2,4-dinitroanisole, nitrotriazolone, and nitroguanidine. Although defense contractors produced this mixture, army civilian workers were to fill the projectiles with IMX-101 at an army ammunition plant. However, a tailored medical surveillance program had not existed for this hazard. As a result, a team (led by Dr. Mirza) searched the scientific and medical literature for a straightforward medical surveillance procedure, but there was none. The U.S. Army Public Health Center toxicologists then conducted literature searches on the observed toxic effects of the individual IMX-101 components in end organs in experimental animal models: a toxicity study. The findings taken together and interpreted for relevance to use in the field enabled the army's team of occupational medicine specialists to design a medical surveillance procedure.

Quality assurance, audit, and vigilance are critical in the overall army occupational health program, both to protect and preserve workers' health and to ensure deployment and contact readiness. The U.S. military has adopted civilian Department of Labor (OSHA) occupational health and safety standards and adapted these to internal mission objectives and tasks to be fit for purpose.

Not infrequently, emergent issues appear that must be addressed on an urgent basis. One example was an issue that arose during the war in Iraq that required immediate attention. The call for this investigation followed an article published by the *New York Times* that reported service members' accounts of their Iraqi deployment experience focused on their exposure to chemical warfare agents and subsequent health experiences. The army quickly assembled a team that developed an investigation protocol and published a guide to provide specific implementation and reporting instructions to be executed by all service branches (i.e., not the army alone). The purpose of our investigation, to ensure that exposed service members received appropriate medical care and follow-up, drove several significant outcomes. One was to identify, contact, and evaluate service members and veterans for potential chemical warfare agent exposures. Eligible participants were offered a medical exam, their experience was documented in the Department of Defense record-keeping systems, and pertinent information was shared with the Department of Veterans Affairs. Last, we provided information about potentially eligible service members and veterans who were identified as eligible to receive help from service-specific human resources representatives. They were then able to be considered for appropriate recognition for injuries that resulted from chemical warfare agent exposure.

The capacity of the U.S. military to handle complicated problems involving large numbers of people is unmatched. In this same example, the investigation team included clinical and nonclinical public health personnel from each service, medical providers who telephonically conducted case interviews, and occupational medicine specialists at the Walter Reed National Military Medical Center who conducted clinical evaluations. Additionally, the army partnered with the Department of Veterans Affairs and regularly participated in their Chemical Warfare Exposure Working Group. Medical personnel evaluated approximately 8,000 service members and veterans for their potential exposure to chemical warfare agents under this effort. Because this was a massive and complicated operation that would serve as a template for similar initiatives in the future, this led to initiatives to improve future medical capabilities in the field to recognize and respond to personnel exposed to chemical warfare agents. These initiatives involved updating army policies, designing training for medical professionals, developing educational tools for providers and the general military public, and presenting and publishing the findings for varied audiences, including executive and congressional leaders and the news media. Internally, the team that did this established tactics, techniques, and procedures for investigating future occupational and environmental hazards, including registries. During this investigation, the army hosted a permanent public-facing website to link current and former service members to relevant exposure information, known health outcomes, and instructions on how to obtain access to medical care. From here, the army piloted a program with employees at the army ammunition plant.

Over time, the Occupational Medicine Division team improved the design of the surveillance protocol by monitoring the performance of the surveillance results, including laboratory analyses and focused examination findings. Substantial cost savings and increased surveillance compliance were realized because of the new science-based approach. The team presented and published their methodology for establishing a medical surveillance program. Further, the division set an internal standard for creating and adapting medical surveillance programs for novel military occupational and environmental hazards.

This is the scale of what OEM physicians are capable of achieving in the military.

Disclaimer

The views expressed in this publication are those of the author and do not necessarily reflect the official policy or position of the Department of the Army, Department of Defense, or the U.S. government. The mention of any nonfederal entity and/or its products is not to be construed or interpreted, in any manner, as federal endorsement of that nonfederal entity or its products.

CHAPTER EIGHT

Academic Occupational and Environmental Medicine

Judith Green McKenzie

Academic OEM developed in response to events that laid bare the evident dangers workers faced as industrialization progressed. Physicians, who had long been called upon to take care of injured workers, now became critical as hazards went out of control with increased mechanization and the cost of payouts associated with lawsuits brought after a traumatic injury exponentially increased (source). As well, society and organized labor had lost patience with the increasing costs of disability and insecurity resulting from serious injury and occupational disease. In the meantime, environmental pollution and public health threats were worsening and required control. Evaluating the health effects of various workplace exposures required more systematic assessment beyond anecdotal evidence, and applying the scientific method to study occupational exposures gained value. This chapter will discuss the context in which academic OEM developed as well as the current state of academic OEM.

The history of OEM in North America is briefly related in chapter 1. In the late nineteenth century, there were very few centers of academic excellence in either occupational or environmental medicine, or in the science of toxicology, and what few there were, were concentrated in Germany and France. The United Kingdom developed programs in this era, but most of the expertise was within the factory inspectorate, and teaching was by experience. Toxicology was the leading science in understanding occupational and environmental chemical hazards and was dominated by German scientists and teachers. However, the United Kingdom was emerging as a center of thought in what later became a systematic discipline of epidemiology. American scientists, practitioners, and professors who wished to master these fields were obliged to study in Europe because they could not achieve competence in the United States. The one exception was injury care, which was advanced in the United States because of lessons learned during the Civil War and management of trauma in the railroads, which were remarkably dangerous at the time for workers, passengers, and residents of railroad communities alike.

That is why Alice Hamilton, introduced in chapter 1, took the route she did to become the preeminent American scientist, regulatory toxicologist, and hygienist of her age. After her medical education at the University of Michigan, she trained in pathology, learned much chemistry, and learned the basics of toxicology and microbiology, which she then pursued in study visits to leading German research universities in 1895 and at the heavily German-influenced Johns Hopkins University in 1896. Thus, she was well prepared in 1910 to import German medical concepts into a system of health regulation and monitoring that was slowly developing on the model of the UK factory inspectorate but at a much lower level of sophistication. This regulatory model, which she decisively shaped and transformed for the United States, was based on research findings and was knowledge and data intensive. It required an academic research and training infrastructure that scarcely existed in the United States at the time. Famously, on the strength of her pioneering scientific work in support of occupational health standards based on toxicology, she became the first woman faculty member at Harvard in 1919. By this time, Harry Mock (also described in chapter 1) had established the first academic teaching clinic at Northwestern University in Chicago and had written his famous textbook *Industrial Medicine and Surgery* (1919). The beginnings of at least the occupational medicine arm of academic OEM in the United States can, therefore, be dated quite precisely to this year.

Because of the danger associated with work and recognition of the injuries and illnesses experienced because of workplace exposures, competent physicians played increasingly important roles in providing care to workers and preventing injury or illness in the twentieth century. These skills needed by "efficient industrial physicians" were discussed in a 1930 article in the *Journal of the American Medical Association* by Sappington and Marbarker.

> The efficient industrial physician should "get out to the plant from time to time . . . making adequate study of the conditions under which men work, namely heating, light, ventilation, toilets, lockers, lunchrooms, shower-baths, drinking water. . . . He studies especially chemical hazards involved in the manufacturing process. . . . Dangers to the eyes, hazards to the skin,

risks of exposure of poisonous gases, dusts, heat, cold and electricity. He recognizes the relative value of the physical exam prior to employment and of periodic exams during the course of employment. The ramifications of mental hygiene in industry are given proper time and consideration. The public health is dependent on the health of the workers. Industry, not medicine, initiated the idea that accidents could be reduced to a minimum and that workers are entitled to the proper working conditions in which accidents and health hazards can be eliminated as humanly possible."

OEM Training Programs

Dr. Harry Mock established the first teaching clinic for occupational medicine, at Northwestern University in Chicago sometime after 1906. The first Occupational and Environmental Medicine (OEM) Residency was established at the University of Cincinnati College of Medicine in 1947 through the Department of Environmental and Public Health Sciences by Dr. Robert A. Kehoe. It remains the oldest continuously running OEM residency in the United States. Three additional OEM residency training programs (TP) were established during the subsequent decade: namely, Harvard School of Public health, Ohio State University Medical Center, and University of Rochester School of Medicine. Of these four, two remain—the University of Cincinnati and Harvard. Of the 53 OEM residency programs that were established in the United States, only 24 remain active. Reasons for this attrition are complex, but one constant theme is lack of adequate funding, which will be explored in more detail later.

Specialty certification in medicine only began in the middle of the twentieth century; before that, specialty recognition was conferred by completion of the training program. The American Board of Medical Specialties (ABMS), the overarching board for all medical specialties, was established in 1933. This nonprofit organization currently represents 24 specialties in medicine. Its 35-member governing board of directors includes representatives from each of the ABMS member boards and from members from the public such as nonphysicians, retired physicians, and other professionals from across the country with a broad range of experience including patient care, health policy, business, and community service.

The American Board of Preventive Medicine (ABPM) was established to "promote the health and safety of the American people through our high standards in the certification and maintenance of certification in the profession of preventive health." ABPM was originally incorporated in 1948 as the "American Board of Preventive Medicine and Public Health, Incorporated," and its name was changed to the American Board of Preventive Medicine, Inc. in 1952. It was approved as part of the ABMS in 1949.

The ABPM was formed on the recommendation of a joint committee with representatives from the Section of Preventive and Industrial Medicine and Public Health of the American Medical Association (AMA) and the Committee on Professional Education of the American Public Health Association (APHA). Around 1950, there was also an initiative to form an American Board of Occupational Medicine (by that name) as a separate entity. At the time, the Industrial Medical Association (now ACOEM) was in a three-way tug-of-war with the AMA and the APHA over control of the "new specialty" (new only as a recognized specialty, old as a field of practice). It was specifically called "occupational medicine" so as to put workers at the center rather than employers. The American Board of Occupational Medicine was soon subsumed under the ABPM in a negotiated compromise.

The ABPM formally classified occupational medicine as a medical specialty (not a subspecialty) in 1955. There are two other ABPM specialties: Aerospace Medicine and Public Health and General Preventive Medicine. Board-certified specialists in these fields often practice OEM at some stage of their career or after retirement from the military. Additionally, there are four ABPM subspecialties, effectively subsidiary multidisciplinary boards: Addiction Medicine, Clinical Informatics, Medical Toxicology, and Undersea and Hyperbaric Medicine. This structure is not unlike other medical specialties.

The Liaison Committee for Graduate Medical Education (LCGME) was established in 1972 and became responsible for the accreditation process for occupational medicine residencies in 1975–1976. The Accreditation Council for Graduate Medical Education (ACGME) took over this accreditation process in 1982–1983 and has been responsible for accrediting all graduate medical training programs (residencies and fellowships) since then. Established in 1982, the ACGME is a physician-led not-for-profit independent organization that sets standards for the United States and some international residencies and fellowships, as well as for their sponsoring institutions. Program accreditation depends on compliance with set standards. There is a voluntary process of evaluation and review based on published accreditation standards, which can then lead to accreditation of the program. In essence, ACGME accreditation provides assurance that the quality standards (Institutional and Program Requirements) of the specialty or subspecialty practice(s) for which it prepares its graduates are met by a sponsoring institution or program. ACGME accreditation is overseen by a review committee (RC), which consists of volunteer specialty experts from the medical field to which the program under review belongs.

Members of the ABPM board of directors are nominated by ACOEM. The initial term is three years, and one may sit for up to three terms. The ABPM board of directors meets twice per year and oversees the ABPM-OM's initial board certification and maintenance of certification process. There is no salary or compensation for members of the board of directors.

Structure and Content of Specialty OEM Training

Occupational medicine training has evolved over the decades. The traditional three-year postgraduate residency is still intact, but new training methods have been sought to meet the changing needs of our society and the changing nature of work. Our specialty has devised and piloted a new innovative Train-in-Place model at the University of Pennsylvania now in existence for over two decades. The first in the nation, this model is now being used by the General Preventive Medicine model at the Centers for Disease Control and the Yale school of Medicine Physician Assistant Train-in-Place Training Program.

The conventional residency pathway to OEM training consists of supervised clinical training and acquisition of a graduate degree with a public health emphasis and coursework relevant to the field, most often the master of public health. For the more common traditional residencies, residents move to the location of the institutions and carry out designated rotations to fulfill the ACGME requirements for medical education in OEM (ACGME website: https://www.acgme.org/specialties/preventive-medicine/overview/).

In the past, occupational medicine (now OEM) residents trained in the residency for two years and completed an additional one-year in-plant training with employers that were approved by the accreditation agency and ABPM. Such employers included NASA, the U.S. Air Force, Kaiser Steel Corporation, Ford Motor Company, Boeing Airplane Company, and American Telephone and Telegraph. During this third year of training, the OEM trainee formed a close alliance with the employers conducting in-plant training where they rotated at the plant: assessing, monitoring, coordinating, and treating occupational health problems in workers. After completion, the positions to which they were recruited were usually in-house corporate physicians. This is one major difference in the training of modern occupational physicians compared with those in the past, in that current trainees, in most cases, carry out training at the academic medical institution to which they are accepted. They may conduct short "away" rotations in a corporate or industrial setting but, in general, will have their home base at the academic medical center. The exception is the Train-in-Place program, which will be discussed later.

Currently, occupational residency programs are one or two years in length as laid out in the ACGME Program Requirements document. Board certification is through the ABPM or the American Osteopathic Board of Preventive Medicine.

The general requirements for admission to an OEM residency is a minimum of one-year postgraduate training (PGY-1) with 10 months of direct clinical care. Training programs beyond this are two years in length where each year is devoted to both OEM and the master of public health degree (MPH). Each year is referred to as the OEM-1 year and the OEM-2 year because most trainees enter at various stages of prior residency training and even after practicing in the field for several years. Some have already attained board certification in another field. In general, more competitive candidates complete more than one clinical year and may be fully certified in a specialty such as internal medicine. The two-year OEM residency training program is competency based, so OEM physicians are expected to possess certain skills and the expertise necessary to successful practice prior to graduation.

Learning objectives for OEM physicians are defined by a set of competencies developed by consensus, most recently in 2021 by ACOEM, and operationalized by the ACGME. These competencies, compiled by thought leaders and professors in OEM, are grounded in various areas such as law and regulations, disaster preparedness, OEM management and OEM administration, and population health, among others deemed essential for successful OEM practice. OEM physicians must be competent in 10 core competencies, with knowledge and skills specific to their area of clinical practice focus (see table 8.1). The OEM competencies developed by ACOEM are a "delineation of core competencies for the profession providing employers, government agencies, health-care organizations, and other health practitioners a solid context of the role and expertise of OEM physicians."

The "OEM Milestones," developed by the ACGME, are complementary to the competencies. The milestones are "competency-based developmental outcomes (e.g., knowledge, skills, attitudes, and performance) that can be demonstrated progressively by residents from the beginning of their education through graduation to the unsupervised practice of their specialties." The milestones have been updated by the ACGME twice since being first developed in 2010 and the ACOEM competencies four times by ACOEM since being first developed in 1998, and most recently in 2021.

Table 8.1   The 10 core competencies of training for an occupational and environmental medicine physician

- Clinical OEM
- OEM-related law and regulations
- Environmental health
- Work fitness and disability management
- Toxicology
- Hazard recognition, evaluation, and control
- Disaster preparedness and emergency management
- Health and productivity
- Public health, surveillance, and disease prevention
- OEM-related management and administration

The nominal duration of OEM residency training, not counting clinical training, is one or two years depending on the trainees' prior training. The program is two years in length for those trainees who have not completed a residency prior. If trainees already completed a residency and completed or substantially completed the master's degree, then they may enter the program as OM-2 residents, in essence, making the program a one-year program for those who qualify. Trainees may opt to stay in the training program for two years, however, to take advantage of more rigorous research training that would be helpful in academia or in OEM positions emphasizing population health management—an important element of any OEM physician's armamentarium. Some trainees do take this option.

Each trainee will have an individualized learning plan to ensure that they achieve the ACGME milestones and the ACOEM competencies. This is accomplished through required rotations—rotations tailored to the resident and didactic offerings. Each trainee must also complete graduate coursework prior to graduation. This entails successful completion of a master of public health or equivalent master's degree or a postgraduate doctoral degree. The content must include five required core courses: epidemiology, biostatistics, health services administration, environmental health sciences, and social and behavioral sciences. There are cases where the trainee may enter the program already having been awarded a master of public health or hold an equivalent master's degree or a postgraduate doctoral degree but not have completed the five core courses. These five core courses must be completed prior to sitting the ABPM-OM examination. The master's degree, if not already completed, is carried out over the course of two years.

All OEM trainees are required to complete at least four months of clinical occupational medicine each year. Other options include research rotations, corporate rotations, rotations at governmental agencies such as Occupational Safety and Health Administration (OSHA), NIOSH, the Environmental Protection Agency (EPA), the Agency for Toxic Substances and Disease Registry (ATSDR), the local Department of Health, international rotations, rotations with clinics that specifically serve public service workers such as policemen and firefighters, and rotations with local employers. Rotations are tailored to each resident's individualized educational plan to ensure that the ACOEM competencies and the ACGME milestones are all met and to accommodate other advanced learning that the trainees need for their career aspirations.

To be eligible for the residency pathway, applicants must have completed at least one clinical training year of an ACGME-accredited or a Royal College of Physicians and Surgeons of Canada (RCPSC) residency. The clinical year is to have been supervised postgraduate clinical training provided as part of an ACGME-accredited graduate medical education program. Clinical training accredited by ACGME International Advanced Specialty Accreditation, American Osteopathic Association (AOA), the Royal College of Physicians and Surgeons of Canada (RCPSC), or the College of Family Physicians of Canada (CFPC) are also acceptable. At least 10 months of direct patient care comprising ambulatory and inpatient experience involving diagnostic workup and treatment of individual patients must have been conducted (https://www.theabpm.org/become-certified/specialties/occupational-medicine/, ABPM, OM).

To sit for the ABPM-OM certifying examination, these individuals must have completed an ACGME-accredited or an RCPSC residency training program in OEM with appropriately supervised experience in the practice of OEM as well as the requisite graduate coursework. If the individual graduated from residency more than 24 months previously, she or he must have been practicing in OEM for at least one of the previous three years.

The complementary pathway is the second pathway to ABPM-OM certification. First offered in 2011, it is designed to accommodate physicians who wish to make a midcareer shift into practice of the specialty. Eligible physicians must have completed two or more years of training in a clinical residency program as well as one year with an ACGME-accredited OEM residency program. The at least two clinical years must have been completed during supervised postgraduate clinical training provided as part of an ACGME-accredited GME program. They are also expected to have completed a year of ACGME-accredited OEM residency training, which must include at least eight months of direct patient care, and also completed the five core postgraduate-level courses in epidemiology, biostatistics, health services administration, environmental health sciences, and social and behavioral sciences. Furthermore, they must have been practicing OEM or been in OEM training for at least two of the past five years. Of note, as of March 1, 2022, applicants through the complementary pathway must have completed a master of public health or equivalent degree additionally, with the five core courses also required. No longer will solely the five core courses suffice.

The special pathway is the third pathway to ABPM-OM certification, where a diplomate currently certified by the ABPM General Preventive Medicine (GPM) or Aerospace Medicine may apply to sit for an initial certification examination in ABPM-OM.

Finally, individuals who graduated from a school of medicine or school of osteopathic medicine prior to January 1, 1984, and have not formally completed all the components described in the other pathways may apply to sit the ABPM-OM through the alternative pathway. A year of supervised postgraduate clinical training provided as part of a graduate medical education program accredited by the ACGME is required. The board will judge their training and experience prior to admitting them to sit for the examination. Applicants must also complete the five core postgraduate-level courses, and the applicant must have been practicing or been in training in OEM for at least two of the past five years. Notably, the alternative pathway closed after the 2021 application cycle and is no longer be available.

Issues in Professional Preparation

Of note, less than half the physicians providing OEM services today have been formally trained. ACOEM data show that of its physician members, 43–47 percent are board certified in OEM. Many are diplomates of other ABMS boards, where 65–71 percent of ACOEM members are diplomates of another specialty. Many ACOEM members are dual boarded. One barrier to formal training is that many who practice OEM do not become aware of it as a specialty until years after graduation from medical school when they are deeply entrenched in practicing OEM or another specialty and relocating would pose tremendous hardship. ACOEM offers high-quality educational programs for physicians seeking to increase their competency in or to review in OEM. For those who seek board certification, this is an inadequate solution; however, the Train-in-Place program presents a potential solution to midcareer changes.

Upon completion, OEM graduates take positions in academia and corporate and governmental settings such as private practice, hospital-based clinics, group OEM practice, legal and regulatory agencies, and consultation. In general, there has been a decrease in corporate positions over the years, likely due to the "increase in the use of automation and a shift from manufacturing to service-based workers with downsizing of traditional corporate medical departments." There has been a shift, whereas many OEM graduates go on to work for national clinical OEM systems, which provide OEM services to local industry, using a centralized leadership structure.

OEM leaders need to be cognizant of increasing globalization and modernization of the workplace. For example, corporate medical directors are no longer solely responsible for U.S. workers but also for employees from other countries who fall under the umbrella of the company they represent. Cultural competence skills are essential (see chapter 6). The changing nature of work is a leading indicator to which OEM educators and leaders must pay attention to have the ability to transition and pivot as needed to meet the needs of the workforce. Burnout, wellness, and resiliency are also important to help reduce expensive worker turnover.

Funding for OEM residencies is complex. Unlike other residencies, funds are not available from the Centers for Medicare and Medicaid (CMS), the main funding source for clinical specialties in medicine. Funding sources for OEM residencies include grants awarded to the program director, who must compete for these grants at each grant cycle (three to five years), institutional funds (which only a small number of programs receive), and some corporate funding (which has become much less available). If the program is unsuccessful in competing for grants, there will simply be no funds available to train the residents. This reality has resulted in the closure of some programs, irrespective of quality.

The rise in the number of OEM programs that coincided with the 1977 OSH Act was no accident, as it reflects the fact that funding became available for OEM residency programs. After a steady rise from 1957, OEM residency TPs reached a peak at 43 in 1995. The number of OEM training programs remained relatively stable between 36 and 43, after which they started to decline in number. Since 1999, at least 18 occupational medicine programs have closed, principally due to a lack of funding. There are currently 24 ACGME-certified OEM residencies in the United States. Coupled with the reduction in OEM TPs, the number of trainees has also declined, despite robust availability of positions and jobs after completion.

Thus, until very recently, OEM training and education faced severe and seemingly refractory challenges. The situation began to change around 2020 and in 2022 when several long-awaited changes actually took place. The official name of the specialty was changed by ACGME to "occupational and environmental medicine" (OEM, as used throughout this book), removing a constant source of irritation because of the discrepancy between the de facto name of the field of practice (OEM) and the official name of the specialty—just "occupational medicine." OEM programs were separately listed in the official ACGME directory apart from preventive medicine in general, and there were no further closures of programs. However, to further increase visibility of the specialty, there are efforts underway to designate OEM (and the other preventive medicine specialties) separately in the directory, where they are now indiscriminately mixed together under the general umbrella of preventive medicine in the directory. This may seem like an obvious change to highlight the identity of each specialty, but repeated efforts to do this failed in the past. Now, however, the ACGME has proposed this change, and it is out for public comment. If it passes, then OEM will be listed separately as any other specialty, such as internal medicine or surgery. OEM will remain under the Preventive Medicine Review Committee umbrella, along with General Preventive Medicine and Aerospace Medicine administrative purposes and economies of scale. This is an example of the small but refractory problems that have greatly slowed changes in the specialty.

At the same time, the market for residency-trained OEM physicians has dramatically increased, causing an acute shortage (as it has many times in the past). This has led to the stark realization that the pipeline for OEM training is choked by funding constraints and artificial bottlenecks out of the control of the specialty of OEM. This is why the seemingly small successes in 2022 were so important: they directly addressed structural issues that have been holding the specialty back. Progress in stabilizing training programs will still be slower than it should be, but the situation is much improved compared to the 1990s.

The future of OEM as a whole is discussed in chapter 13.

Alternative Training Models

One approach to breaking through the bottlenecks and barriers to training is to prepare OEM physicians in different, nontraditional ways.

An important but now-dated study by the Institute of Medicine of the National Academy of Sciences (now the National Academies of Science, Engineering, and Medicine) reviewed the severe shortage of specialists in OEM and the bottlenecks to training. As many physicians enter the field of OEM midcareer, the academy report recommended new routes to OEM certification. This endorsement has led to innovation in new training models.

Because of the difficulty in maintaining conventional residency structures at a time of diminished support and intense demand for all postgraduate medical trainees to perform clinical services, models have been developed for OEM training. For the ACGME-approved "Train-in-Place" OEM residency, residents undergo supervised clinical training at a local vetted OEM site with supervision by an ABPM-certified physician without having to move to an academic medical center.

This Train-in-Place OEM residency program at the University of Pennsylvania (UPenn), which was established first at Thomas Jefferson in 1995, and moved to UPenn in 1997, was the first such program in the nation. It was created specifically for midcareer physicians practicing in the field, allowing them the opportunity to be formally trained in OEM. This innovative residency pathway allows physicians to train where they practice and live, without incurring the costs of relocation. A Train-in-Place program was one way to increase the number of OEM physicians, especially those individuals who seek to transition from another field to OEM. An essential element of this program is supervised training in a community setting combined with intensive training at an academic institution. Trainees work where they live, at a vetted clinical site, with supervision by a board-certified preventive medicine physician, precluding the need to relocate. This also allows for a higher output of graduating residents per training dollar and facilitates continuing employment of trainees at their sites. The program has graduated over 150 trainees to date, who comprise about 10 percent of newly certified diplomates of the ABPM in OEM over the past decade. In a sense, this is somewhat similar to the historical model of training, where the third year of OEM training occurred at corporate or industrial sites, almost coming full circle.

NIOSH is mandated to provide an adequate supply of qualified personnel to carry out the purposes of the Occupational Safety and Health Act, and the agency has played a critical role in keeping training opportunities open and preparing leadership faculty for the future. Increased support through NIOSH would be welcome, but NIOSH is a small agency in the federal system and has not been able to keep up given the lack of funding.

NIOSH-supported training project grants (TPGs) have played a key role in helping meet this mandate. By 1977, OSHA offered education and training grants through NIOSH, and the first nine education and research centers (ERCs) were awarded with the goal of helping prepare the future OSH workforce to respond to new challenges posed by the changing nature of work. This also funded OEM residencies. NIOSH funds were also used for OEM residencies that were not a part of the ERCs. Over the next two decades, following the OSH Act, the number of occupational medicine residencies increased from 7 documented ACGME-certified programs in 1977 to a high of 43 ACGME-certified programs in 1995. The 18 NIOSH ERCs are at Harvard University, University of Cincinnati, Johns Hopkins University, University of Texas Houston, University of Minnesota, University of North Carolina, University of Washington, University of Illinois at Chicago, and University of Arizona. NIOSH training grants support academic programs at ERCs, enabling students to obtain specialized training in OSH disciplines besides OEM—namely, occupational and environmental health nursing, industrial hygiene, occupational safety, and other closely related disciplines.

Research Training

Through the National Institute for Occupational Safety and Health (see chapter 1), occupational health research became more formalized and better supported. In addition to conducting education programs, directly or through grants, to provide an adequate supply of safety and health specialists to carry out the purposes of the OSH Act, NIOSH had another role. This role is to create a research program to generate objective scientific research findings in the field of occupational safety and health that can enable the OSHA to formulate safety and health standards. NIOSH started by publishing Criteria Documents for Recommended Standards on Toxic Substances (which were essential sources of information), funding ERCs as centers of excellence for occupational health training and education (incorporating industrial hygiene, occupational medicine, and occupational health nursing, but sometimes also safety sciences), and over the next few decades led pioneering research on worker safety and health concerns, awarding research grants, which allowed the slow development of a permanent research infrastructure with reliable, albeit inadequate, funding.

The National Occupational Research Agenda (NORA) was launched in the 1990s as an innovative public-private partnership among industry, labor, and government to develop research priorities and is now in its third decade

(Howard, 2020). More than 500 individuals and organizations outside NIOSH contributed to NORA's development. The NORA research agenda focuses on the top 10 most important topics for workplace health and safety. This list is updated to reflect the times. NORA sets an agenda for research and improved workplace practices in the following sectors: agriculture, forestry and fishing, health care and social assistance, oil and gas extraction, public safety, wholesale and retail trade services, transportation, warehousing and utilities, construction, and manufacturing and mining.

Environmental medicine research also became more formalized with the National Institute of Environmental Health Sciences, which is an institute within the National Institutes of Health (NIH), and the U.S. Environmental Protection Agency.

Acknowledgments

Sonia Brown, MD; Brianna McKenzie; and Jamie Curran—all of the University of Pennsylvania—assisted Dr. McKenzie in preparing this chapter.

CHAPTER NINE

Case Studies

Manijeh Berenji, Natalie P. Hartenbaum,
Chang Rim Na, and Tee L. Guidotti

Every case of occupational and environmental injury and disease is preventable. Every such disorder has a condition behind it that can be corrected, and every case is a failure of prevention. Every condition that results in a case has a story behind it of why the hazardous condition was allowed to exist, who was accountable, and what the implications are for the worker or community resident, for the workforce or the community as a whole, and for the employer or the local community. Of course, workers live in and are part of the community, as are their families, so the dividing line is not distinct. At the same time, every case has a human face.

Occupational and environmental injuries and diseases span virtually the whole of medicine. The list of diagnoses in chapter 2 demonstrates that occupational and environmental medicine (OEM) is a highly diverse field. However, as in all specialty areas of medicine, some problems (such as low back pain) are very common in practice, while others are rarely seen. On the occupational medicine side, the more common injuries include low back injuries (usually short term and easy to treat but sometimes initiating chronic low back problems); hand injuries; sprains, strains, and other soft-tissue injuries (most often of the shoulder, knee, and ankle); injuries associated with slips, trips, and falls; and poisonings (which are always counted as injuries in workers' compensation). There are very many occupational diseases, by the definition of workers' compensation (a disorder caused by a process, not an acute event), with an occupational association through cause, aggravation and exacerbation, or multiple factors. These include asthma, dust diseases of the lung, dermatitis (skin rashes), types of cancer, noise-induced hearing loss, and many others. The most common causes of death in the workplace are falls; being struck by objects; electrocutions; and being caught in machinery, in a collapsing trench or excavation, or between moving objects. Some musculoskeletal disorders are not classified as injuries because they develop over time without a specific traumatic event and are so classified as "diseases," including chronic low back pain and repetitive strain injuries.

Environmental diseases, on the other hand, are much less obvious, and identifying causation is much harder. Even more than occupational diseases, diseases associated with environmental exposures tend to look like everyday cases of the same diagnosis. Identifying the cause requires further investigation and analysis.

These fictionalized cases illustrate some of the problems, both clinical and managerial, that OEM physicians and other physicians who treat injured workers have to address. All cases have been changed substantially to prevent identification but remain true to the essentials of their medical history. They are not "typical" or textbook cases but representative of the problems encountered in this type of practice. All cases are "occupational" rather than "environmental," because disorders associated with ambient (outdoor) environmental causes almost never have distinguishing features and declare themselves by an increase in frequency or timing—for example, asthma following an air pollution event.

Acute Low Back Pain

Manijeh Berenji

A 55-year-old woman worked at a fulfillment center in large metropolitan area as a warehouse worker. The job involved much repetitive bending and stooping. She sustained an initial injury to her low back while loading a pallet for transport. Her pain was localized in the lower back, with no "red flags" (no radicular or myelopathic symptoms or signs of inflammation, neurological compromise, cancer, or infection). She was treated conservatively with ibuprofen (a nonsteroid anti-inflammatory drug, or NSAID), physical therapy, and work restrictions (no push/pull/lift/carry greater than 20 pounds, no repetitive bend/stoop, discussion with her supervisor). She subsequently improved over two to three months. But since the initial inciting event, she has had multiple flare-ups (three to four times per year), primarily axial (truncal) low back pain with intermittent radiculopathy (shooting pain from nerve root irritation) in the right L4-L5 and L5-S1 distributions (in other words, typical sciatica). An MRI showed mild to moderate degenerative disc disease with degenerative changes of the vertebrae and mild spinal canal narrowing. Comorbid conditions include obesity. She has managed with additional physical therapy, home exercise program, an anti-inflammatory drug (naproxen), pain control drug (gabapentin) and a TENS unit. The time lost from work, her reasonable fear of reinjury, the absence of alternative placement with her employer, and limits on allowable physical therapy in her workers' compensation insurance have made her employment precarious. It is unlikely that she will be able to keep doing her job; her supervisors would like for her to quit but cannot fire her for a work injury, and she cannot afford to retire on limited disability benefits.

Comment: This case illustrates two important realities.

The first is that most *acute* back pain, meaning back pain that comes on suddenly, can be dealt with readily with pain medication such as an NSAID (thus avoiding analgesics such as opioids), home stretching and physical therapy as indicated, targeted work restrictions, and continuous monitoring of the patient, at which point, the patient may return to normal work. The exceptions are when there are certain medical signs indicating a more serious problem (called "red flags") and when acute pain transitions to a chronic problem. Acute back pain care is, therefore, aimed at treating the immediate symptoms with the most optimal, evidence-based pain management and rehabilitation protocols available. The end goal being returning the worker to normal activity as soon as is reasonably possible. It is critical to engage the worker throughout the process so as to avoid the development of chronic pain, which is much more difficult to manage. Some means to do this include core strengthening exercises, regular exercise, and supervised weight loss programs.

Chronic Low Back Pain

Tee L. Guidotti

A 50-year-old male office worker experienced an incident in which he strained his lower back getting out of a chair and experienced the sudden onset of excruciating low back pain. He was not lifting any heavy object at the time and was turning as he rose.

He had no fever or systemic symptoms that would suggest infection or cancer or congenital spine problem. He was unable to stand upright because of the pain and muscle spasm but was able to walk while leaning to one side with an abnormal gait and shortened stride, if he was not rushed. On examination, he showed muscle spasm and tenderness at the area of pain. Clinical tests involving traction on the sciatic nerve were positive on the left. There were no signs of neurological deficit (abnormal sensation or weakness). He did not smoke (back pain is more common among smokers).

He was treated with a short course of an opioid pain reliever (oxycodone), which was then rapidly tapered off. He was then encouraged to move around and walk as much as he could tolerate.

He has since had occasional twinges of pain radiating down the back of his left leg, with stiffness and constant soreness in his lower back made worse by standing for long periods, prolonged sitting, or repeated bending. The pain was blunted but not entirely relieved by acetaminophen (Tylenol®).

An MRI of the lumbar spine showed wide bulges in the discs between L3-L4 and L4-L5 (designating which lumbar vertebrae), both pushing toward the left against the nerve roots exiting from the spine on that side. The right side was normal. There were signs of degenerative changes (arthritis) in the facet joints at both levels. (A facet is the side joint between two vertebrae that allows bending and twisting movements.)

He was diagnosed with lumbar disc herniation and "facet syndrome" and sent for physical therapy, with a goal of "core strengthening." He was advised to continue his physical therapy regularly at home between visits and after his supervised treatments ended, because this would reduce the frequency and severity of pain episodes. He was instructed to continue his daily activities as tolerated and under no circumstances to seek prolonged bed rest, although it helped to relieve the pain. He was strongly discouraged from pursuing surgery.

On this regimen, his opioid pain reliever (analgesic) was cut back until he was using only NSAIDs. He was reassured that occasional twinges of discomfort were inevitable but did not represent serious reinjury or worsening of his condition. He was skeptical at first but grew more confident as he saw improvement. He returned to work and was able to tolerate occasional discomfort without fear. Every few years he had an episode of severe pain across the lower back, which he dealt with by short-term rest and a short course (days only) of analgesics stronger than NSAIDs.

Comment: Chronic low back pain is one of the most common problems in OEM. When pain, particularly back pain, goes on for longer than three months, it transforms from an acute injury into a different medical condition called "chronic pain syndrome." When this occurs, it becomes self-perpetuating and very hard to manage because increasing doses of analgesics do not work as well and may even make the condition worse. So, the main objective of managing chronic low back pain is to avoid doing harm, by steering the patient away from drugs such as opioids (except very short term for acute episodes) and directing the patient toward evidence-based in-person and virtual behavioral interventions (including coping strategies, motivational interviewing), core strengthening, and other nonpharmacological methods to manage pain in the long term. This regimen can be difficult for some patients to adhere to because chronic pain can alter an individual's neurological framework (including pain perception and tolerance levels).

The consequences are very high, however. Ongoing reliance on opioids to manage chronic pain has contributed to the current opioid-dependency epidemic in the United States with avoidable deaths and mostly unsatisfactory outcomes.

The key to this case was not the specific diagnosis. Disc herniation, where the shock-absorbent pads between vertebrae degenerate and are displaced, is very common and often unrelated to pain. In this case, it is compressing the nerve roots of the sciatic nerve, giving rise to a typical syndrome called "sciatica." The additional diagnosis of "facet syndrome" is just one of several "mechanical" causes of low back pain that have similar features and nonspecific treatment. After ruling out a deeper problem by looking for "red flags" (symptoms or signs of potentially serious disease), his physician tried in every way to back off intensive treatment, avoid surgery (which often ends badly), and to use conservative measures such as physical therapy to manage the problem without drugs.

Carpal Tunnel Syndrome with a Difference

Manijeh Berenji

A 50-year-old right-handed certified nursing assistant working at a long-term care facility was assigned to total care of residents, providing assistance with all activities including bathing, toileting, and helping in and out of bed. The facility had only one mechanical patient lift (an apparatus that raises patients out of bed safely, saving considerable strain and preventing injuries to staff). She had been having chronic joint pains including bilateral shoulders/elbow/wrists with intermittent numbness and tingling of right second and third digits, and mild thenar (thumb muscle) atrophy of right hand.

Initially, it was assumed that she had carpal tunnel syndrome due to repetitive strain injury—in other words that the demands on her upper extremities put a repeated strain on her hands and forearms. However, she also had comorbid conditions including fibromyalgia, diabetes mellitus type 2 (non-insulin dependent), overweight but not obesity, and hypothyroidism. Additional workup for inflammatory markers revealed high ESR, CRP, positive anti-nuclear antibody, positive antibody to ribonucleoprotein. These suggested underlying medical issues. She was started on treatment including NSAID, gabapentin, physical and sports massage therapy, and referral to rheumatology for further workup of what was diagnosed as mixed connective tissue disorder, which is very uncommon. She ceased working at the nursing home.

Comment: Carpal tunnel syndrome is a common problem that is not always related to work demands. Other common causes include obesity, diabetes, and pregnancy. In her case, however, it was a rather rare and unexpected disorder requiring special tests to identify. This is a reminder to always be on guard for "zebras" (medical slang for the unusual or unexpected diagnosis).

Acute Musculoskeletal (Soft Tissue) Strain/Sprain with Successful Rehab

Manijeh Berenji

The worker was a 45-year-old female, right-hand dominant, city-bus driver with right wrist strain. She injured her right wrist while she was braking hard to stop the bus when a car cut in front of her. Over the next few days, she started to have increasing wrist pain and swelling along the first dorsal compartment (the sheath in the wrist that thumb tendons pass through). She was evaluated at a work injury clinic, given prescription-strength NSAID, immobilized by splinting, given work restrictions with no push/pull/lift/grip/grasp greater than five pounds of force, and referred for occupational therapy. She made only slow progress, monitored with routine follow-up every four weeks. She was accommodated (see chapter 3) with advanced work restrictions and reduced work hours operating the bus but had setbacks and continued to have deficits in active flexion of her right wrist. An MRI done six months after the initial injury demonstrated mild tenosynovitis along the muscles of the thumb (abductor pollicis longus and extensor pollicis brevis) with soft-tissue swelling, but the mechanically important triangular fibular cartilage was intact. She was referred to a new occupational therapist with expertise in work injury rehabilitation and provided additional vocational counseling. The workers' compensation carrier approved care for rehabilitation and return to work.

Then she lost her husband as well as a cousin in an incident involving gun violence. In reaction to this tragedy, she had to cease work and treatment for work injury, and she went through prolonged bereavement and mild depression. She went on short-term disability for six months. Her primary-care provider contacted her workers' compensation carrier about the worker's status and coordinated care with her personal health insurance. He connected her with a psychiatrist with expertise in grief and trauma who started her on antidepressants. After three months, she started to transition back to part-time work with restrictions and then to full-time work one year after initial injury.

Comment: This case illustrates an important principle in occupational medicine, which is that there is never just one thing going on in a worker's life. Life happens to worker-patients. In this case, the course of rehabilitation was interrupted by tragedy but in the end was successful. Many people find the structure, routine, and social setting of the workplace to be supportive and helpful in returning to a normal life. That, of course, depends on the workplace, the individual, and the policies of the employer.

Occupational Musculoskeletal Disorder of the Upper Extremity

Manijeh Berenji

The worker/patient was a 41-year-old employee of a garment manufacturing company for 12 years when she experienced the onset of left shoulder and neck pain. She subsequently noticed numbness in an ulnar nerve distribution (palm and back side of her left hand), primarily involving the fifth digit (little finger). This was worse when she used her hands repeatedly. She was given wrist supports, but these made her condition worse. She also noticed the onset of right-sided discomfort, and numbness affecting digits four and five of her right hand. She was evaluated with nerve conduction studies, which showed entrapment of the ulnar nerve on both sides and a carpal tunnel syndrome of her left wrist. She is right-handed.

She underwent surgery twice, once for release of a nerve entrapment at her left elbow and wrist and in February 1989 for release of nerve entrapment at her right elbow only. Since then, she has improved much with respect to the pain in her upper extremities but still has pain in her left shoulder and neck, particularly with exertion.

Her duties at the company involved working on a sewing machine stitching jeans. She worked hunched over the machine, using her left arm and hand repetitively and vigorously to handle the heavy fabric while it was being sewn. She had to grip the denim very tightly and continuously through the operation. She noticed little vibration, however, as she did not touch the machine but held on to the garment by the fabric.

A claim to the workers' compensation carrier was initially denied on the grounds that her conditions were related to other medical problems, specifically a thyroid condition. The patient had undergone treatment of her thyroid for early thyroid cancer and has done well on thyroid replacement since.

On physical examination, the scars from her surgery were visible. An Adson's maneuver (a preliminary test for constriction of major arteries in the shoulders involving throwing the shoulders back and turning the head to the side while palpating the radial pulse) was negative, as was Phalen's test (a preliminary test for carpal tunnel syndrome involving a hand maneuver that compresses the medial nerve at the wrist).

She appeared depressed and tearful, and her English skills were poor. The patient is a relatively recent immigrant to North America with her family. She did not speak English fluently, although she was enrolled in an English as a second language course.

She experienced considerable relief following surgery, precisely as would be expected from nerve entrapment associated with overuse and repetitive motion. She continues to have residual pain in her neck and shoulder localized to the site primarily involved in her work.

She is permanently/partially impaired by her residual chronic pain and neck and shoulder discomfort. It was strongly advised that she not return to work requiring heavy and repetitive use of the upper extremities. Her lack of command of English and her limited educational level make it difficult for her to obtain alternate employment.

Eventually, she was awarded permanent disability following an appeal. The consulting physician offered to refer her to a physician specializing in chronic pain control and coping with the sequelae of injuries but she declined, stating that her depressive reaction was strictly a matter of frustration at not having her problem recognized.

Comment: Nerve entrapment syndromes resulting from repetitive strain and overuse are common, and the garment industry is notorious for these problems. The constant gripping and repetitive movement in an awkward position are very compatible with the subsequent development of this patient's nerve entrapment problems and certainly the musculoskeletal complaints affecting her neck and shoulders. Vibration also makes the condition worse in many cases. It is particularly noteworthy that her problems are particularly severe on her left side, although she is right-handed. This is easily explained by the requirements of her job, and there is no other plausible medical reason for this localization.

Screening clinical tests, such as Adson's test (which was a true negative in this case) and Phalen's test (which was a false negative in this case) are just that: for screening. They are not definitive but, if positive, can suggest that the disease is present. The definitive test in this case for carpal tunnel syndrome is nerve conduction studies, which measure the conduction velocity of nerve impulses along the median nerve.

Furthermore, it makes little sense that her musculoskeletal and nerve entrapment problems would be associated in any way with her thyroid condition. In the first place, the presentation of any thyroid disease, including extreme hypothyroidism, in this form in isolation would be such a remote possibility as to be inconceivable. Radionuclide ablation of the thyroid with appropriate replacements is an extremely benign treatment with few side effects.

There is no reasonable doubt that her nerve entrapment and musculoskeletal pain is a direct consequence of her work. If there is any thought of her neck pain being associated with a thyroid disorder, this is not credible. Nothing else in the patient's medical history suggests an alternative cause for her musculoskeletal pain.

Musculoskeletal disorders of this type, affecting soft-tissue structures primarily, can persist for quite long after the offending motion and load at work have ceased.

Truck Driver Returning to Work after a Heart Attack

Natalie P. Hartenbaum

A 69-year-old, commercial motor vehicle operator (CMV) who works for a nationwide trucking company but only drives within his home state, has been cleared by his cardiologist to return to work six weeks after an inferior wall myocardial infarction. An echocardiogram demonstrated normal wall motion, with the exception of inferior wall hypokinesis, no valvular abnormality, and an ejection fraction of 50 percent. An exercise tolerance test done prior to discharge showed that he was able to reach 6 METS on a Bruce protocol test with no ischemic heart symptoms or signs. The driver is currently asymptomatic and anxious to return to work. He initially asked his personal physician to complete the examination form but was told that his primary-care provider could not do it. He then went to an occupational medical clinic for a formal recertification examination.

Comment: One of the most common and consequential responsibilities of OEM physicians is to evaluate workers in safety-sensitive positions, most commonly truck drivers. Medical examinations for CMV drivers are regulated by an agency of the U.S. Department of Transportation (DOT), the Federal Motor Carrier Safety Administration (FMCSA). Other "DOT examinations" cover workers in aviation, rail transport, maritime, and oil and gas pipeline workers.

The two key features of these evaluations are a medical evaluation and screening for drugs and alcohol. There are two aspects to the evaluation. The first is a medical examination and screen, which is primarily designed to ensure that the operator can safely drive or otherwise operate the vehicle and is not subject to a medical disorder that could result in sudden incapacitation. The second is to ensure that the operator is unlikely to be driving under the influence of drugs. The "medical review" function for drug testing is complicated and strict and, for FMCSA, nominally applies only to interstate drivers but is often used by employers to ensure that their entire workforce is drug-free. Physicians must qualify through training and examination as "medical review officers" to conduct drug screening and, as a result, many, if not most, OEM physicians practicing in a primary-care capacity already have this certification and are knowledgeable about drug and alcohol effects and the many ways that a small fraction of operators (mostly, truck drivers) have attempted to evade or foil testing.

The commercial driver medical examination (CDME) process has undergone many changes over the years. Since 1970, a CMV operator was required to be examined and certified at least every two years and meet FMCSA medical standards. For many years, the commercial driver medical examinations for a CMV operator operating in interstate commerce, could be performed only by doctors of medicine or doctors of osteopathy. In 1992, the qualifications were expanded to include any "person licensed, certified, or registered, in accordance with applicable State laws or regulations, to perform physical examinations." This included but was not limited to doctors of medicine, doctors of osteopathy, physician assistants, advanced practice nurses, and doctors of chiropractic. More recently, FMCSA-designated medical examiners are required to be trained and certified in accordance with the FMCSA's National Registry of Certified Medical Examiners. The determination of whether the driver is interstate (and therefore must meet federal medical standards) or intrastate (and therefore may meet state but not necessarily federal requirements, can still drive CMVs) is based on the material being transported, not where the individual drives.

When determining whether the individual meets the federal requirement, the medical examiner must review the medical standard but also consider other guidance issued by FMCSA such as medical advisory criteria, interpretations, and frequently asked questions (FAQs) and, until recently, the *Medical Examiner Handbook*. Other resources the examiner should review include FMCSA-sponsored Evidence Based Reviews, Medical Review Board (MRB) reports, and other medical literature.

For the case in question, the applicable medical standard and relevant portion of the medical advisory criteria are as follows:

> 49 CFR § 391.41(b)(4): A person is physically qualified to drive a commercial motor vehicle if that person; Has no current clinical diagnosis of myocardial infarction, angina pectoris, coronary insufficiency, thrombosis, or any other cardiovascular disease of a variety known to be accompanied by syncope, dyspnea, collapse, or congestive cardiac failure;

Medical Advisory Criteria

a) The term "has no current clinical diagnosis of" is specifically designed to encompass: "a clinical diagnosis of" a current cardiovascular condition, or a cardiovascular condition which has not fully stabilized regardless of the time limit. The term "known to be accompanied by" is designed to include a clinical diagnosis of a cardiovascular disease which is accompanied by symptoms of syncope, dyspnea, collapse or congestive cardiac failure; and/or which is s [sic] likely to cause syncope, dyspnea, collapse or congestive cardiac failure.

b) It is the intent of the Federal Motor Carrier Safety Regulations to render unqualified, a driver who has a current cardiovascular disease which is accompanied by and/or likely to cause symptoms of syncope, dyspnea, collapse, or congestive cardiac failure. However, the subjective decision of whether the nature and severity of an individual's condition will likely cause symptoms of cardiovascular insufficiency is on an individual basis and qualification rests with the medical examiner and the motor carrier. In those cases where there is an occurrence of cardiovascular insufficiency (myocardial infarction, thrombosis, etc.), it is suggested before a driver is certified that he or she have a normal resting and stress electrocardiogram, no residual complications and no physical limitations, and is taking no medication likely to interfere with safe driving.

c) Coronary artery bypass surgery and pacemaker implantation are remedial procedures and thus, not medically disqualifying. Implantable cardioverter defibrillators are disqualifying due to risk of syncope. Coumadin is a medical treatment which can improve the health and safety of the driver and should not, by its use, medically disqualify the commercial motor vehicle driver. The emphasis should be on the underlying medical condition(s) which require treatment and the general health of the driver. The Federal Motor Carrier Safety Administration should be contacted at (202) 366-4001 for additional recommendations regarding the physical qualification of drivers on coumadin.

The most recent approved guidance for returning to work from the FMCSA for a driver with myocardial infarction (MI) recommends that there should be a two-month wait and evaluation by a cardiologist prior to returning to commercial driving. The individual should have no significant side effects from medication. An echocardiogram should be done to assess ventricular function, and the ejection fraction (EF) should be at least 40 percent. An exercise tolerance test (ETT) was recommended four to six weeks (or could be done while in the hospital) after the MI and should be repeated at least every two years, more often if indicated. It was recommended that for the ETT to be acceptable, the individual should be able to reach 6 Metabolic Equivalents (METs; Bruce protocol Stage II or equivalent) and attain a heart rate greater than or equal to 85 percent. Upon returning to work, the driver who has had an MI should be recertified annually and should remain asymptomatic.

The medical examiner (physician) makes the final determination based on the individual's current status and guidance issued by FMCSA and current best practice, and considering the risk of sudden or gradual impairment or incapacitation over the duration of the certification issued.

In this case, the driver's personal physician appropriately declined to perform the CDME, as it must be conducted by a health-care provider on the NRCME. The driver would be required to meet FMCSA medical standards (interstate operations). The waiting period, ETT, and cardiac echocardiogram recommendations were met, and the driver could therefore be medically qualified for up to one year (provided there are no other medical issues that could impact medical qualification).

Accordingly, the driver returned to work with no difficulty once the correct procedure was followed.

A Commercial Driver for a Common Carrier with Positive Random Test for Marijuana

Natalie P. Hartenbaum

A 60-year-old bus driver for a regional public transit organization had a history of osteoarthritis. On a random FMCSA drug-screening test (otherwise known as a DOT drug screen), he tested positive for marijuana (tetrahydrocannabinol, THC). During the medical review officer (MRO) interview, he denied use of marijuana but reported that he uses pantoprazole for GERD and CBD (cannabidiol, cannabis oil) for his joint pain. The MRO explained that neither was a legitimate explanation for a positive result on a federal drug test and that the test would therefore be reported as positive. The employee was irate, sending both the MRO and the employer documentation that both pantoprazole (Protonix®, a proton pump inhibitor) and CBD could cause a positive test for marijuana.

The employer is seeking additional guidance from the MRO. The MRO authorized a confirmatory test (mass spectroscopy) on the urine sample, which is routinely retained by the testing laboratory. That confirmatory test, which is highly accurate, showed no evidence of THC.

He kept his job.

Comment: It is true that certain drugs can cross-react and cause a positive test for THC. Pure CBD does not, but there are many impurities in available CBD products that can.

Regardless of state law, federal law does not accept marijuana as a legal drug. DOT and FAA regulations prohibit use of marijuana in safety-sensitive positions, regardless of the legality of its recreational use in certain state jurisdictions. Therefore, a confirmed positive test would have been disqualifying for FMCSA CDME certification.

Tile Setter with Asthma

Tee L. Guidotti

The patient was a 40-year-old man who had his own business as a tile setter. He developed intermittent wheezing, cough, and shortness of breath while at work that gradually lasted longer and longer and interfered with his life after leaving work and changed its pattern. Lung function tests showed moderately severe reduction in airflow (obstruction), only partially reversible with bronchodilators. He was therefore treated for asthma. He continued to work as a tile setter because that was his business.

Over a period of a year, he required increasing bronchodilator medication to maintain his functional state and noticed the shortness of breath becoming steadier and persisted into the night. His shortness of breath tended to be worse in the evening and early morning and often awakened him from sleep. He noted that he was irritated by dusts, particularly those resulting from carpentry work and drywall installation at the construction projects where he was laying tiles. His condition was much worse in cold weather. Half-face mask cartridge respirators appeared to help but were difficult to wear for long periods in his work.

He had no known allergies. He has not smoked for 10 years, when he quit his 10–15 cigarettes per day habit. He relates that his breathing is better off work and on holiday, becoming abruptly worse over a period of several hours once he returns to work and gradually worsens over several days thereafter.

He kept a diary of his symptoms at the suggestion of the referring physician. He has found that his work habits profoundly affected his bronchospasm in that the longer he stays at the job site, whether supervising employees or doing the work himself, the worse his reaction, but if he limited his presence to only a couple of hours at a time, he could avoid the most severe attacks. The agents in the workplace, which appear to be most reliably associated with his bronchospasm episodes, are cedar dust, acrylic, and solvent-based glues. Latex (water-based) glues did not seem to trigger his response. Exposure to dust of any type, whether sawdust, drywall, dust, or cut-tile dust increased his cough but did not trigger asthmatic attacks and did not seem to be specific in their response.

Two issues remain to be clarified, however. The first is the contribution of nonallergic, irritant exposures to his airflow obstruction. The second is the degree of variability in his peak flow during the day. These issues need to be assessed in order to manage his condition because they determine whether he can remain at his job. If he is reacting to a specific agent, his problem might be managed by elimination of the agent from his working environment but is likely to continue if he cannot avoid it. If there is a nonspecific contribution from irritant agents, utilizing personal respiratory protection may solve the problem. Through the process of elimination (because direct testing can be tricky, and there is a risk of inducing sensitization), it was determined that he was sensitive (allergic) to bonding material used in setting the tile. Unfortunately, this is indispensable for the work.

By this time, he had other tile setters working for him but found that he could not visit locations where the tile was being installed or inspect their work without shortness of breath.

The implications were quite unfavorable. He is experiencing permanent partial disability from occupational asthma, and continued exposure to workplace antigens and irritants is likely to increase the severity and resistance to treatment of his asthma.

He filed a claim with the workers' compensation carrier, which was accepted. He was considered to be totally and permanently disabled from his usual occupation as a tile setter but able to work in other jobs. It was suggested that he investigate the possibility of wholesale or retail sale of specialty tiles or similar products. At this point, the worker's future employment prospects were no longer a medical problem.

When he was advised that he had to leave the trade in order to prevent long-term airways obstruction, he had to reevaluate his options. Fortunately, he had accumulated a nest egg and contacts in the industry and so went into business as a tile importer.

Comment: This worker has sensitizer-induced asthma, with the possibility of some exacerbation due to dust. Sensitizer-induced occupational asthma tends to be seen mostly in settings with a few chemicals (such as the isocyanates) that are present in many common products. Once established, it is difficult to control because although it responds to regular asthma treatment, the worker often cannot return to the job or any other setting in which the chemical is used. In the case of a nurse sensitized to latex, for example, that may mean sharply reduced career options. In the case of this worker, he had the resources to become a supplier to others in his field; few workers are as fortunate.

Occupational (work related) asthma is now the most common occupational respiratory disease in North America. It comes in three broad categories, sometimes with some overlap in a particular case: sensitizer-induced occupational asthma, irritant-induced occupational asthma, and work-exacerbated asthma. Sensitizer-induced asthma is caused by allergy to a particular low-molecular-weight chemical (such as trimellitic anhydride) or a particular large-molecular-weight substance, such as flour or latex. (Asthma is common among bakers.) Irritant-induced asthma is caused by a chemical irritant or concentration of dust that triggers nonspecific responses in the airways. Work-exacerbated asthma occurs when an individual with existing asthma experiences a return or worsening of symptoms due to exposure in the workplace. There are also special types of asthma with their own characteristics and conditions in which asthma is part of the reaction but not the main problem. Irritant-induced and exacerbated asthma can often be managed with improved ventilation or personal respiratory protection (respirators), but sensitizer-induced asthma is usually much harder to manage. It often takes very little of the sensitizing chemical to trigger the response, so that often the worker has to leave the job entirely.

This worker was suffering from one of several characteristic presentations of occupational asthma and would be classified as a late responder. That is, it behaves somewhat differently from the more familiar asthmatic response that is mediated by a classic acute allergic reaction. His primary response to inhaled agents is displaced by several hours and appears in the evenings instead of during the day. This is not uncommon and sometimes results in the patient initially presenting with the complaint of a sleep disorder.

Catastrophic Trauma from a Safety Hazard

Manijeh Berenji

The patient was a 20-year-old man who was working at a meat-processing plant shortly after his arrival as an undocumented worker from a rural area of El Salvador. He received no training in the safe operation of equipment before being assigned the seemingly simple task of loading a large grinder with meat.

The meat grinder he was using got stuck for some reason. In order to solve the problem, he turned off the apparatus and stepped onto the platform on which it was mounted, intending to dislodge the cutting blade. As he was trying to straighten out the blade, the meat grinder turned back on, and he stumbled. His leg was drawn into the grinder. Blood loss was severe.

He was transported to the nearest major trauma center, where a team of trauma, orthopedic, and vascular surgeons attempted to salvage his lower extremity, but it was too mangled. This was not possible and the surgeons had to perform a hemipelvectomy, in which the right leg and half of the pelvic girdle, including the hip, was removed. (Hemipelvectomy is an uncommon procedure for trauma and is normally performed for advanced cancer in the pelvis.) Being young and having no other medical problems, he recovered physically after the surgery and was provided with a prosthesis, so that he could walk with crutches. He underwent physical therapy and occupational therapy. Complicating his situation was the language barrier, since he spoke little English.

His employer was unable to accommodate his work restrictions, and no return to other work was possible due to his undocumented status. He returned to his home country six months after the injury, with limited prospects and an impoverished family.

Comment: This case is a dramatic and tragic illustration of a common problem, complicated by many social factors.

Undocumented workers do not have the protection of workers' compensation (or other health insurance), a contract with employers specifying conditions of work or return to work after injury, or reliable enforcement of occupational health and safety regulations. Their ability to protect themselves is also limited by language barriers, lack of education, and often by cultural barriers and neglect. In this case, he was assigned to unsafe work, and when a problem arose, he tried to solve it himself in the only way he knew how, with horrendous results. A highly disproportionate number of fatalities or serious injuries occur among workers who are new on the job.

In a workplace with a functioning safety program, the unsafe conditions would have been corrected by a safety professional, there would have been more management oversight, worker training would be required, and there would be standard procedures (called "lockout or tag out") to ensure that power was cut off, access was restricted, and equipment was locked in a safe position before any attempt was made to correct a mechanical problem.

Now he returns to a community ill-equipped to meet his needs and itself in crisis, where he is unlikely ever to support himself.

An Endemic Infectious Disease Causes an Occupational Illness

Chang Rim Na

A 53-year-old male corrections officer who works at a prison in the San Joaquin Valley of California presented with a history of fever, nonproductive cough, and chills. He also complained of diffuse muscle aches in both ankles without any swelling or history of trauma. Physical examination was unremarkable except for tachycardia (fast heart rate) at 100/min. His respiratory rate was 26/minute, which is nearly panting. His lab results were normal, with one test pending. Chest film showed bilateral pulmonary infiltrate without pleural effusion (consistent with a limited pneumonia-like condition).

A serologic (antibody-detection) test for coccidioidomycosis eventually returned and showed that IgM as well as IgG were elevated. The diagnosis of coccidioidomycosis was made, and the patient was started on fluconazole (Diflucan®). The patient filed a workers' compensation claim on the basis that his outdoor exposure as a correctional officer was the cause of his illness. He stated that outside of work he did not engage in gardening or activities involving digging and did not moonlight doing construction work.

When asked for details about his occupational history, he stated that he often works outdoors as a correctional officer while monitoring inmates in the exercise yards and accompanying them while they do roadside work where the conditions are dusty. He reported that for about a month before his symptom onset, the prison yards had also experienced some high winds. Workplace inquiry revealed that several other workers at the prison had acquired coccidioidomycosis in the similar time frame. Based on these findings, it was determined that, within reasonable medical probability, his exposure to coccidioidomycosis was work related (occupational or "industrial"), and his claim was accepted.

His symptoms slowly improved, but he had lingering fatigue for months. He had become deconditioned, losing strength and stamina during his recovery. He was referred to physical therapy for "work hardening" (a type of physical therapy that emphasizes strength and capacity building to match the job the worker will eventually return to). After completing work hardening, he was eventually able to return to full duty as a correctional officer.

Comment: As discussed in chapter 3, the occupational health professions typically recognize work-related hazards as being physical (including physical energy, mechanical, and ergonomic), chemical, biological, or psychosocial. However, some hazards are tied to location, where they often cluster with other common or severe local hazards. *Coccidiodes immitis* is a fungus that is found in soil in many arid parts of the world but particularly in the Central Valley of California and the southern Sonoran Desert of Arizona and northwestern Mexico. The disease can be completely asymptomatic (but with telltale changes on chest film), a flu-like disease (called "Valley fever") or rarely a life-threatening disseminated (general) infection. It is certainly a biological hazard, but not one that arises directly from work. It occurs most often when the ground is disturbed by construction, agriculture, gardening, or archaeology. Therefore, it is more useful to think of it as a disease of location than a biological hazard related to the work process.

Correctional officers maintain order and supervise inmates in prisons and jails. They are at high risk for workplace violence and injury as well as exposure to communicable disease. These communicable diseases had historically included tuberculosis and HIV/AIDS but, more recently, COVID-19.

Cancer in a Firefighter

Tee L. Guidotti

A 45-year-old professional firefighter and hazardous materials (hazmat) responder had worked in this occupation for 13 years. He was in robust good health until he developed a refractory headache and intermittently blurry vision, which progressed over four months. These symptoms turned out to be a metastatic tumor to the brain. This was treated with steroids to shrink the tumor, while his physicians searched to find the primary, which was in the kidney and was confirmed on biopsy to be renal cell carcinoma. He was treated with nephrectomy to debulk the tumor, giving him a chance of palliation with radiation therapy and interleukin immunotherapy.

His past medical history included the following: In 2008, he had passed a kidney stone. He never smoked. He had not reported to have abused alcohol, analgesics, or prescription drugs. He did not have diabetes or hypertension. There was no family history of renal cell cancer, only breast cancer in female relatives.

He submitted a workers' compensation claim for recognition of his tumor as an occupational cancer. The claim was initially rejected but then accepted on appeal with submission of supporting documentation, including published scientific papers.

He died of his cancer about six months later.

Comment: In analyzing the causes of an occupational disease, such as cancer, there are two steps. The first is "general causation": Is it possible for the exposure to cause the disease in question? The second is "specific causation": Is it more likely than not (the usual standard) in this particular case?

There is considerable evidence that firefighters are at increased risk for some cancers, including renal cell carcinoma. This is not surprising because despite utilizing respiratory protection, firefighters are exposed (via inhalation and skin absorption) to a variety of carcinogens associated with fire smoke and with diesel exhaust. It is also well established that many of these same exposures are specifically linked to renal cell carcinoma. Thus, although the issue continues to be disputed, the weight of evidence therefore appeared to be satisfied for general causation. However, demonstrating general causation often requires extensive literature review and expert opinions.

Hydrocarbon compounds, known as polycyclic aromatic hydrocarbons (PAHs) are present in combustion materials and include several specific carcinogens: benzo(a)pyrene, chrysene, benzo(a)anthracene, benzo(b)fluoranthene, dibenzo(a,h)anthracene, dibenzopyrene, and 5-methylchrysene. These occur in mixtures as products of incomplete, low-temperature combustion, never as individual compounds in isolation. PAHs are found in high concentrations in soot, which is the large-particle phase of smoke, and are absorbed through the skin. Other confirmed carcinogenic compounds to which firefighters are exposed include benzene and its associated "solvent" chemicals, trichloroethylene (which is known to be present in fire smoke but its levels are poorly measured), asbestos, and dioxin (a powerful cancer promoter). Evidence is also strengthening for perfluorooctanoic acid, which is present in flame-suppressing foam previously used in firefighting and is now being withdrawn. The International Agency for Research on Cancer (IARC) recognizes the carcinogenic potential of these chemicals and of exposures related to firefighting work in general.

Specific causation is more difficult in this case but is made somewhat easier because other exposures such as cigarette smoking and risk factors such as hypertension and obesity are not present in the history.

The most difficult question in this case was whether sufficient time had elapsed since his first exposure. Ordinarily, it is assumed that a solid tumor takes 20 years from initiation to clinical detection, but this "latency period" is in fact highly variable, and for some cancers, including renal cell carcinoma, the latency can be relatively short, especially when there has been heavy exposure in the early years of exposure. Therefore, a causal association could not be discounted in this case. The workers' compensation appeals board decided to accept it.

Claims in cases such as this are almost always challenged by employers or their insurance companies. The rule to be followed in almost every such case is whether it is more likely than not ("to a reasonable medical certainty" or "reasonable medical probability") that an exposure at work caused or contributed to the cause of the condition. This is inevitably countered with the argument that there is no proof of causation in the individual case. It is impossible to prove causation in such cases beyond a doubt since one cannot go into the DNA of a person to determine what happened 20 years before. Such disputed cases require opinions from experts with extensive documentation and analyses.

Such preparation rapidly becomes very expensive, which largely defeats the purpose of workers' compensation, which was invented in part as a way to streamline the process and make it more accessible to workers with limited resources. For this reason, most states have passed "presumption" legislation for firefighters and police, which in most cases leads to automatic acceptance of such claims unless there is a clear alternative cause.

CHAPTER TEN

Core Controversies

Tee L. Guidotti

This chapter does not focus on specific issues with respect to occupational and environmental hazards, although some are used as examples, rather on the systemic lines of tension and long-standing controversies that define the field. Occupational and environmental medicine (OEM) is a lively field for value-laden controversies. Such controversies are less often about medical practice, however, than about mission and responsibility, ethics, levels of safety and protection, justice and compensation, and the social role of (specifically) occupational medicine, not to mention the risk of specific hazards and how best to manage them.

OEM as a "Critical Science"

OEM is a paramount example of what has been called "critical science," although it is not usually discussed in those terms. Critical science can be described as the "mode" of science that acts for the public interest and documents problems of technology and society, using scientific approaches to do so. Other examples include ecology and environmental sciences, technology assessment, complexity theory (especially as applied to so-called wicked problems, in which attempts at a solution change the nature of the problem), and sociotechnical systems (where both social or cultural change and technological change are required to solve problems). Although the term is usually applied to highly complicated and charged environmental issues such as climate change, the deeply enmeshed issues of economics, social justice, acceptable risk, and technology may be considered a wicked problem by the strict definition.

Scientists and the public usually make a sharp distinction between two modes of science: basic and applied science. Basic, in this sense, does not mean "simple"; it means "fundamental." Basic science is often thought of as science for its own sake. Applied science is the application of science to achieve an intended goal. It builds on basic science and contributes to technology and engineering by finding ways to apply scientific knowledge and research methods to solve concrete problems. Technology, taking up where applied science leaves off, develops the science into a specific application or product. These two modes of science are well recognized, although they are not as separate as is generally assumed. However, there are other possible modes of science. One of them is a science that would document abuses or problems arising out of technology and social actions and monitor the effectiveness of solutions. That is critical science.

The prominent philosopher of science Jerome R. Ravetz (b. 1929, American working in the United Kingdom), described critical science in the 1960s as an emerging mode of science and conceived of it as a critique of technology and applied science using the methods of basic science (meaning fundamental science without reference to immediate application). Critical science is more like basic science than applied science because it is fundamentally about discovery and solving a puzzle rather than achieving an objective or application. What defines it as critical science is that the problem under study is of human creation and results from advances (real and apparent) in technology. Critical science can perhaps best be understood as the use of basic (fundamental) science to provide a check and correction on unrestrained, ineffective, or harmful tendencies of technology and applied science. In this sense, it is feedback on where technological innovation and development are taking society, the economy, and human health.

Science itself can be a check on the misapplication of science and technology. The premiere example of critical science, which inspired new thinking on the role of science, was a set of studies undertaken in 1961 by physicians Eric and Louise Reiss (1920–2011), assisted by the then-unknown environmental scientist Barry Commoner (1917–2012) and other colleagues. They collected baby teeth from American children in St. Louis to demonstrate that levels of strontium-90 bound in the teeth had risen steadily as a result of above-ground nuclear weapons testing during the Cold War and then spiked abruptly and massively after 1963 as a result of atmospheric testing in the Pacific. The results persuaded the American president John F. Kennedy and Soviet Union premier Nikita Khrushchev to conclude the first Nuclear Test Ban Treaty in that year. The "Baby Tooth Project" became the nucleus for organizing several early nonprofit environmental groups concerned with sustainability—most notably, the Scientists' Institute for Public Information, which included such eminent names as anthropologist Margaret Mead (1901–1978) and microbiologist Rene Dubos (1901–1982), both of whom were highly influential advocates of science as a critique of technology and society and its use in supporting advocacy. On the occupational medicine side, the work of Alice Hamilton (see chapter 1) is likewise an example of critical science. She was far from opposing technological and economic progress—far from it—but she used the methods of science to identify problems that required technical solutions and regulations to minimize harm, manage risk, and allow that progress to continue without unacceptable cost.

Basic science is the mode of science that pursues the development of new knowledge and is driven internally by problems and issues that arise from the discipline. Basic science is not just a matter of making discoveries and piecing together bits of information. Basic science accumulates facts and builds models of the universe as a means to an end, which is a more complete understanding of the material world. Practical applications certainly arise in abundance from basic science, but attempts to channel basic science into desired outcomes ultimately defeat the purpose because they tend to impede exploration that results in new insights. These new insights, supported by empirical evidence, piece together a worldview that provides a more complete map of reality, a more stable platform from which to begin explaining things, and a point of departure for practical applications. Sound basic science is based on a process of probative testing of sequential hypotheses and ruling out what is not true (called "falsification"), because it is contrary to the evidence obtained in an experiment or through observation.

Applied science works toward an external goal or useful application, such as cure for a disease or an advance in biotechnology or an engineering breakthrough or a new product. In every case, applied science lays the groundwork for technology by building on knowledge and the conceptual framework created by basic science. Because applied science is narrowly channeled and directed toward an objective, it is not very good at achieving new insights, although there are occasionally unexpected discoveries. It is also not very good at anticipating adverse consequences: in practice, in fact, people in the field tend to be relentlessly optimistic. The adverse consequences of a new chemical introduced into the workplace, a new process that works in the lab but is rushed to the factory floor, or a newly designed facility or chemical that causes environmental pollution are often difficult to predict and even more often simply overlooked in the drive to get the job done. The very strength of applied science, which is that it is goal oriented, limits its capacity to open new doors.

The most naive view of science assumes that the individual unit of scientific progress is the discovery and that progress is incremental and builds on an accumulation of facts. It assumes that the scientific literature is the place where all of this is written down. The reality is that science is about proving reasonable conjectures (hypotheses) false and then moving on to the next hypothesis until the general outlines of what is true are exposed. It is not heaping up a bunch of facts and drawing an inference; that is the way one makes the hypotheses but not how one tests them.

Conventionally, the popular view of scientific research is that it is a systematic way of gathering facts: methodical, logical, coherent, comprehensive, and dispassionate. The process of generalizing from facts (induction) provides the usual image of scientific discovery held by nonscientists, for whom experimentation is basically seen as an exploration to see what can be found. Emotion and belief should not play much of a role, except to motivate the scientist. Science is seen by most people who do not do it as progressing toward an objective or end result accumulating facts to "prove" a particular truth or to validate a theory. A "breakthrough" is a new discovery or observation that leads to new understanding by making known a previously unknown fact. The scientific community is believed to be grounded in these objective facts and therefore should demonstrate consensus on important principles. The public perceives objective truth as immutable and the scientific method as a progression toward increasing certainty in describing reality. These ideas are stereotypes and only half-truths. For one thing, there has to be a reason to do research, so the investigator who does the work does not begin complete free of expectations and incentives; there also has to be a reason for someone to pay for doing the work. Most new chemicals or potential exposures are hardly investigated at all for health effects, unless there is suspicion. In OEM research, that is usually because there is reason to suspect that something is a hazard, so it can be evaluated, replaced, or regulated.

One of the enduring metaphors of science is exploring the darkness with a lantern. Science is actually more like exploring a deep cave with a flashlight instead of the diffuse light of a lantern. One sees what is in the narrow beam of light, not the big picture. Funding agencies, even those that fund basic research, mostly want results and solutions to problems. They want what is in the beam of the flashlight; what remains in darkness remains so. If a scientific topic is not very interesting or is not well funded or has never been highly controversial, basic knowledge is usually lacking. There are, therefore, huge gaps of ignorance lying in-between the well-supported or commercially attractive domains of scientific investigation.

Skepticism—disagreement with advocacy positions in either sustainability or health—is the hallmark of science. A skeptical attitude toward the argument, the facts, and the framework does not necessarily mean rejection. Good scientists must be skeptical: skepticism is an essential characteristic of science that sets it apart from belief and other ways of knowing. All too often, advocates interpret penetrating questions or critical comments or expressions of disbelief to mean rejection of their cause or issue, when they are actually invitations to prove or bolster the argument. However, there is also a tendency, very clear in the history of occupational and environmental health research and OEM, that junk science emerges to undermine, bias, or deny the scientific process.

Good policy and good decision-making must be based on sound science. In OEM and other technical affairs, good policy and responsible actions depend on sound science. If the science behind it is sound, there is no guarantee that the policy will be good and effective, but it is more likely to be. If the science behind it is poor, then the policy will not work, because even if by dumb luck the right option is chosen, it cannot be justified, and so in the face of opposition, the decision probably will not stand.

Scientists can inform the debate but cannot expect to control it, nor does society want them to. Scientists are not technocrats, who make decisions in their expert wisdom: they are creators of public knowledge for the purpose of understanding the world. It is by a process of assertion and counterassertion on a broad scale, often with disappointingly little information, that our society makes decisions and sets out on its path toward social action. The OEM physician, therefore, needs skepticism and critical skills, like training in epidemiology, toxicology, and risk science, to navigate the uncertainty and to know what to do and advise. The OEM physician must also understand the problem facing workers and community residents who are at risk. This is why the effective OEM physician, especially those working at the second and tertiary tier of practice (see chapter 7) must be deeply science literate as well as clinically competent (see chapter 5 for some examples).

The field of OEM research is a hot spot for problems with the integrity of science and, as a consequence, a constant arena for controversy, questioning, challenge to motives, and dueling experts. However, as distressing as this can be at times, real problems are being addressed. Scientific research, properly conducted and interpreted in good faith, is still the best guide available to resolving problems in OEM (see chapters 12 and 13).

Mission and Responsibility

OEM is a little more complicated than other specialties and specializations in other fields of medical practice. Medicine, in general, is focused on providing diagnosis, treatment, and preventive care to individuals who are sick and injured. Everyone understands this. Public health is focused on keeping people healthy and functional, in groups, as a population or community. OEM does both. OEM is also more focused than most of medicine on documenting exactly what happened, the circumstances in which the events happened, how it affected the injured worker or the environment, and how to prevent the problem from happening again. Not so many people understand this.

In occupational medicine (the "occupational" side of OEM), the "treating physician" is the name given to the provider who actually renders care (diagnosis and treatment) to the injured worker. The treating physician might be an OEM physician but is much more likely to be a family physician, an emergency medicine physician, or a surgeon. The OEM physician is more likely to play a role in workers' compensation, in the management of the case by the employer, or in determining if health and safety regulations have been followed. The OEM physician is indeed very concerned with diagnosis and treatment but is more directly involved in determining the cause of the injury, rehabilitation, the long-term prognosis, and safe return to work. This sometimes leads to misunderstandings when primary-care physicians think that their immediate care of the injured worker is all there is to "occupational medicine"—they may even call themselves practitioners of "occupational medicine" when what they are doing is only a small (but necessary) piece of the big picture.

Quality of medical care is one area that all practitioners can agree on: better care has better results. In occupational medicine, this means early and safe return to work with no or minimal residual impairment. Occupational medicine was among the very first medical specialties to formulate comprehensive guidelines for how injuries and acute illness should be treated and managed in order to get the best results and minimize the risk of permanent disability. Some physicians do not like this, however, and are very vocal about their disagreement. They may feel that they are "being told" what to do, that their personal discretion as professionals is constrained, or that they are being forced to standardize the provision of care without regard to differences from case to case. However, the reason for guidelines, and their general (if sometimes reluctant) acceptance by most health-care providers, is that they do get better results, the right tests get done, and the right information is collected and that injured workers can know what to expect.

Ethics in Occupational Medicine

The same ethical framework that applies to OEM is shared with other professions concerned with the protection of the health of workers and people living in a community, but the most controversy usually comes from the occupational side. The emphasis in this section is on ethics in occupational medicine. The issues on the environmental side are not unique to medicine or even human health, except for environmental justice. This chapter does not cover the ethics of environmental health, as this is a vast field that is well beyond the scope of this book, incorporating: environmental ethics (which centers on environmental justice and displacement of costs and losses from those who profit onto communities that do not benefit), "deep ecology" (as opposed to anthropocentrism), ecological ethics (which may recognize the planet itself as an entity), the ethics of specific environmental health professions (such as epidemiology and toxicology), and the many schools of thought that address ethics in environment from different points of view (religious traditions, ecofeminism, cultural traditions). Each has rich literature and is widely discussed elsewhere.

Medical ethics is intended to be universal, but its application is not immutable or free of cultural bias. Two generations ago, for example, it was considered unethical to alarm patients who "could not handle it" with a cancer diagnosis or to prescribe agents of limited therapeutic value more often seen by society as drugs of abuse, such as cannabis. Now we are more direct with patients, and palliation allows such practices because abuse is not an issue. There are numerous other examples of changes in the interpretation of ethics in medicine.

Medical ethics applies, of course, also to occupational medicine, but clarifying the nature of the ethical problem is often more difficult in OEM than in general medicine because of the legal context, the trade-offs among the legitimate interests of various parties, and the number of stakeholders involved. Occupational medicine has had many years to grapple with ethical problems and has developed an extensive and well-documented literature on bioethical guidelines.

Ethics in the tradition of Western philosophy derives from two traditions: deontology (normative, or absolute) and utilitarianism (consequence based, or relative). The traditions weigh competing ethical duties differently. Most ethics in medical and health professions is deontological, derived from a shared sense of absolute commitment to patient autonomy, doing no harm, striving to do good, and distributive justice (table 10.1). From these principles flow subsidiary ethical rules such as truthfulness, privacy, confidentiality, and fidelity. Occupational health protection, however, often requires relativism and utilitarianism because at its core are fundamental problems of balancing interests and rights. Medicine, in general, has continued to favor deontological ethics, but in the modern world of health-care delivery, legitimate interests are increasingly balanced against one another: what the person receiving health-care services (traditionally a "patient," but now considered a "client") needs, what that person wants, how much care will cost, who will authorize it, the public health risks to others, who is entitled to information, and who is empowered to make decisions about providing for and paying for care. The traditional physician-patient relationship (see chapter 7) has been modified for general medicine by managed care and for occupational medicine by workers' compensation, regulation, and case management. For occupational medicine, the deontological approach has likewise proven inadequate.

Table 10.1   The four principles of deontological medical ethics

- There should be respect for the autonomy of the individual ("autonomy").

- Physicians should do no harm ("nonmalfeasance").

- Physicians should strive to do good ("beneficence").

- All individuals have equal rights and responsibilities ("distributive justice").

The bioethical framework in occupational medicine is more complicated than in personal health care, in part, because there are many more parties with a legitimate interest in actions and information regarding workplace hazards, worker injuries, and level of disability, if any, resulting from an injury. The absolutes of the deontological approach cannot balance the legitimate competing interests of all parties. There are also issues of the individual interest of the worker and the common good of the workforce and society with respect to information provided to government regulatory agencies (mostly federal and state occupational health and safety agencies). In occupational medicine, the practitioner often has multiple responsibilities to the worker, to the employer, to insurers (mostly workers' compensation carriers), and to government regulatory agencies. For most, but not all, injuries and illnesses, the workers' compensation system, a no-fault insurance plan, imposes its own rules and procedures and requires sharing of information.

The person being provided the service may not even necessarily be a patient, because so many services are provided for prevention, fitness for duty, and surveillance. In occupational medicine and occupational health nursing, the health-care provider may not have a *patient-provider relationship* with the recipient of care at all. In general, the legal test for the presence of a patient-provider relationship is whether there is an expectation of treatment, the patient stands to benefit individually (not just as a member of a group) from the service, and the employer did not initiate the evaluation or service (and was therefore not in the role of "customer" or "client"). The ethical test would be similar. Many services, such as independent medical evaluations for workers' compensation claims are intended to document necessary information on a case rather than to provide treatment, and the physician may not always accept what the injured worker says as accurate.

Codes of ethics now exist for all the occupational health professions (and for many others that only incidentally touch on occupational health). They are consistent in emphasizing seven basic obligations:

- To provide a safe and healthy workplace environment for the worker
- To maintain professional competence
- To report problems and advise on solutions

- Employers to maintain the confidentiality of the worker's medical records
- To avoid being placed in conflicts of interest
- To avoid discrimination, intended or otherwise
- To maintain ethical standards of professional behavior

Ethical codes such as the American College of Occupational and Environmental Medicine's Code of Ethics explicitly or implicitly address these basics, and so do other medical societies and the codes of other occupational health professions. They do not necessarily coincide in all the details nor are interpreted the same way from profession to profession and country to country. Some small risks exist that they will contradict. There is also a consensus code that informs and subordinates these individual codes: the International Code of Ethics for Occupational Health Professionals (2011). This overriding code is promulgated and kept up to date by the International Commission on Occupational Health (ICOH) (http://www.icohweb.org/core_docs/code_ethics_eng.pdf). The international code applies to any professional who works in the domain of occupational health and applies to the standard of practice and ethics for every profession or discipline touching on occupational health.

Relativism, which is sometimes used in a pejorative sense, holds that ethical principles are meaningful only in relation to one another and to the facts of the situation. It accepts that there may be conflicting obligations and conflicts between legitimate but competing rights and responsibilities. In medicine generally, especially primary care, physicians are taught that the desired interest of the patient and his or her family is foremost and that care is centered on the patient. In occupational medicine, the facts have primacy. For example, the information obtained may argue against a disability claim or time off work or return to work. The OEM physicians is likely to follow the facts and interpret the uncertainties one way, whereas others may feel an obligation to advocate and interpret the uncertainties another way. Relativistic ethics is the only clear way to resolve these issues, but the nature and priority of competing obligations and rights must be clear. Therefore, much of the ethics of occupational health involves analyzing a given situation to identify these competing interests.

There are no great bioethical issues raised by malfeasance on the part of employers or failure to protect workers—it is simply and unambiguously wrong. Just as a serious and unequivocal crime does not raise issues of legal interpretation, willful neglect or intentional failure to comply with occupational health and safety regulation does not raise issues of ethics. They simply cannot be defended. The great scandals of the past and those emerging in the present, such as suppression of scientific information on hazards such as beryllium and asbestos, failure to inform workers of their exposure to serious hazards, and cover-ups of health outcomes among employees, have no ethical defense. Similarly, violations of occupational health standards and safe practices are not deep ethical problems: they are wrongful acts, whether infractions, negligence, or willful crimes, and they are to be dealt with under the law, not argued about.

When a workplace injury occurs, it is a legal requirement that it be reported. It may be reported by the employer or, more often, by the physician who attended the injured worker (on the form universally called the "doctor's report"). This sets into motion an imperfect adjudication system that relies on accurate reports and information to function fairly.

Some employers underreport injuries or suppress information on severity. It is not uncommon for employers to push occupational health professionals to treat minor injuries on-site as "first aid," even if the injury should be seen in an emergency room or to put pressure on the physician not to place restrictions on the worker in writing so that the injury will not be "recordable" (on OSHA's 300A form). Some employers even ask injured workers to show up anyway when they should be recuperating and have them do light-duty tasks or even sit in a corner doing nothing productive in order to avoid having to report a "lost-time injury" to OSHA or their workers' compensation carrier. Employers that do this often have poor safety performance and do so because they are afraid that an OSHA inspection will count these issues against them, uncover new problems, or that their premiums for workers' compensation coverage will go up. Failure to report injuries is a major reason that the injury count has fallen dramatically (but falsely) in recent years and explains why fatalities on the job have not decreased proportionately. Fatalities cannot be hidden or easily explained away by another cause.

The truly sensitive issues in occupational medicine come when there are competing interests that are legitimate. Given the complexities and particularistic nature of these relationships, occupational health presents unique ethical issues that have only approximate counterparts elsewhere in medicine and bioethics.

Some issues are so fraught that there is special legislation governing the use or acquisition of medical information. For example, the Genetic Information Nondiscrimination Act of 2008 restricts the use of genetic biomarkers, family history, and genetic testing to prevent abuse, discrimination, and screening for employment and fitness for duty.

The employer is responsible for providing a safe and healthy workplace (a legal requirement in the United States under the Occupational Safety and Health Act) and is almost always held to a higher ethical and legal standard than the employee, who holds little power in the relationship. The employer needs to have a well-defined and explicit policy, and there needs to be a systematic program for carrying out that policy. The employment relationship is not only an economic one but a fiduciary relationship in which employers have a responsibility to the worker to maintain a safe workplace. A physician employed by a company has a limited—highly circumscribed—fiduciary role to that company, restricted by individual confidentiality, and normally navigated by providing group information in which individuals cannot be recognized or challenged by an imminent (not theoretical) risk of harm to others. There are frequent situations in occupational medicine when a conflict is entirely legitimate, such as the duty of the physician to record information accurately even if it disqualifies a worker from a safety-sensitive position or pension eligibility and to disclose unfitness for duty (but not the diagnosis) against the worker's will. Some of the ethical conflict is hidden behind a legal solution in the form of contract law, since employers may require compliance with occupational health surveillance and protection, or under statutory law—for example, governing safety-sensitive positions in interstate common carriers.

A physician may have a physician-patient relationship with a worker at one time but not necessarily at another—particularly, if the health provider is a treating physician in the community but sees the worker on another occasion for independent medical evaluation or fitness-for-duty evaluation. Such situations sometimes cannot be avoided, especially where the medical community is small, but the physician should still respect the limits of his or her role.

Occupational health professionals are expected to maintain confidentiality of personal and business information but must not withhold information necessary to protect the safety and health of workers or the community. This means that medical information is often widely shared in occupational medicine, as it is in insurance evaluations, independent medical evaluations (common in occupational medicine but also in tort litigation), utilization review, forensic medicine or under subpoena, and operational (combat) medicine in the military. It is a natural consequence of the role of the physician in data gathering for health protection, documentation, decision-making, and conflict resolution. The OEM physician has a responsibility, however, to control this to the extent possible and to ensure that information is not improperly shared, particularly with employers, and without legal authority.

Confidential health information is provided to licensed health professionals with the understanding that it will be kept confidential and never shared with management without the worker's explicit permission or a legal requirement to do so. The employer is not entitled to know the diagnosis of the worker's personal health problems or the medical cause of a limiting condition of a candidate for employment. Unless the injury or illness arose as the result of work, for which this information must be shared as part of the workers' compensation claims process, the diagnosis is not to be disclosed without permission of the worker. Health-care providers who are not trained in occupational health often violate this confidentiality in reporting fitness to work, not knowing it is wrong to do so. Large employers with well-trained human resource departments generally do know not to request confidential health information regarding workers. Some managers still obtain this information inappropriately, and it is hard to keep secrets in smaller workplaces.

Managers for the employer are entitled only to a statement of *fitness for duty*, for which there are only three acceptable options: whether the employee is (1) *fit* to work in their usual job duties, (2) *unfit*, or (3) *fit with accommodation*, which then requires or obliges the employer (when invoked under the Americans with Disabilities Act [ADA] and similar legislation) to determine whether a "reasonable accommodation" can be made. A "reasonable accommodation" is a practical adaptation that can be made at a cost appropriate to the resources of the business, such as a hearing device, a change in work hours or location, or special protections or magnifying devices for the visually impaired. Accommodation, where feasible, is a legal requirement under ADA. The worker's individual functional capacities and disabilities should be considered, with accommodation to remove barriers to full participation, to the extent feasible, for disabled workers.

Workers' compensation is a no-fault insurance system that provides health care and income replacement for workers injured on the job, for the period of recovery for those who are temporarily disabled, or as an award proportionate to the rated degree of impairment and to employability for those who are permanently disabled. OEM physicians have a responsibility to collect objective information. Without this assurance, the system cannot weigh the evidence properly; there is no right, duty, or privilege to share or withhold information to favor the injured worker.

There is often a hidden divide between OEM physicians and the "treating physician" (in workers' compensation vocabulary), who usually sees the injured worker as a "patient," like others in their practice, and naturally wants to keep the "patient" happy. (This is especially true when health-care systems closely monitor patient satisfaction ratings.) Treating physicians, who are the workers' personal or treating physician, understandably identify and side with their patient, especially if they do not know the workplace. This is particularly likely to occur if the physician believes, as many do, sometimes with justification, that insurance companies and employers are biased against the injured worker. Sometimes, treating physicians are reluctant to get involved in the paperwork, and occasionally, they exaggerate or intentionally misrepresent details in the belief that they are acting as "advocates for their patients." The net effect, however, is to further complicate an imperfect system, engender additional mistrust, and undermine the integrity of the system.

Sometimes what a worker wants is also not in their own interests or in the interest of others. Examples include driving a vehicle with poor eyesight or an uncontrolled seizure disorder, workers in safety-sensitive positions who have a sleep disorder, law enforcement officers with suicidal or homicidal ideation, or persons who operate heavy equipment but are at risk of sudden incapacitation from medical cause. As in any provider-patient relationship, the ethical principle is that neither the *confidentiality of medical information* nor the duty to warn others of possible risk is absolute, but disclosure of confidential information without permission is only acceptable in cases of imminent and serious physical harm. To the maximum extent possible, the OEM physician tries to avoid such situations, persuading the worker to disclose the information voluntarily or by making a judgment of "unfit" for duty (without disclosing the cause to the employer—it may be required to be disclosed to a legal or regulatory authority). This situation is usually easier when it involves driving a vehicle that requires a driver's license, because of laws requiring impairment to be reported to the state.

Working outside a patient-provider relationship is the norm in insurance practice, screening examinations for participation in sports, and medical forensics and occurs frequently in occupational health but is unusual in other health-care settings. The ideal is "pure objectivity," in which the physician or other professional is playing the role of disinterested expert obtaining facts and evaluating the case dispassionately, much as a forensic expert might. A clear example of this ideal is when a physician (of any specialization) is asked to conduct an "independent medical evaluation" (IME) to offer an opinion in a workers' compensation case, but not for treatment. It also occurs when the physician is reviewing test results for surveillance or health monitoring and not for diagnosis or patient care or when fitness for duty is evaluated. In such cases, there is no physician-patient relationship, but there is always an overriding ethical obligation to provide care in an emergency—for example, if a worker has an acute medical event during an examination and to inform the worker of findings when a test indicates a serious medical problem of which the worker is unaware. The physician has an obligation to inform the worker when no physician-patient relationship exists and the implications. For example, when an IME is performed, the opinion is not shared directly by the physician with the worker (who in such situations is normally a claimant or plaintiff), and no treatment will be offered, unless there is an emergency in the course of the evaluation, and medical advice is usually not offered unless there is a finding suggesting an imminent health threat of which the worker is unaware.

This has given rise to the idea of "dual capacity" and the physician (or other occupational health professional) as "dual agent," with an ethical responsibility to both the worker and to a third party, usually the employer or an insurer. Dual capacity has been the source of numerous allegations of conflict of interest in the past, and many occupational physicians have failed to balance their responsibilities as dual agents wisely, either always siding with the employer or favoring the worker, instead of following the evidence and the facts of the case. However, dual capacity is always a balancing act, and conflicts arise inevitably when health professionals are brought into an organization to protect the health of workers and to resolve health-related issues. Situations of dual capacity are more difficult to navigate in a corporate setting, because the occupational health provider's "customer" or "client" clearly has an interest in the outcome that cannot be separated from the employment status of the health professional. It is, therefore, essential that the worker be informed unambiguously that the physician or other professional is acting in the service of the third party and what his or her role is. This disclosure should be documented, for legal protection. The OEM physician should then act with professional detachment and objectivity, given his or her role.

Third parties often have legitimate interests in the health of workers. Employers have a right to know whether an employee is fit for the duties of the job (but not to know their diagnosis, if any), whether an employee is fit to return to work after an absence (whether work related or not), and whether the test results of employees (as a group) suggest a hazard in the workplace that is not adequately controlled. Workers' compensation claims may be disputed and the claimant, the employer, and the carrier are all entitled to relevant health information about the injured worker. Government agencies have a right to access information to ensure that laws and regulations are complied with. In these situations, the worker, whether a patient or not, cannot prevent sharing of information, within narrow definitions of relevancy.

The relationship between worker and health-care provider (physician or nurse) is also governed by authority other than ethics: laws, occupational health and safety regulations, workers' compensation rules and procedures (backed by a decentralized body of workers' compensation law), and contract obligations between the employer and the employee.

Issues in Environmental Medicine

As stated often in this book, the role of environmental medicine is still being sorted out within OEM. That it is indivisible with occupational medicine in theory is clear, but how it relates in practice is not. Environmental medicine lacks a payment or compensation system like workers' compensation and does not have anything like the clinical and specialist networks that serve occupational cases. The environmental side of OEM is currently driven by compliance with public health and pollution regulations, "toxic tort" legal actions (especially class action lawsuits), and research on environmental problems.

The most salient and refractory controversy on the environmental side of OEM pertains to "chemical sensitivity" and illness without reliable diagnostic features (see chapter 3). The scientific issue is whether there is disease, collection of diseases, or mechanism of injury from environmental exposure that does not follow conventional understanding of toxicology, immunology, behavior, or infectious disease. It is certain, however, that there are many patients (using the term advisedly) who do come to the physician's office with nonspecific complaints such as fatigue, inability to concentrate (often called "brain fog"), and highly variable (and often inconsistent) symptoms that, at times, cannot be connected to physical signs and who generally show no evidence of disease on clinical tests. "Nonspecific illness" is a term increasingly used in mainstream medicine as a rubric for such patients. The management of nonspecific illness is a very common problem in medical practice generally, but such patients often, perhaps usually, seek an explanation in the environment they live in for why they do not feel well (see chapter 3). One of the usually unspoken obligations of the OEM physician is to avoid reinforcing false beliefs among patients with fixed or unproven belief systems and to avoid making the problem worse by encouraging maladaptive behaviors or holding out false promises.

CHAPTER ELEVEN

Classic Research in Occupational and Environmental Medicine

Tee L. Guidotti

Occupational and environmental medicine (OEM) sits at an intellectual crossroads. It draws its insights and knowledge from research in biomedical sciences, epidemiology, toxicology, engineering, chemistry, physics, ecosystem biology (for environmental medicine), and behavioral sciences. It gives back as much as it takes by returning insights in toxicology, applied physiology, etiological (causation) epidemiology, clinical medicine, and health-care organization. As a result, OEM contributes to knowledge and practice far beyond its own scope. OEM, including the broader field of occupational and environmental health, is not just *multidisciplinary* (involving many technical fields). It is highly and increasingly *interdisciplinary* (requiring collaboration among technical fields). Since the problems OEM deals with range across technology and the economy, research in OEM has a vast scope. Table 11.1 lists perhaps the 10 most important and obvious achievements of research from or pertaining to OEM.

The fundamental purpose of OEM is to reduce harm on the job and make the workplace safer, to have the environment enhance rather than threaten health, to give people the means to improve their own health and avoid disease, and to reduce the risk of long-term harm from work or where a person

Table 11.1   Major achievements of OEM research and closely related fields

1. *Recognition of occupational diseases and application of biomedical and clinical sciences to the problem.* This was absolutely critical, not only for the injured worker but also to establish occupational causation and to document that such disorders were preventable. Without recognition, occupational disorders could not be targeted for prevention or compensated fairly.

2. *Industrial hygiene.* Industrial (or "occupational") hygiene began as an integral part of what physicians did in the field. Over time (by about 1940), it became a separate field of specialization. By the 1950s, it became recognized as a profession separate from medicine, and the rest, as they say, is history.

3. *Respiratory protection and support of ventilation.* Occupational health protection led naturally to studies in respiratory physiology and interest in ventilatory support. Thus, it was the Drinker brothers (Phil and Cecil), pioneers in both occupational hygiene and physiology, who were largely responsible for developing the iron lung, which saved countless lives when it was needed in great numbers during the polio epidemic.

4. *Health promotion in the community and worksite.* We think of worksite health promotion as a modern innovation that built on preventive medicine and health education, but major employers were deeply engaged in practical health promotion in the earliest days of occupational medicine. Much of it was directed toward women workers, immigrant families, and the health of the working class and so extended to community education.

5. *Concepts of asthma.* In the 1960s, ideas about asthma had stagnated, treatment had become formulaic, and the role of chronic inflammation was not appreciated. The early work of Jack Pepys and others using the model of occupational asthma (particularly, the slow, leukotriene-mediated response) gave the field a shove and pushed it forward to consider the need for anti-inflammatory treatment. Right behind the intellectual contribution to asthma research is the contribution of occupational medicine to understanding fibrotic lung disease, but it has had less success in changing outcomes.

6. *Emergency trauma surgery.* In the nineteenth century, railroad surgeons developed several innovations because serious trauma and life-threatening injuries were common, often in remote locations. They developed mobile hospitals (outfitted railroad cars) and surgery packs (instruments bundled for types of operations and prepositioned for emergency use), which are still used today in hospitals, but with the improvement of sterilization! The contribution of railroad surgery to trauma care is probably second only to military surgery.

7. *HMOs and health-care networks.* The railroads set up chains of health clinics and hospitals along their routes in the nineteenth century, some of which survive today as major health-care systems. Kaiser, of course, was the prototype of HMOs and arose from medical services for workers and their dependents.

Table 11.1 (*continued*)

8. *Cancer epidemiology.* Early studies of cancer causation were usually occupational, because of the high risk and the inspiration of Percivall Pott. Many of the early epidemiologists studying cancer were physicians, although not necessarily occupational physicians. Ideas about chemical carcinogenesis and subsequent experimentation largely arose out of early studies of occupational causation of cancer.

9. *Air pollution epidemiology and toxicology.* Starting with the Donora episode in 1948, early episodes of air pollution were investigated by U.S. Public Health Service scientists who had learned their methods and developed their ideas about toxicology from occupational studies. The exquisite sophistication of air quality epidemiology would not have occurred without people such as John Goldsmith, who started out as a pioneer in social and occupational medicine.

10. *Environmental and occupational toxicology.* Modern ideas and methods in toxicology, including methods for animal experimentation and analysis, clinical tests and indicators, databases for human health effects (e.g., IRIS), and so on truly began with occupational physicians, including pioneers such as Alice Hamilton, who contributed greatly to the broad field of toxicology as well as its regulatory applications. Lead was the breakthrough example—a hazard that, when understood, led to broad insights and to practical models for control.

lives. The secondary purpose, achieved largely by doing all this, is to make the workplace more productive and the environment more sustainable, both in the sense of reducing threats and achieving health gains. The way OEM has done this is by researching the problem and partnering with other fields to find solutions to problems, in addition to diagnosis, treatment, and impairment evaluation of individual injured workers.

The research agenda for OEM was initially driven mainly by priorities of industry: for example, to investigate hazards, to make workplaces physically safer, to support regulation, and to prevent hazards in the workplace or community from causing disruption to economic or technological development. This is reflected in figure 11.1, which illustrates a view of research from mid-century, or approximately, 1960. The assumption was that hazards were going to be introduced anyway and OEM would trail behind to mitigate the problems they created and offer solutions. The viewpoint changed over time to put workers and community residents at the center of research priorities and to emphasize technology assessment and precaution. As a consequence, OEM research today is more forward looking, proactive, and interdisciplinary, on both the occupational and environmental sides.

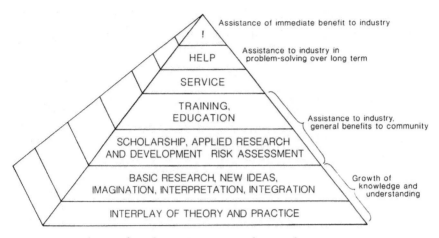

Figure 11.1. Schema of academic OEM research at midcentury representing conventional view at the time, showing how applied research, building on basic research, assisted in problem-solving for industry. (Figure by Tee L. Guidotti, 1985).

This has made research and research careers in OEM unusually innovative and open to collaboration among scientific disciplines, including the social and behavioral sciences. Contributions to practice are regularly made by scientists from all medical specialties. However, unlike other fields of medicine, developments in OEM research are driven largely by technology and changes in the economy and hardly at all by new treatments or drugs.

During the COVID-19 pandemic, for example, OEM physicians had to master or at least understand the intricacies of virology and immunology to determine guidelines for worker protection and fitness for return to work (especially after "long COVID"). Those who worked in health-care settings organized vaccination campaigns alongside infectious disease specialists. However, they had almost no other role in the treatment of sick patients. This is typical. In 1918, OEM physicians ("industrial physicians" in those days) managed strikingly similar problems involving pandemic influenza in the workplace and community. Before, and continuing well after the 1918 pandemic, the infectious disease problem of the workplace was tuberculosis (TB). In fact, many occupational medicine practices came out of the experience of dealing with TB, and research on how TB was spread through the air was in the mainstream of both occupational and environmental medicine.

The main scientific and technical fields that have driven OEM forward have been (roughly in this order): the introduction of scientific (rather than purely empirical) clinical medicine, the slow emergence of exposure science (which required refinements in analytical chemistry and measurement technology and is still emerging), experimental toxicology (particularly after the turn of the nineteenth century), applied personal protection technology (particularly after World War I), "chronic disease" epidemiology (a late-blooming science that came together in the mid-twentieth century), human factors research (now called "ergonomics"), risk science (which systematized the application of science to regulatory policy), and prevention science (which underpinned preventive medicine and public health but was hard to apply to occupational medicine until the era of health promotion). These streams of scientific thought brought to OEM new knowledge, skills, and opportunities.

A good example is "exposure science." Physicians were initially trained to make their own measurements and invented methods as they went along, mostly using basic analytical chemistry. However, this role was taken over by "real" chemists and engineers who had more sophisticated techniques. By the mid-twentieth century, physicians were more or less out of the picture, and the technological advances were being made by engineers and chemists. Once the methods were available to make basic measurements, it became possible to do statistical analysis and develop strategies for getting the most relevant information. This became the cornerstone of modern *occupational (or industrial) hygiene,* and environmental science and was called *exposure assessment.* Engineers developed technology to automate monitoring (an engineering problem), which allowed rational and precise regulation, so that standards (such as OSHA's "permissible exposure limits") could be developed and compliance could be confirmed. Later, exposure assessment (particularly, on the environmental side) adopted an arsenal of new techniques from genomics and biochemistry that came to be called "biomarkers." This opened the door to a new and more sophisticated "exposure science," to characterize environmental influences on the body over a lifetime or at biologically important times of life (called by some earnest practitioners "the exposome"). Exposure science has developed quickly in the last few years and is increasingly tackling epigenetic gene modification in response to environmental exposures or stress. The arc of exposure science—from early "wet chemistry" to measure what is in the workplace or environment at one point in time to now pondering the traces of past and present exposure over the lifetime of the individual and variability in populations—is enabling advances in other occupational and environmental health fields, such as pollution control, occupational (industrial) hygiene, epidemiology, environmental engineering, and the study of gene-toxicant interactions and is contributing insights that will be valuable in basic cellular and molecular biology.

Early health studies were based on direct observation. Experimental research, in the early years, followed many of the same methods shared by early drug research and the emerging science of toxicology, the science of the body's response to chemicals. OEM has benefited enormously from experimental toxicological research, which has defined mechanisms of injury at the cellular level and suggested, by extrapolation, exposure limits for the prevention of disease. These are always controversial, inevitably tightened as more is learned about the toxicity of a chemical, and uncertain, requiring many assumptions for estimating comparable human thresholds. However, experimental toxicology using well-studied animal models (mice being the great majority of animals used these days) has proven remarkably accurate in predicting health effects for human beings, understanding how the chemical works, and establishing dose ranges that approximate human toxicity levels, especially for cancer. Such studies are not perfect and have to be interpreted with a clear knowledge of similarities and differences between the animal model and human physiology, but they are also good indicators of what happens in the human body. Concern for animals has led to changes in the design of these studies so that fewer animals are required, good laboratory practices are followed (with consequences if they are not), and the most use possible is made of data that are produced by animal studies. Test-tube (in vitro) studies are used whenever possible as a substitute for animals, but such methods cannot replace all animal studies. Many studies simply require an intact organism, in all its complexities. A key issue in animal studies (and an even greater one in in vitro studies) is how to compare the results and scale the level of exposure to human beings. At some point, human data become essential for confidence that exposure levels are protective or that exposure-induced disease does or does not occur in people.

Historically, the foundational human research that underlies OEM has come mostly from the study of individual cases. Most human studies in OEM, particularly in the early days, were driven by targets of opportunity or in response to disaster. Exposure levels in the workplace and pollution levels in the environment were so high that relatively crude methods worked acceptably well to identify most of the worst hazards and to confirm that the workplace and environment held many serious hazards.

Later, studies were conducted to demonstrate what levels of exposure should be considered acceptably *safe*, in order to set standards. The usual methods of experimental research were impossible to apply in OEM, and scientists had to be innovative and often clever. The reason for this is that it is almost impossible to conduct a large-scale experiment in the workplace or the environment. In the laboratory, the scientist can set up controlled situations with, for example, one group of people, animals, or cells exposed to a pollutant or hazard and another unexposed to serve as a control group. Except in the most benign situations (such as comparisons of health promotion interventions), this can rarely be done in the workplace due to ethical restraints on exposing workers to a known hazard that is not intrinsic to their job or to levels that exceed the permissible exposure level (in the United States) or recommended occupational exposure levels. That is why occupational epidemiological studies usually compare rates of disease at two plants, one where a given chemical is used or a hazard is present, and another that uses a different product or process. This method (formally called quasi-experimental because the comparison population is not a true control group) has been used many times—for example, in studies involving exposure to benzene.

Because workplaces are never identical, there are always challenges in interpreting the results and accounting for bias. In environmental health studies, this can be approximated by comparing one community with a problem to another without the same problem. This can be difficult because, in the real world, communities usually differ in other ways as well and have different problems that may introduce bias. Sometimes, these differences actually offer opportunity.

In the 1970s, a series of studies using this comparison method was initiated by the then-new Environmental Protection Agency to assess the health effects of air pollution; it may have had its greatest success in the identification of the effects of the oxides of nitrogen (a constituent of photochemical air pollution) precisely because there was a single predominant source of emissions in Chattanooga, Tennessee, and no other point sources in the area, so the effect could be isolated. Even then, investigators had to determine whether the communities that were affected were similar were enough to the comparison communities, and they had to overcome problems, including the failure of the instruments they were depending on for exposure measurement. In the end, they persevered, found other ways to validate exposure, and then something unusual happened. A serious and widespread epidemic of influenza hit the region, affecting all the communities being studied (and most of the country). That normally would have been a setback for a study based on comparing respiratory illness symptoms (not to mention for the people who became ill!), but the investigators made good use of this "natural experiment." They used the opportunity to determine if the communities exposed to nitrogen dioxide had more cases with each wave of influenza, showing clearly that nitrogen dioxide has an effect on the immune system.

Disasters have unfortunately driven some of the most important advances in OEM. In the 1920s, workers producing tetraethyllead (TEL) as a new (antiknock) additive for use in gasoline quickly began showing severe, disabling, and irreversible neurological disease. This tragedy forced a reevaluation of the toxicity of lead and other metals and measures for the protection of workers, but even so, TEL was adopted as the standard gasoline additive by the industry. Lead later became a serious environmental hazard in air pollution, as it had been for years in lead paint. Leaded gasoline was banned in the United States in 1986 but remains in use in other parts of the world.

OEM Research

Research in OEM began with observation, such as the early findings of Ramazzini and the recognition by the already-eminent surgeon Percivall Pott in 1775 that chimney soot was carcinogenic (and, by extension, established that chemicals could cause cancer). As OEM progressed, it adopted more sophisticated research methods of experimentation (hypothesis testing), statistical analysis, and interdisciplinary methods (applying and integrating methods and insights across disciplines). Most OEM investigators are at least multidisciplinary (capable of approaching a problem from different points of view), most often in a field of clinical medicine and epidemiology. Much of the best research in OEM, of course, is performed by other scientists who specialize first in a particular discipline or approach and may apply their knowledge and methodology to other problems as well as workplace and environmental disorders. These other scientists most often have PhDs. It is difficult, but not impossible, for a scientist to perform high-quality, significant research in OEM alone, and so it is most often done by inter- or multidisciplinary teams.

The specific research achievements of occupational and environmental medicine are far too numerous to list here. They include numerous studies of particular hazards, particular occupational diseases, particular approaches to diagnosis of special disorders not often seen outside the workplace, and particular approaches to the prevention of injury and disease, emphasizing those that do not require behavioral change. Although most of the early work in OEM research was performed by physicians, scientists of all types have contributed insights, knowledge, and methods within occupational and environmental health research. Many practicing OEM physicians, particularly in universities and research institutes, conduct research or lead research groups, but they are as or more likely to be members of a team that includes other scientists outside clinical medicine, especially if the problem is big, complicated, or specialized. These other scientists are usually epidemiologists (who study patterns of health problems and their risk factors in populations), toxicologists (who study the effects of chemicals or other exposures on the body and the body's defenses), exposure scientists (often occupational hygienists, who measure exposure to chemicals and other hazards), behavioral scientists (particularly for stress-related disorders), engineers (who understand the problem), and environmental scientists (who can describe the pathways or pollution and environmental conditions). Increasingly, research is involving social scientists to understand the complexities of why the problem exists and how people respond.

Unlike other fields of medicine, however, OEM research has not emphasized treatment. There are differences in emphasis between OEM research and that of other medical and public health specializations. In general prevention, physicians persuade or at least encourage patients to change their personal lifestyle risk factors. That approach usually fails in the workplace and is completely ineffective for environmental conditions in the community. That is because the diseases and injuries in question are the same or similar to conditions that are unrelated to occupational or environmental exposures. Ethical research cannot allow intentional exposure to hazards that may cause harm and provide no anticipated benefit. There are very few situations in which people who are exposed to chemicals can be studied ethically, even as volunteers: drug clinical trials, natural "experiments of nature" (usually disasters), volunteers (only in the safest situations and closely monitored), in the workplace, and in the community where they live and would be exposed anyway.

Because the workplace is one of the few situations (within occupational and environmental standards) in which hazards can be modified and the results tracked, OEM research is a very valuable source of information on mechanisms of toxicity and response, as well as on the hazards themselves. Environmental exposures affect entire communities, including children, and represent one of the few situations in which the responses of children can be studied. That is why the study of occupational diseases has been important broadly in many areas of general medicine, such as asthma, dermatology (especially contact dermatitis), audiology and hearing loss, chronic musculoskeletal disorders, reproductive biology (specifically infertility and miscarriage monitoring), and cancer causation. One example is the eminent physiologist John Scott Haldane (1860–1936), whose studies of respiratory physiology, carbon monoxide, sewer workers (exposed to hydrogen sulfide), both high-altitude and diving medicine, and lung diseases (especially silicosis) improbably fit together into a coherent whole that led to the invention of the military gas mask, the (civilian) respirator (mask and protective device against toxic gases and dusts), the oxygen tent, mine safety lamps, and the clinical measurement of blood gases.

Alice Hamilton, the first female professor at Harvard, a pioneering academic detective, was instrumental in publicizing the causal association between white phosphorus used in American match factories and phossy jaw in 1900 (*Exploring the Dangerous Trades*). Sesquisulfide, discovered by a French chemist, was found to be a safe substitute for white phosphorus, employing one of the hierarchies of controls—substitution (NIOSH Hierarchy of Controls). Alice Hamilton went on to write a seminal textbook, *Industrial Toxicology*, establishing the toxicological/scientific basis for occupational medicine (OM) and inventing regulatory toxicology in the United States. Harry Mock, the secretary-treasurer for the American Association of Industrial Physicians and Surgeons (AAIPS), was another early OEM academic. He established the clinical basis of OM, "invented" work-site health promotion, and wrote a seminal textbook, *Industrial Medicine and Surgery*.

OEM research in the United States, as with OEM training, started with the "industrial physician" (see chapter 8). Acute and chronic cases of lead toxicity was being seen in workers of General Motors (GM) automobiles, as lead was being mixed with gasoline, starting in the 1920s, because it served as an effective antiknock agent. Charles Kettering, the head of research at GM, hired Robert A. Kehoe, an instructor in the Department of Physiology at the University of Cincinnati, in 1924, to examine health issues related to the production of tetraethyllead (TEL). In 1925, Kehoe became the chief medical adviser of Ethyl Corporation. He assembled a multidisciplinary team of physicians, analytical chemists, toxicologists, industrial hygienists, and engineers to study TEL and Freon. His research spanned decades. Two decades later, in 1947, Kehoe established the first Occupational and Environmental Medicine Residency at the University of Cincinnati College of Medicine.

With the rise of the use of TEL in gasoline, lead toxicity also emerged as an occupational hazard. This, however, created a catastrophic acute toxic emergency in 1924 among workers handling TEL, a chronic toxicity problem for other workers handling lead in the plants, and an environmental problem with emissions of lead into air from automobile exhaust.

Since these beginnings, OEM research has now become established with at least reliable sources of funding from NIOSH and the National Institute for Environmental Health Sciences (NIEHS), which is an institute within the National Institutes of Health (NIH). Significant journals such as the *Journal of Occupational and Environmental Medicine* and *Environmental Health Perspectives* have provided a forum for sharing ideas and disseminating findings.

Through the National Institute for Occupational Safety and Health (see chapter 1), research became more formalized and supported. In addition to conducting education programs, directly or through grants, to provide an adequate supply of safety and health specialists to carry out the purposes of the OSH Act, another role of NIOSH was to create a research program to generate objective scientific research findings in the field of occupational safety and health that could enable OSHA to formulate safety and health standards. NIOSH started out by publishing criteria documents for a Recommended Standard on Toxic Substances List, funding educational resource centers as centers of excellence for occupational health training and education, most in industrial hygiene, occupational medicine, and occupational health nursing but also in safety sciences. The next few decades led pioneering research on worker safety and health concerns and awarded research grants, which allowed the slow development of a permanent research infrastructure with reliable, if inadequate, funding.

The National Occupational Research Agenda (NORA) was launched in the 1990s as an innovative public-private partnership among industry, labor, and government to develop research priorities and is now in its third decade

(Howard, 2020). More than 500 individuals and organizations outside of NIOSH contributed to NORA's development. The NORA research agenda focuses on the top 10 most important topics for workplace health and safety and is updated to reflect the times. NORA is responsible for research and improved workplace practices in the areas of agriculture, forestry and fishing, health care and social assistance, oil and gas extraction, public safety, wholesale and retail trade services, transportation, warehousing and utilities, construction, and manufacturing and mining.

Examples of OEM Research

This section is by no means comprehensive but will serve to illustrate the extent of OEM research. The examples chosen are arbitrary, selected to tell interesting stories as well as to illustrate OEM research.

The most obvious topic of research in OEM is the recognition of occupational diseases and the application of biomedical and clinical sciences to the problem. Prior to the modern scientific age, astute observation by practicing physicians did rather well in identifying problems and not badly in inferring their causes, but the methods were limited. Contemporary research in OEM uses essentially all scientific tools available to study important problems. Physician-scientists and later investigators in related fields needed to establish occupational causation for suspected occupational disorders, backed up by evidence and some idea of the mechanism (nature of the effect), in order to develop preventive measures.

Without research to document the connection between a hazard and a disease outcome, occupational and environmental medicine would be a series of anecdotes without scientific evidence. Most of the work to establish these connections in the last century has come from either epidemiology (the study of diseases and their risk factors in populations, groups of people, or communities) or toxicology (the study of what chemicals do to the body and how the body handles chemicals). This process of practical recognition followed by systematic investigation was absolutely critical, not just for the injured worker but also to document that such disorders were preventable and to set standards to achieve prevention. Eventually, in the 1970s and 1980s, a century after the need was obvious, research to support standards, together with risk analysis in engineering, spun off its own discipline, called risk science (risk assessment), which developed a systematic approach to evaluating the probability of adverse effects and estimating the uncertainty in the estimates, determining how people understand and process ideas about safety and risk (risk perception), talking about risks (risk communication), and developing policy and practical management options (risk management). One reason this took so long is that assessing risk required a relatively sophisticated understanding of hazards and the probability of bad outcomes, which was beyond the capabilities of laboratory toxicology and the new methodologies of calculating disease risk that epidemiology had in the mid-twentieth century. Until midcentury, epidemiology was still developing basic methods for the study of "chronic disease" (as opposed to "infectious disease," in the terminology of the time).

Over time, by about the 1910s, OEM developed a robust network of laboratories and research groups, particularly in the United Kingdom, Italy, and later, France and the United States. However, experimental toxicology had a serious limitation because animals (mostly mice today, but mostly rats in the early days) were the subjects and, in some cases, did not respond the same as human beings; it was also difficult to know how much exposure would cause the same health problem in a person. The rise of epidemiology as a statistical science of human populations filled that gap, mostly in the 1920s and 1930s. By the 1950s, environmental epidemiology was becoming a distinct area of emphasis. Occupational epidemiology lagged because the field was already dominated by the toxicological approach to problems, which appeared to be more precise, and because of limitations in exposure measurement. Occupational epidemiology finally came into its own in the 1970s, and research methodology became more standardized, informed by toxicology. In the latter part of the twentieth century, OEM research increasingly adopted methods drawn from behavioral science, social science (especially, as it has to do with why these conditions exist), and stress physiology.

Toxicology

As noted, OEM research in the late nineteenth and early twentieth centuries concentrated on experimental toxicology instead of epidemiology. Toxicology deals with the effects of chemicals (and some other hazards, such as radiation) on the body but also how the body handles chemicals, how it absorbs them, distributes them around the body, metabolizes or processes them, and eventually excretes them and the pattern of elimination. Toxicologists relied on animal testing for evidence of harm and the mechanism of action and developed screening and diagnostic tests for human use, particularly to monitor occupational exposure.

Modern ideas and methods in toxicology, including methods for animal experimentation and analysis, clinical tests and indicators, databases for human health effects, and calculations of allowable exposure based on scientific evidence often began with occupational physicians, including pioneers such as Alice Hamilton, who contributed greatly to the broad field of toxicology as well as its regulatory applications. Toxicology has paralleled the rising sophistication of biomedical science since then and most recently has adapted the science of genomics and epigenetics (the "editing" of DNA expression in response to chemical interactions and stress) with the realization that much chemically related disease is the result of an interaction between individual genetic makeup and the toxicity of chemicals, not toxicity alone.

Lead was the breakthrough example, a hazard that, once understood, led to broad insights, practical models for control, and many clinical tests, most of which were inferior to the simple measurement of lead in blood once that became routinely available. In adults, lead poisoning causes many disorders and brings a risk of brain and nerve damage. In children, lead toxicity can range from a spectrum of subtle learning disorders to catastrophic nervous system damage, depending on dose. Research on lead established the role of laboratory studies, the importance of chemistry, and the importance of a bridge between the laboratory and application of lessons learned to preventing disease in the workplace. It was also one of the earliest hazards to be regulated in the workplace, providing a precedent for setting and enforcing exposure standards. Because lead also affected children, quite severely, it was an early example of the crossover between occupational medicine and environmental medicine and demonstrated their essential unity.

Another example is benzene, which was known to cause aplastic anemia at the turn of the twentieth century and was recognized three decades later to cause a form of leukemia; the evidence came at first from individual human cases (usually fatal) and then was confirmed by animal studies. The findings of the first animal studies were questioned (mostly by industry—benzene was a very valuable solvent widely used at the time) on grounds of relevance to humans (the cancers showed up in a different organ) and because the mechanism of how benzene caused cancer was not clear. Better-designed studies and details of the biochemistry of benzene metabolism, which is very complicated, have clarified the situation and shown that there are actually several mechanisms. After early work by Peter Infante, a new generation of epidemiological studies has determined that the risk of leukemia after exposure is actually greater than previously suspected and that other forms of leukemia and related cancers are linked to benzene exposure. Similar stories can be told about dozens of chemicals that have been studied as possible causes of cancer.

Although cancer risk remains the major public concern over chemical hazards, only about 90 of the tens of thousands of chemicals in use have actually been shown to cause cancer and about double that are strongly suspected of being carcinogens. Most of these are old hazards. One would think that they would be gone because we know about them, but they keep coming up, through carelessness and oversight, new applications, and neglect.

Perhaps the classic achievement of experimental toxicology in the early years of the twentieth century was the demonstration that crystalline silica dust—which results from the grinding, cutting, or drilling of quartz in rock, as in mining, sandblasting, and (today) polishing artificial granite countertops—caused silicosis and, later, that it caused cancer. The early research used methods largely repurposed from studies of tuberculosis. Experimental studies, particularly at the Saranac Lake Laboratories and notably by Le Roy Upson Gardner and Anthony Lanza, established that silica dust caused the same disease (silicosis) in animals as in miners, sandblasters, and other exposed workers—a profuse form of fibrosis (scar tissue) in the lung. Much later, silicosis and exposure to silica dust was found to cause cancer. The conventional wisdom among lung physicians and scientists studying the problem had been that it did not, but a persistent graduate student named David F. Goldsmith (son of John Goldsmith) insisted that the evidence showed otherwise. He fought for 20 years to get the association recognized, which it was in 1997, confirmed with both epidemiological and toxicological evidence.

Concurrent with the early studies of silicosis, pathology studies in the United Kingdom were showing a similar but less potent pattern of scarring for coal workers' pneumoconiosis (CWP, "black lung"). The two often occurred together. Similar methods and studies were applied to other dust diseases of the lung, most controversially, asbestos. The three main dust diseases (silicosis, CWP, and asbestosis) each have different patterns of fibrosis (scarring) in lung tissue (they look completely different under a microscope), different effects on susceptibility to other lung diseases (silicosis predisposes to tuberculosis), associations with other organs (CWP, when advanced, can be associated with a form of heart failure) and cancer risk (asbestos is highly carcinogenic). Silicosis was a much feared disease, and there was considerable but fruitless research to find an antidote, cure, or preventive agent. In the 1940s, some mining companies made workers breathe in aluminum powder, which not only did not work but was subsequently found to put the aging workers at risk for neurological impairment.

Cancer toxicology and carcinogenesis studies, which are the basis for setting standards through regulation, arose out of a clinical observation that belatedly turned into a laboratory science. The eminent eighteenth-century surgeon Percivall Pott (a major figure in orthopedic surgery) famously identified the first occupational cancer (scrotal carcinoma in chimney sweeps), an observation that (after a long delay) led directly to the earliest experimental studies of cancer causation, in the early twentieth century. The current understanding of chemical carcinogenesis, as well as carcinogenesis bioassays to identify cancer-causing chemicals by testing, arose out of this line of investigation. (Almost all such studies are conducted on rats or mice.) Research pioneers such as Wilhelm Hueper and Umberto Saffiotti developed the modern bioassay for carcinogenesis, which has proven remarkably accurate in predicting human risk. While still not perfectly predictive, the correlation between cancer causation in humans (as demonstrated by epidemiology) and in experimental studies is so close that a chemical proven to cause cancer in animals is almost certain, once differences in species are accounted for, to cause cancer in human beings in similar tissues at some level, and vice versa. Research over the last few decades has sought to reduce dependence on animal studies by using other ("test tube") methods such as tissue culture but has not achieved the same success as with the animal testing cancer bioassay.

Epidemiology

In the late nineteenth century, physicians started using statistics to quantify disease risk and track clues to possible causes. The most famous of these studies is the story of the "Broad Street Pump," a fascinating bit of detective work by the early anesthesiologist and public health pioneer John Snow. In 1854, and again in 1857, during the periodic outbreaks of cholera that disproportionally killed poor and working-class residents in one particular area of London, Snow mapped the occurrence of cholera cases and found that they initially clustered around a particular source of water on Broad Street in Soho. There were many more cases in the area served by the company operating this particular pump than occurred in a similar disadvantaged area served by another water company nearby. Snow also determined that at least some of the few cases among residents in the other area had in fact sometimes gotten their water from the water company using the Broad Street Pump. Already very interested in water quality and health, Snow correctly surmised that cholera could be transmitted by polluted drinking water (from sewage carrying waste from cholera patients). Against considerable opposition, he personally intervened to convince initially skeptical town officials to remove the handle from the pump, so nobody could gain access surreptitiously, following which the local epidemic abruptly stopped. Later, he showed that after the first water company changed the location of its water intake upstream, cholera disappeared among users. This story marks the beginning of environmental epidemiology and many firsts: including the recognition of cholera as an infectious disease, one of the first analytical studies of a disease outbreak, one of the first successful interventions that provided convincing evidence of causation, and an early successful example of environmental regulation by the government.

In the twentieth century, epidemiology was still used primarily for infectious disease outbreaks until few studies began to address chronic (long term) diseases in populations—most notably, on pellagra (a nutritional disorder due to vitamin B3 deficiency). The rapid development of statistical science and the invention of inference (significance) testing in the 1930s, provided the tools for a more versatile and mature science of epidemiology, led by Wade Hampton Frost (whose primary interest was waterborne disease) at Johns Hopkins and others, applying methods of both "acute disease" (primarily, infectious disease) and "chronic disease" (primarily, cancer) as the specific problem required. (These distinctions no longer hold much relevance.) Occupational epidemiology belonged primarily to the newly emerging branch of chronic disease epidemiology, which developed first under the influence of Frost and later the Oxford-based school of British epidemiologists, who were concerned with cigarette smoking and lung cancer risk and inventing ways to study the relationship. Environmental epidemiology, which started off with water and infectious disease, came to be dominated by problems of air pollution and toxic substances, which were considered chronic disease problems. Today, epidemiology is the primary way that both occupational and environmental disease problems are studied. While there is far too much research in occupational and environmental epidemiology to describe its full scope here, two examples of OEM epidemiology will illustrate the field.

Early studies of cancer causation were usually occupational, because of the high risk in occupations and because exposure to chemicals in the workplace could be more easily measured. Many of the early epidemiologists studying cancer were physicians. One of the most impressive bodies of work in epidemiology was produced by Irving Selikoff, who studied asbestos and cancer. Despite opposition from industry, the overwhelming evidence he and his colleagues pulled together eventually led to an effective ban on asbestos, falling cancer rates from exposure to the dust, and insights into cancer biology, including the important principle that some carcinogenic exposures interact (a principle often called "synergy").

Air pollution epidemiology branched into a major field within epidemiology in the 1940s and 1950s. Starting with a lethal Donora, Pennsylvania, air pollution episode in 1948, early episodes of air pollution were investigated by U.S. Public Health Service scientists using methods originally developed for occupational studies. Over time, studies of the community effects of air pollution grew more sophisticated by refinements in the methods of epidemiology applied to large communities—the pioneering work of researchers like John Goldsmith, who started in social and occupational medicine, and Carl Shy, who led critical studies for the U.S. Environmental Protection Agency (EPA). Following passage of the Environmental Protection Act in 1970, EPA itself conducted and funded essential studies on which standards were based. Until the 1980s, it was not clear whether air pollution was important as an overall determinant of health. The number then used to interpret risk looked small compared to other causes of death. Later studies, led by Douglas Dockery at Harvard, demonstrated that the toll of deaths and illness from air pollution was much greater than had been imagined. Deaths attributable to air pollution were much greater when calculated as a fraction, and many of the deaths from other causes (such as heart disease) were in fact caused by air pollution (often in combination with other factors). This ushered in the modern era of air pollution epidemiology.

Respiratory Protection and Support of Ventilation

Occupational health protection led naturally to studies in respiratory physiology, purification of contaminated air, and the development of practical respirators. Most of the early technology built on devices (not very effective) to filter out dust for the protection of miners. Later developments built on military technology (World War I) for surviving chemical warfare. Some of the greatest names in science, such as John Tyndall (physicist), Alexander von Humboldt (biologist and among other things, a mining engineer), and JS Haldane (physiologist), worked on this problem. This technology required deep insights into the physiology of the respiratory system, and this led naturally to an interest in ventilatory support and assistance, which was also an urgent medical problem for patients who could not breathe on their own. The Drinker brothers (Philip, a hygienist, and Cecil, a physician and dean of the School of Public Health at Harvard) were pioneers in both occupational hygiene and physiology at Harvard. Philip was primarily responsible for developing the iron lung, which saved countless lives (including the lives of tens of thousands of children) when it was needed in great numbers during the polio epidemic.

Health and Wellness in the Community and Work Site

Work-site health promotion and wellness programs are often thought of as a recent innovation arising from late twentieth century preventive medicine and health education, because they became popular in the 1970s. However, major employers have been deeply engaged in practical health promotion from the earliest days of occupational medicine. Much of it was directed toward women workers, immigrant families, and the health of the working class and so extended to community education. Harry Mock was a leader in this movement at the turn of the twentieth century (see chapter 1).

More recently, the field was led by Dee Edington of the University of Michigan, who, together with physicians such as Wayne Burton (medical director at several large financial institutions where there were few confounding factors), demonstrated that worker-centered programs to reduce risk of death or illness and to maintain wellness and productivity actually work. To make it practical, Eddington boiled down the extremely complicated findings of cardiovascular disease epidemiology to a simple, highly robust risk factor score that could be used by employers to predict risk and track change.

Distinct in research methodology but related to wellness was the introduction of stress research into OEM. The study of how the body responds to both traumatic and psychological stress was mostly pursued as a laboratory problem in physiology until the early 1950s when psychological stress was increasingly recognized as a risk factor for heart attacks (myocardial infarction). Research then suggested that chronic (long term) stress was a risk factor for heart disease, but the field of research in occupational health was hampered by inconsistent definitions, the popularity of unproven theories, and resistance to the idea that the workplace had to be changed to reduce stress among workers. Above all, research findings appeared contradictory or inconsistent. Then sociologist Robert Karasek developed a new theory that resolved many conflicting issues by postulating that it was not just workload that created stress in the workplace but also perceptions of control and the capacity to keep up. The concept also lent itself to a different strategy for measuring stress in two dimensions. This "job-demand-control model" correlated well with observed rates of myocardial infarction and the risk of cardiovascular disease. There have since been other behavioral theories that add to the predictive power of the model, but Karasek broke the problem open for OEM and the management of stress in the workplace as a hazard like others.

Clinical Medicine

In the early nineteenth century, railroads had to hire surgeons because trains were very dangerous for workers, serious accidents involving passengers put them at risk of lawsuits, and they had operations in remote areas. Railroad surgery became a sophisticated specialty and over the years produced innovations in medical care such as mobile hospitals (outfitted railroad cars) and surgery packs (instruments bundled for types of operations and prepositioned for emergency use), which are still used today in hospitals. The contribution of railroad surgery to trauma care is probably second only to that of military surgery, historically. Railroad surgery and medicine also experimented with innovations in health care, setting up hospital systems in both major cities and remote locations, many of which survive today.

One of the major contributions of OEM research to medicine generally was how studies of asthma among workers led to changes in the concepts of asthma as a disease. In the 1960s, ideas about asthma had stagnated. Treatment had become formulaic, and the details of what happened in asthma were not understood. Jack Pepys, at the University of London, and others broke the impasse, starting in the 1950s, through findings from research into occupational asthma, which pushed clinical care forward with the result that regular anti-inflammatory therapy to match episodic bronchodilator treatment is now the standard of care. Pepys and his team also made major advances in understanding other immunological disorders, particularly of the lung, based on observations and studies of affected workers.

Metrics for Disability and Rehabilitation

OEM investigators have developed some remarkably innovative approaches to practical problems in occupational medicine, specifically. One of them is the standard methodology for assessing impairment (loss of body function) as the first step in assessing disability (the loss of capacity for work and life). Insurance companies needed a way to assess and measure the permanent harm done to an individual's ability to earn a living and perform the activities of daily living. Just describing it was not enough, because distinctions that were small medically (such as strength, range of motion, and ability to use the index finger or thumb) often had major implications for a person's ability to do their job or get through the day. Comparing impairment among injured workers was also important to the consistency and efficiency of the workers' compensation system, which was intended to provide partial wage support for disabled workers as well as to cover their medical care expenses. By the 1950s, there were many systems of measurement, classification, and ratings in use, varying by company, country and state or province, and purpose (those intended to guide clinical care or rehabilitation were not sensitive enough to predict work performance). In 1956, the American Medical Association created a task force to address the problem and developed the *AMA Guides to the Evaluation of Permanent Impairment*—a handbook that standardized all this, across organ systems, on the basis of measurements that could be done in a physician's office. The *AMA Guides* are now in their sixth edition and constitute the most widely used system in the world. This was one of the earliest and may still be the most successful way of quantifying functional impairment.

Another example is the practical problem of measuring abnormalities on chest films in order to track progression or predict impairment from dust diseases of the lungs (pneumoconiosis) in disabled miners, asbestos workers, or other workers. In 1950, a standardized approach with a highly innovative feature was formulated under the sponsorship of the International Labour Organization (ILO, a United Nations body, like the World Health Organization). The innovation consisted of a rating scale (1 through 3+) that allowed a "second look." The person reading the film gave a primary rating (say, 2 for moderately severe profusion) but was asked to take into account their second impression (say, 1 for disease that could have been read as mild or that was less than the typical 2). The combined rating (2/1 in this case) factored both a semi-objective reading and the accompanying psychological uncertainty into a single scale that correlated remarkably well for given dust diseases with deposition of dust in lung tissue and respiratory impairment. The ILO Classification of the pneumoconioses has been extended to other imaging technologies and is used worldwide for research, following progression of disease, and establishing eligibility for compensation.

OEM Research as a "Critical Science"

OEM research is a paramount example of what has been called "critical science." Critical science can be described as the "mode" of science that acts for the public interest and documents problems of technology and society, using scientific approaches to do so. Other examples include ecology and environmental sciences, technology assessment, complexity theory (especially as applied to so-called wicked problems, in which attempts at a solution change the nature of the problem), and sociotechnical systems (where both social or cultural change and technological change are required to solve problems).

Scientists and the public make a distinction between two modes of science: basic science and applied science. Basic, in this sense, does not mean "simple"; it means "fundamental." Basic science is often thought of as science for its own sake. Applied science is the application of science to achieve an intended goal. It builds on basic science and contributes to technology and engineering by finding ways to apply scientific knowledge and research methods to solve concrete problems. Technology, taking up where applied science leaves off, develops the science into a specific application or product. These two modes of science are well recognized.

The prominent philosopher of science Jerome R. Ravetz (b. 1929, American working in the United Kingdom) described his concept of a mode of "critical science" that documents abuses or problems arising out of technology and social actions. He conceived of it as a critique of technology and applied science using the methods of basic science.

Critical science can be understood as the use of basic science to provide a check and correction on unrestrained, ineffective, or harmful tendencies of technology and applied science. In this sense, it is feedback on where technological innovation and development are taking society, the economy, and human health.

In OEM and other technical affairs, good policy and responsible actions depend on sound science. If the science behind it is sound, there is no guarantee that the policy will be good and effective, but it is more likely to be. If the science behind it is poor, then the policy will not work, because even if by dumb luck the right option is chosen, it cannot be justified and so probably will not stand.

Scientists can inform the debate but cannot expect to control it, nor does society want them to. Scientists are not technocratic rulers, who make decisions in their expert wisdom: they are creators of public knowledge for the purpose of understanding the world. It is by a process of assertion and counterassertion on a broad scale, often with disappointingly little information, that our society makes decisions and sets out on its path toward social action.

The more the information, the more likely it is that the ultimate decision will be rational, although there are no guarantees.

The field of OEM research has been a hot spot for problems with the integrity of science and, as a consequence, a constant arena for controversy, questioning, challenge to motives, and dueling experts. However, as distressing as this can be at times, real problems are being addressed, and scientific research, properly conducted and interpreted in good faith, is still the best guide available to resolving most controversies on safety and health risk in OEM.

CHAPTER TWELVE

Contemporary Research and Looking Ahead

How-Ran Guo

Chapter 11 discusses classical research in occupational medicine on traditional topics; the crossover between occupational and environmental medicine, which is resulting in a synthesis; and how research developed in OEM. All these areas of research are still very active, in part, because so many problems have not been completely resolved (lead, silica, and noise, even though the solutions are not difficult) and, in part, because new problems have been created by changes in the manufacturing process or by the introduction of new chemicals. The current direction of OEM research includes those areas and also a range of newly emerging or reemphasized problems that have attracted greater attention in recent years.

This chapter emphasizes these more recent priorities on the OEM research agenda, but the older priorities should never be forgotten.

Hazard Characterization

Perhaps the most active area of research in OEM is in the identification and characterization of hazards. This is done in two ways: by epidemiological research and by experiment, particularly using laboratory methods in toxicology.

Epidemiological methods have wide acceptance and utility in setting standards and in legal actions and are relied upon in most standards-setting and decision-making as the most relevant human health data available. In recent years, epidemiological studies have been combined with methods that look at measures, or "biomarkers," of exposure, of biological effects, and of susceptibility. The biomarkers under study rapidly progressed from toxicological cumulative dose estimates and genetic characteristics to genomic methods—looking at gene activation and the interplay of genes and gene products. This has proven to be a very fruitful line of research that has wide application in population studies but, to some degree, has raced ahead of studies related to exposure. The current critique of studies examining the interaction of genes and chemical or other exposures ("gene-toxicant interactions") is that the science is heavily weighted on the side of identifying genetic mechanisms and remains much less developed for exposure assessment. Both tendencies skew understanding of the contribution of each and have led, in the views of some, to the widespread belief in some circles that genetic predisposition and biological propensity play a more important role than chemical exposure in determining disease outcome. It is particularly true in environmental toxicology, where exposures tend to be lower than in occupational settings. This is not really so much a dispute as a question of emphasis and a desire to achieve a more well-rounded understanding of toxic effects on which to base exposure standards.

Exposure science, which has only recently emerged as a science in its own right, attempts to quantify as much as possible the exposure of humans both in a particular time frame and over a lifetime. Traditional methods of doing this are based on measuring the concentration of chemicals or their metabolites in biological samples (such as those of body fluid, tissue, or exhaled air) or environmental samples (such as those of air, water, soil, or food), either summing the total exposure or isolating the exposure from a particular source, such as the workplace, a process, or the living environment. Contemporary research looks at more varied, robust, and often indirect measures of exposure, such as induced biochemical changes; DNA damage; or epigenetics, the modification of expression of the genome that is influenced by environmental factors. The ideal would be to characterize "the exposome," the cumulative record in the cell or organism of all exposures an individual has experienced in a lifetime, and thus, to assess biological effects. This ambitious undertaking and progress has, of course, been uneven but has led to substantial insights into more subtle effects of toxicity and risk.

Laboratory methods include animal studies, which almost exclusively use rats or mice these days. Methods have been developed to minimize the number of animals used, but the framework of occupational and environmental health standards in use today worldwide is based on extrapolating risks from defined anchor points, such as the lethal dose or concentration for 50 percent of animals (LD_{50} or LC_{50}) or unit doses of toxicity such as q^* in the EPA's

Integrated Risk Information System (IRIS) database. Despite concerted efforts to find alternatives, these end points are exceptionally robust and reproducible, which is why they are still used. As methods become more sophisticated in identifying biomarkers of effect and the exposome becomes a reality, toxicological methods are being developed to deal with lower and lower exposure levels, novel exposures, and biological mechanisms of damage repair, adaptation, and compensation. Again, genetic injury is at the cutting edge and is probably the model for such studies. This appears to be the overall direction that occupational and environmental toxicology will continue to follow for some time to come.

Of course, at any time, there are numerous chemicals and other exposures of current interest that are under study. For example, the perfluoroalkyl substances (PFAS) are significant occupational exposures (such as from fire suppression foam) and environmental hazards in water (due to effluent from manufacturing), foods, and consumer products, which are associated (mostly in laboratory studies to date) with a variety of potential health concerns—principally, cancers, reproductive effects, and immunological alterations. As in all such cases, findings have been disputed, but the evidence for at least some effects being significant for humans has only been growing stronger over time. Many chemicals are under study by the National Toxicology Program (NTP), the lead federal agency for hazard characterization for chemicals. It operates by collaborating with other federal agencies to identify priority chemicals and then designing efficient toxicity studies. The whole priority list is long but never complete because of new nominations, and the priorities may change as needed. It includes, for example: nanomaterials, pesticides (including glyphosate), artificial fibers and synthetic turf (as used in playgrounds), PFAS, drugs, botanical dietary supplements, and food-related chemicals (such as artificial butter flavorings, which have been associated with a very serious lung disease), as well as a number of old and common exposures for which unresolved questions remain, such as polycyclic aromatic hydrocarbons, sulfolane, and hexavalent chromium.

In addition, NTP develops new and more sensitive methods for toxicological evaluation, which can then be more generally applied. These include alternative methods to animal testing.

Although not a specifically medical undertaking, current research and technology development in "green chemistry" is one way to greatly reduce the toxic burden in both the environment and the workplace. Green chemistry is a systematic approach to substituting methods, feedstocks, process chemicals, and end use so that the level of chemicals of all types currently used is much reduced and the amount released is minimized. This effort is led by chemists and chemical engineers, not physicians, but it is an example of the public health approach to primary prevention (see chapter 3).

Musculoskeletal Disorders and Ergonomics

As a developing country advances to a developed country, the proportion of workers engaged in the service sector becomes larger and larger. Consequently, physical, chemical, and biological hazards in the workplace become less and less prevalent, and ergonomic hazards (including psychosocial hazards) become more and more important. The most common occupational diseases attributable to ergonomic hazards are those of the musculoskeletal system. In addition, as people live longer, aging becomes a major factor contributing to musculoskeletal disorders. Under such a circumstance, the diagnosis of occupational musculoskeletal disorders and other occupational diseases attributable to ergonomic hazards is quite challenging. Ergonomic hazards are also prevalent in environments outside the workplace. In many developed countries, back pain is the most common occupational disorder, and ergonomic hazards, especially those arising from body movement and posture, account for the vast majority of work-related back pain. Although numerous studies have been conducted on back pain, data on dose-response relationship between ergonomic hazards (mechanics, repetition, force, etc.) and occurrence of back pain are still limited, making the determination of its association with work difficult. This is also true for other prevalent musculoskeletal disorders such as trigger finger, carpal tunnel syndrome, tennis elbow, and rotator cuff syndrome. The urgent need of solid scientific bases for the diagnosis and prevention of occupational disorders caused by ergonomic hazards has been recognized for a long time but not yet met.

The diagnosis of an occupational disease requires confirmation of both the exposure and the disorder. For musculoskeletal disorders caused by ergonomic hazards, both are difficult. Many tools, mostly in the form of a checklist with scores, have been developed to characterize and quantify body movement and posture involved in work activities. The key indicator methods (KIM) comprise a set of such tools, and some researchers have tried to correlate them with musculoskeletal disorders. The Functional Movement Screening™ (FMS™) was initially used in sport players, and some researchers have also tried to correlate its score with musculoskeletal disorders. However, most of the studies validating associations between scores and occurrence of musculoskeletal disorders are cross-sectional by design, which could not determine whether the body movement and posture were the cause or the results of the symptoms. A major reason for this is that it takes a longitudinal study to collect reliable data, but the latent period between the exposure and onset of remarkable symptoms or signs is usually quite long, even in the scale of years. Over a long period of time, a worker is quite likely to change work activities and even change jobs, sometimes due to musculoskeletal disorders. Another major obstacle in validating associations between the scores and musculoskeletal disorders is the complexity of body movement and posture involved in work activities, which makes the precise characterization and quantification very difficult. While the U.S. government failed to adopt an ergonomics standard, the American Conference of Governmental Industrial Hygienists (ACGIH) has constructed a threshold limit value (TLV) on the basis of epidemiological, psychosocial, and biomechanical studies that is intended for jobs performed for four or more hours per day, but for "mono-task" jobs only. Using an analysis of video records, a prospective longitudinal study found the dose-response relationship between the TLV for hand activity level and the risk of carpal tunnel syndrome was not linear, indicating the complexity of the relationship.

The confirmation of musculoskeletal disorders is also difficult in many cases. For example, back pain is the most common occupational disease in the United States, but the majority of patients do not show remarkable findings. In fact, many patients do not show any evidence of the disorders in any medical imaging. A portion of them are attributable to psychological factors, as in cases with psychosomatic symptoms. Even in cases that are truly caused by abnormalities of the musculoskeletal system, medical imaging and electrophysiological examinations often fail to confirm the illness. However, identifying the cause of the disease—that is, separating cases caused by psychological factors from those caused by abnormalities of the musculoskeletal system—is essential to successful treatment and prevention. An ideal solution is to develop biomarkers for disorders of the musculoskeletal system. In the practice of occupational medicine, such biomarkers will also be useful in identifying cases of malingering.

Most cases of occupational musculoskeletal disorders are cumulative traumas in nature and attributable to repetitive movement, awkward posture, or both. These two common ergonomic hazards can usually be resolved by reengineering or automation, using machines. Better yet, automation can usually increase productivity while preventing musculoskeletal disorders in workers, although a trade-off is the reduction of manual jobs. However, machines have their limitations, and the lack of flexibility and the inability to deal with unexpected situations are two major ones. With the introduction of robotics and artificial intelligence, these two major limitations can be overcome. The application of robotics to dangerous and repetitive jobs should be the focus of research in the prevention of musculoskeletal disorders attributable to ergonomic hazards, but safety is a major challenge.

Particulate Matter and Nanomaterials

Particulate matter (PM) is a mixture of solid particles and liquid droplets found in the air. PM in the ambient air, experienced as air pollution, has become a great public health concern in recent years. The most obvious target of the health effects of PM is the respiratory tract. In addition to nonmalignant respiratory diseases, PM can cause lung cancer, and the International Agency for Research on Cancer (IARC) has classified PM as a group 1 carcinogen (carcinogenic to humans). However, among the deaths attributable to PM, those from cardiovascular diseases exceed those from respiratory diseases. PM is associated with various cardiovascular diseases including ischemic heart disease, arrhythmia, and heart failure, as well as cerebrovascular diseases. Epidemiological studies also showed that PM was associated with endocrine diseases such as diabetes and neurological disorders such as Alzheimer's disease and Parkinson's disease. It may also affect the immune system and lead to inflammatory responses. Furthermore, some epidemiological studies have observed associations between PM exposures and mental disorders such as autism, not just physical illness. In comparison with the volume of literature on the health effects of PM in the ambient environment, studies on those of PM in the working environment are limited, even though pneumoconiosis caused by dust has been recognized as an occupational disease for centuries. Recent studies of fire smoke, diesel exhaust, and the occupational disease risk of firefighters have thrown new light on the effects of PM in occupational settings.

In some industries, PM is also an important safety issue, not just a health hazard. For example, fine particles—PM with diameter of 2.5 μm or smaller ($PM_{2.5}$)—are the main cause of reduced visibility (haze) in some parts of the world, and visibility impairment is a common risk factor for accident and injury.

The size of PM is directly linked to its potential for causing health effects, as it determines the range that PM can reach in the respiratory tract. Engineered nanoparticles were introduced to the industry just several decades ago. While the chemical components vary widely, they have drawn much attention as a single entity simply because of their size. With their small size, nanoparticles are able to penetrate various barriers such as cell membranes and deposit in organelles such as mitochondria. They can travel throughout the body and have the potential of causing damage that humans have never encountered. A property closely related to the small size is the relatively large surface area, which is an important factor for toxic effects. Although data on their adverse health effects are limited, it is a serious concern whether innocuous materials such as carbon may cause serious diseases such as cancer when they are in the form of nanoparticles. When the size of the same material is down to the nanolevel, its shape, density, physicochemical stability, and surface modification are regarded as the main causes that elicit an altered physiological response or cytotoxicity. As the global market for nanomaterial-based products is rapidly growing, there is an urgent need for studies exploring the occupational safety and health issues related to their manufacturing process.

Occupational Mental and Behavioral Disorders

Mental health has been a great concern in the workplace for decades, but it was not until 2010 that the International Labour Organization (ILO) included "mental and behavioral disorders" in its list of occupational diseases, under "occupational diseases by target organ systems." Unlike disorders of other organ systems, however, most mental and behavioral disorders do not have clearly identified etiology. Consequently, it is hard to assess their associations with work, except for those caused by chemicals and brain injuries. In fact, post-traumatic stress disorder (PTSD) is the only mental/behavioral disorder specified in the list. By definition, identification of the "stressor" is an essential diagnostic criterion of this disorder (American Psychiatric Association, 2000). Therefore, if the stressor is from the work environment or activity, it is reasonable to recognize the case as an occupational disease. As a feature of the revised ILO list, an open item was added to each category, and so *other mental or behavioral disorders not mentioned in the preceding item where a direct link is established scientifically, or determined by methods appropriate to national conditions and practice, between the exposure to risk factors arising from work activities and the mental and behavioral disorder(s) contracted by the worker*" was added to this category. Nonetheless, it is challenging to recognize any other mental or behavioral disorder as an occupational disease. With well-defined etiology, PTSD should be a good breaking point to achieve a better understanding of the mechanisms of mental and behavioral disorders. One promising direction is the study of biomarkers on mental stress such as the saliva cortisol level, which links stressors to physiological changes.

Studying biomarkers is also important to the surveillance of mental and behavioral disorders in workers, no matter the disorder is work related or not. Currently, most surveillance programs for workers are literally "physical checkups," and a major reason is the lack of objective and reliable tools. Except for substance abuse, the tools available for screening mental and behavioral disorders are mostly self-reported questionnaires, and honest answers to the test questions are crucial to make them work. With a better understanding of the etiology of mental and behavioral disorders, reliable biomarkers of the disorders may be identified and applied to surveillance programs and even to their diagnosis.

In addition to occupational mental and behavioral disorders per se, psychosomatic symptoms are also very important in the practice of occupational medicine. They may reduce productivity and even lead to sick leaves. In workers who take sick leaves due to diseases or injuries, no matter work related or not, psychosomatic symptoms may delay or terminate their return to work. Besides ruling out physical conditions, a more efficient and reliable approach to identify psychosomatic symptoms is desirable. Hopefully, with a better understanding of the etiology of mental and behavioral disorders, such an approach can be achieved.

Shift Work and Burnout

In a broad sense, "shift work" refers to working on a schedule outside the regular working hours, 9:00 a.m. to 5:00 p.m. in most countries. The regular working hours are set mainly depending on sunlight, which means that shift work usually involves night shifts. Therefore, the first wave of shift work should have come along with the improvement of lighting, which makes illumination in the workplace during the night similar to that in the daytime and thus extends work schedule to nighttime. The second wave of shift work should have come as a result of the Industrial Revolution, when workers took turns to work with machines to maximize the production. With globalization, shift work has become a requirement of business operation across time zones, instead of just a measure to increase productivity, in more and more industries, especially in the service sector. In the United States, more than 21 million (17.7%) wage and salary workers worked alternate shifts on a regular basis in 2004 (McMenamin, 2007), and in the European Union, up to 20 percent of the working population was involved in some forms of shift work in 2007. The numbers should have increased over the years. In developing countries, with outsourcing services from countries with higher wages to those with lower wages becoming increasingly common, the demand for working night shifts has expanded further. Because not so many people can or are willing to work night shifts on a regular basis, the number of workers engaged in rotating shifts has been increasing.

Shift work is associated with many diseases. Most obviously, shift work may lead to sleeping disorders because of the disruption of the circadian rhythm. Studies have also linked shift work to metabolic syndrome, which is the development to varying degrees and combinations of insulin-resistance and, therefore, may increase blood sugar, obesity, cholesterol, and blood pressure, leading to consequences such as cardiovascular disease and diabetes. It has also been linked to the functioning of liver, kidney, and thyroid, as well as disorders of these organs. Furthermore, there are studies showing associations between shift work and cancer.

In addition to causing diseases, shift work may increase injuries and threaten the safety of the workplace. It is also associated with decreased productivity and a diminished quality of life. As shift work has become a necessary evil associated with globalization, occupational safety and health professionals need to identify working schedules that are less harmful to workers while meeting business needs at the same time.

An emerging problem associated with shift work is extended working hours. In addition to safety issues, a major concern associated with working too many hours is so-called *karoshi*. The term was first applied by the Japanese to describe the most serious outcome of working too many hours—death, or sudden death to be exact. In fact, most of these cases can be attributed to cardiovascular and cerebrovascular disorders, and so the term "overwork" is used in the East Asia to describe less serious cases that are not fatal. However, such conditions have not been recognized as occupational diseases in most countries in the world. A review of systematic reviews with meta-analysis in 2020 found that stroke is the only outcome that had moderate-grade evidence associated with long working hours, which showed a dose-response relationship, while there was only low-grade evidence supporting such associations for coronary disease and other outcomes including depression and selected complications of pregnancy. The evidence came from a meta-analysis of 603,838 individuals in 24 cohorts in the United States, Europe, and Australia. Therefore, Western countries should pay more attention to the health effects of long working hours than they used to.

Another health condition associated with long working hours is "burnout," which has been around for a long time, especially among health-care professionals themselves. Like *karoshi*, this condition has not been identified as a disease entity. In fact, aside from physical illness, "burnout" is also used to cover mental illness related to overwork, which may be introduced by stressors other than long working hours. In Japan, suicide due to stress from overwork is regarded as an occupational disease and has received much attention. More studies are needed to construct the scientific basis of "burnout" and establish its diagnostic criteria and prevention strategy. In fact, with the COVID-19 pandemic, many studies on burnout of health-care professionals have been conducted recently. While this is an occupational health issue, more importantly, it is a patient safety issue also affecting the quality of care.

Infectious Diseases and Working from Home

Infectious diseases that can be transmitted person-to-person may spread widely in the community or along routes of exposure that bring people together, through social networks, schools, shared living, and face-to-face interactions.

As a practical matter, contagious infectious diseases mainly threaten workers in the health-care industry. Some countries do not even recognize an infectious disease acquired during the course of taking care of the patient by a health professional as an occupational disease, although transmissible infectious diseases are clearly occupational diseases when they are contracted in the workplace by health professionals. It is sometimes difficult to distinguish between infectious diseases occurring as a result of exposure in a health-care setting or in the community in which the health-care worker lives, especially when there is already a widespread transmission. However, when a localized outbreak of a serious contagious disease occurs, it is almost unavoidable, despite universal health-care precautions, that patients seeking care will expose health-care workers to the pathogen, especially at the very beginning of the outbreak.

Although hospitals and health-care services concentrate the risk in the workplace, contagious infectious diseases in the community pose a threat in all walks of life, and with the COVID-19 pandemic, people around the world have generally realized the damage they can introduce. In fact, long before this pandemic, contagious infectious diseases have been claiming human lives as an occupational hazard for centuries. In particular, with the appearance of multiple-drug resistance strains and transmission, tuberculosis (TB) is a reemerging occupational hazard in the United States. Other than that, the threat of viruses has become more and more serious in recent decades. At the same time, parasitic diseases such as malaria remain an occupational hazard affecting millions of workers in certain parts of the world.

Even with proper personal protective equipment (PPE) and vaccination programs, with threats like the COVID-19 pandemic, working from home appears to be an effective solution to protecting workers while keeping the business running. In fact, before the pandemic, working from home had become increasingly popular with the advancement in distance communication and the emergence of home offices. Health issues, such as those arising from social isolation and ergonomic hazards, should be an emerging area requiring greater research.

Personal Protective Equipment

As discussed elsewhere in this book, PPE is the mode of protection in which the worker wears a device or protective clothing that shields them from contact with the hazard. PPE is considered a last resort when it comes to protection but is sometimes the best that can be done. In the past, however, ensuring and facilitating the use of PPE was often more challenging than developing the PPE in the first place. Nonetheless, the two major reasons why a worker may be unwilling to use PPE are inconvenience and interference with work. Therefore, there is an emerging need to develop better PPE, not just for safety, but also for health. Hopefully, with the COVID-19 pandemic as a vivid example for both health-care workers and "essential workers" throughout the economy, the compliance of workers in using PPE correctly can be greatly improved, and employers even outside of health care will be more vigilant.

In the health-care setting, development of PPE plays a disproportionately important role because the opportunities for protecting workers as a group (the "public health approach" as described in chapter 3) are more limited than they might be in mining (where PPE is used to protect against silica dust but there are also effective methods of ventilation and dust suppression, for example).

Aging Workforce

With declines in the total fertility rate (which fell from 2.9 to 2.5 births per woman between 1994 and 2019) and the extension of life expectancy (rose from 65 years in 1994 to 72 years in 2019), population aging is taking place throughout the world. In 2020, there were an estimated 727 million persons aged 65 years or over worldwide, and the global number of persons aged 65 years or over was projected to more than double by 2050. In the United States, more than 10,000 people turn 65 every day, and in 2021, the number of people aged 65 years or over was 56.4 million, which is expected to be 82.3 million in 2040. On top of that, increased levels of education among younger generations keep them longer at school and work longer periods of time in order to save enough for retirement. They are living healthier lives and so are able to work longer. Consequently, the workforce is aging.

In terms of occupational health, there are many problems emerging as the workforce is aging. To physical hazards, the elderly are more vulnerable than younger people. For example, they are more likely to suffer from heat-related disorders because of the decreased ability to regulate body temperature, reduced cardiac function, and so on. To biological hazards, their immunity declines with age. For chemical hazards, they accumulate more body burden as they work more years and stay at work long enough (beyond the latent period) to develop illness while still on the job. In addition, their abilities to metabolize chemicals decline with aging. For ergonomic hazards, the situation is even worse. While the elderly have changes in the natural course of aging, minor traumas in the musculoskeletal system can be accumulated and add to those changes, which may become symptomatic and even disabling during the tenure of working. Besides illness, declines in sensory organs and the neurological system make them prone to accidents. Even for healthy elderly, they often feel frustrated as they find their performance in both daily work and personal activities decline, and the situation gets worse in those who have illnesses. Psychosocial support is very important in keeping them in the workforce, especially from their superiors and colleagues at the workplace.

Although aging is an inevitable and overall irreversible process, modifications of the work environment and activities can keep workers in the workforce longer and healthier at the same time. Research in the field of ergonomics plays an essential role in dealing with an aging workforce. While hardware such as smart tools and robots should be developed, software such as management and psychosocial factors should be studied.

CHAPTER THIRTEEN

The Future of Occupational and Environmental Medicine

Tee L. Guidotti, William G. Buchta, Tanisha Taylor,
Denece Kesler, Robert K. McLellan,
Robert Bourgeois, and Bill Bruce

The field of occupational and environmental medicine (OEM) covers a vast range of activities such as direct patient care, optimizing the health and safety of entire workforces, consulting, and responding to toxic and biological exposures and environmental issues. Individual practitioners, scholars, and thought leaders may approach these topics or issues in a variety of ways, depending on their type of practice. There is an ongoing dialogue within the field over important concepts as well as emerging problems and hazards. No chapter or book can possibly capture the range of opinions, priorities, and ideas. This chapter presents views of the future of OEM that are widely held and frequently discussed. The opinions expressed in this chapter do not necessarily reflect the personal views of each author or the official position of ACOEM on a given topic and, of course, cannot reflect the subtlety and nuance of each topic. For physicians entering OEM fresh, it may be the first time in one's professional career that medicine is not limited to the hospital or clinic but expands to the whole world, including the world of work, as many varied workplaces as exist in the economy, and living in all human environments, natural and built.

OEM physicians play diverse roles and must function on many levels including direct patient care, policy development and leadership, public and population health, and medicolegal issues, to name a few. Increasingly, this will also involve serving as a leader in responding to health affairs in their respective organizations, sometimes as a consultant, sometimes as an executive, and sometimes as a practitioner.

There will always be a need for the specific skills that define an OEM physician: the cognitive skills, the specialized knowledge, functional assessment of workers, causation analysis, and management skills applied to health. Because of their unique training and long-term familiarity with workplaces and environmental issues, OEM specialists are better positioned than other medical specialties to champion workplace wellness, prevent or mitigate work-related injuries and illnesses, improve worker health, and deal with environmental issues. The environmental medicine side of OEM will increase in importance and recognition as a field of medicine in support of public health but will probably not become a distinct area of clinical practice. The two will remain conjoined and will continue their slow integration into one medical specialty, in which the workplace is one "environment" and the community is another.

OEM was a leader in developing evidence-based medicine, developing the *ACOEM Practice Guidelines* to help physicians of any specialty deal with occupational injuries and illness and their outcomes (some states require their use). However, state and federal regulations have sometimes lagged behind the science, such as when evidence of harm from hazards based on new research accumulates before regulation catches up or there is general awareness. Examples in the past include asbestos, lead, radium, and perfluorocarbons. This is because the implementation of occupational health science and regulations depend on acceptance of the evidence for risk and on balancing social, economic, and political factors in a largely political arena in which scientific evidence is not the only consideration. How OEM will respond in the future can be predicted by how it responded to change in the past: by championing worker health, anticipating the risk of exposures at work from innovations and changes in process, focusing on prevention rather than exclusively on diagnosis and treatment, and giving medicine a central role in identifying disease and surveillance.

OEM is shaped and driven on the occupational side by changes in technology, the economy, the organization of the workplace, the profile of the workforce, the needs of individual workers for a system that protects them and their families, and regulation. On the environmental side, it is shaped by changes in technology and the economy as well but also by new research (documenting previously unsuspected injury), ideas of environmental justice, and public tolerance for "externalization" of costs (when costs are offloaded onto workers or the community who do not receive the benefit) in the form of pollution, health risk, and unsustainable development, which in turn is reflected in legal actions against polluters.

A good example is close to home for physicians: health care. Hospital, clinic, and medical center environments are exceptionally complicated and potentially hazardous workplaces and of particular interest with diverse exposures and hazards including biological (viruses and bacteria), physical (radiation), drugs and other care-related chemicals, and violence, in addition to all the chemical and safety hazards that are common to any large workplace, not just health care.

The COVID-19 pandemic has highlighted the profound role of OEM physicians in health care in dealing with challenges involving infectious disease on a very large scale—not patient by patient, which is the traditional role of a physician, but supporting services to entire communities, entire health-care institutions, and entire civic institutions such as schools. OEM physicians protected frontline health-care workers and sometimes were at the front line themselves. Their experience, training, and insight were needed first regarding testing, exposures, personal protective equipment, and organizing vaccinations and later in managing return-to-work challenges. In many instances, OEM physicians used available data from reasonable studies, local and regional testing numbers, and the needs of employers to manage and change these mitigation and screening methods to keep the essential workforce viable. While much of the country was locked down, most essential workers were able to work safely and stay healthy. As we venture into the next century, workplaces will become increasingly more complex, with increasing use of robotics and automation, including in operating rooms.

The interface between humans and technology, including artificial intelligence and working around robots, creates new work challenges. The field of ergonomics has been the traditional domain for "human factors" and the capacity to control and keep up with technology and the working environment. Physical safety around ever more powerful and autonomous devices has been the domain of safety science, but the OEM physician will be involved at a deeper level than just patching up injuries. Automation will further complicate the economics of work, jobs as we know it will be replaced, new jobs created, and more opportunities will arise as a result of the "gig" economy of short-term work assignments. OEM has the capacity to evolve to a more personalized, individualized preventive science, based on the capacity of the worker and the needs of workplaces on issues such as safety, ergonomics, infection control, fitness for duty, and return to work.

Change within OEM comes from changes in the big wide world, by real changes in technology, economics, and employment that matter to real people. Of all medical specialties, OEM is closest to what makes society tick and what makes the world go around. That has meant that it is not as flashy or dramatic as some areas of clinical practice—it does not settle for sick care alone but works diligently to keep bad things from happening in the first place, to limit the harm if they cannot be prevented, and to restore workers to good health and normal function when the worst does occur. This is not the stuff of movies and television dramas that feature dramatic rescues, glamorous action, and public attention. OEM practitioners settle for the satisfaction of knowing that they have made things better, safer, and fairer. In the end, that is more valuable than fame and glory.

Physicians who have training in and insight into occupational and environmental health problems add value in the occupational health system (especially in workers' compensation and managing health in large enterprises) and can clearly see the issues on the environmental health side, where there is a public health system to protect the community as a whole but no system for individualized specialty care. The environmental side of OEM is expanding due to climate change and other new environmental issues, and many OEM physicians address environmental issues as part of their OEM practice. As these environmental issues impact workers, for the time being and foreseeable future, environmental medicine will remain an extension of occupational medicine practice.

How OEM Got Where It Is

In order to understand the most likely future for OEM (the ideal future is another subject entirely), it is helpful to know how it got to where it is, picking up from chapter 1.

OEM (as "industrial medicine") had a long history, culminating in the Progressive Movement around the turn of the twentieth century. Since then, much more than other medical fields, it has been pulled in different directions and has struggled to reconcile the contradictions. These contradictions are resolving but slowly, and they may still define some of the culture, identity, and motivation of physicians in the field.

The first and most obvious juxtaposition is tension between the interests of the employer and the interests of the workers. In the nineteenth and early twentieth century, it was hard to make a living as an occupational (in those days "industrial") physician without working for a company, and bosses were usually not respectful of a physician's independence or medical ethics. However, there were many exceptions, and more enlightened companies that did value worker health and safety, physicians' independence, and medical ethics. There was no environmental medicine to speak of.

During the period when asbestos and radium were found to cause cancer, some physicians and medical investigators tried to conceal this reality. However, others, the ones who are celebrated today, were responsible for revealing what widespread and very dangerous hazards they were. The issue revealed the presence of one group of experts who either sold out or were in denial about the risk and another group of experts who accepted the evidence. Those who remained true to the evidence were led by Irving Selikoff, who was a leader in both occupational and environmental medicine and called for OEM to stand for integrity and the primacy of scientific evidence. Attracted by this vision and with training funded by the new National Institute for Occupational Safety and Health (from 1970), hundreds of physicians and other occupational health professionals entered the field with a new commitment, much like the Progressive Movement the better part of a century before. The field was transformed, although it still struggles from time to time with these contradictions.

The OEM physician's skills, training, and recognition through licensure have ensured the survival of the field over the years, despite the Depression, despite efforts to snuff it out in the 1950s on the notion that general practitioners could do the work just as well, and despite the great "outsourcing" starting in the 1980s, when many big companies closed their occupational health services, with mixed results. When physician positions in the industry were being terminated in the 1990s, their functions were often taken over by nurses or other professionals, to the consternation of OEM physicians who felt that their jobs were being taken from them. In reality, the jobs would probably have been lost anyway because many companies wanted to cut costs and gain more control. The number of OEM physician jobs actually increased during this time because they moved out of large companies and into the community, where they became available to many more small- and medium-scale employers.

After the opposition to occupational medicine in the 1950s and 1960s broke down (coinciding with but not caused by the rise of managed care), there followed a long, messy, dispiriting sorting-out period in medicine generally and OEM in particular.

During this time, occupational medicine changed greatly. The Occupational Safety and Health Act of 1970, together with growing pressure for reform of workers' compensation systems at the state level, underscored the importance of occupational medicine, and the Americans with Disabilities Act (ADA) of 1990 provided a framework for occupational justice. However, aspects of occupational medicine practice that had previously been considered drawbacks turned out to be advantages in the long run, particularly the independence of the field from personal health insurance and hospital cost-cutting. Heightened interest in environmental hazards created a niche for occupational medicine practitioners and teachers to become more visible in addressing environmental problems, such as indoor air quality and concern in communities for toxic hazards, which led to a modest revival of interest in mainstream environmental medicine but also a much larger wave of interest in unscientific and alternative medical practice.

The ADA and subsequent amendments recognized the need to put workers with disabilities on a more equal and fair footing. It has improved OEM physicians' ability to base fitness-to-work decisions on essential job functions and bring employees back to work or keep them at work, which is increasingly important, given our aging and diverse workforce. The critical nature of safe and early return to work and stay at work is a basic principle of caring for the injured worker within OEM.

The number of OEM physician jobs rebounded in the 2000s as employers faced the reality that some functions simply required special training and medical credentials. By that time, however, some OEM training programs (residencies for physicians intending to specialize) had closed for lack of funding, and the pipeline of trained specialists had decreased, so there was a worsening shortage of OEM physicians just at the time that demand for qualified physicians was exploding.

There is still a profound imbalance between the capacity to train OEM physicians and demand for them. OEM is currently dealing with a constricted "pipeline" or supply of practitioners for the future. Over the years, OEM training has mirrored the balance of individual and population practice, but maintaining residency programs has been a challenge, due primarily to inconsistent funding. Because of the time and expense that it takes to start and run a training program and a shortfall in funding from federal and other sources for residency programs in OEM (funds that are available to other medical specialties), there are far fewer training programs than are needed. The benefits of having a strong OEM presence during COVID have precipitated a renewed interest in increased sustainable federal funding for additional OEM residents. Enhancing the number of OEM graduates depends on the success of these efforts.

However, recent changes to OEM training requirements allow programs to include a first postgraduate year (PGY1) year of training to facilitate medical school graduates and the option for midcareer physicians to transition to OEM with advanced standing. Residents usually have completed another residency program or have had significant prior clinical work experiences, a benefit to OEM. Although many practicing OEM physicians have not completed an OEM residency program, they provide a significant amount of clinical OEM care in the United States at a high level of competency.

The discipline of OEM also does not rely solely on the pipeline residency program graduates to fill needed physician openings, otherwise one would be left to ask how OEM could survive with so few graduates each year. The answer is that OEM is one of the best opportunities for practitioners embarking on a second career in medicine. Physicians who plan on an OEM career may choose other specialty residencies depending upon their focus areas of practice. Many physicians enter OEM from internal medicine, family medicine, or emergency medicine to name a few. Often, military physicians enter the specialty as a second career.

OEM as a Field of Practice

OEM tends to move in 20- to 30-year cycles. OEM is entering a new era, more favorable to specialty practice, addressing new occupational hazards introduced by changing technology and focusing on environmental issues of medical concern.

OEM is a unique field of medicine and a unique medical specialty. There is virtually no inpatient, hospital-based component of occupational or environmental medicine, although there are occupational health services for hospital employees in every medical center. It may be highly research and knowledge intensive in advanced practice (see chapter 2), but direct (clinical) patient care may be done by other physicians (e.g., in family or emergency medicine). However, the clinical medicine component is not "simple." For example, when taking care of the workers' compensation (WC) patient, understanding the differences between outcomes and approaches in WC versus non-WC is challenging and requires quite a bit of training and understanding.

Most of medicine exists because people get hurt and need relief. Most of public health exists because people quite reasonably fear getting sick and want to be protected, together with their families. OEM exists for many reasons, chief among them that society has a conviction that people should not put their lives on the line just to make a living or due to the environment they live in, and if they do become injured on the job or in their community, they deserve justice and ideally compensation. For OEM, these practical tools include effective diagnosis and treatment, to be sure, but they also include the skills and knowledge to investigate and explain the cause of the problem, the ability to see down the road to what recovery will look like, how to assess and limit impairment, and how to prevent problems from happening in the future.

There are OEM physicians who serve as chief medical officers or medical directors, as experts in court, as experts for government agencies and as advisers to regulatory bodies and who teach about health risks. Others serve as consultants who assess injured workers and patients for occupational and environmental disease, managers for prevention services, and specialists who handle the occupational and environmental health problems of private and public enterprises. Currently, there are numerous OEM-trained physicians who provide direct patient care full time or as part of their job duties.

Basic health care can be performed by other health professionals such as occupational health nurses, nurse practitioners, or physician assistants. One aspect of the future of OEM lies in defining what the OEM physician does best and knows best, with a view toward how specialists should be influencing the practice of all health professionals providing occupational health care. The medical specialty society representing occupational medicine, the American College of Occupational and Environmental Medicine (ACOEM), has accomplished this task by formulating and then validating a set of essential competencies for specialty practice. ACOEM then developed a comprehensive set of clinical guidelines to improve quality of care and provides learning opportunities for physicians to learn the basics of occupational and environmental medicine, regardless of their original specialization and training.

Physicians can enter practice at this basic level without OEM specialty credentials, and many of these physicians bring knowledge and skills from other specialties (such as surgery and internal medicine). Much of what a career OEM physician specialist does is virtually invisible to medical students or other physicians because it involves designing and evaluating health programs, monitoring groups of workers for evidence of ill-health or exposure to hazards, measuring levels of impairment for compensation, managing health risks at the level of populations (rather than individuals), and reviewing risks in order to determine causation and prioritize prevention. There is no exact counterpart to any of these functions in the rest of medicine. An injured worker might be seen initially by a treating physician and then followed up by an OEM physician, but most health-care systems in the United States are not set up for that. As a result, care is fragmented; providers understandably do not wish to lose track of their patients, and if the OEM physician is not the treating physician, he or she is relegated to a supporting role.

There are predictable changes on the horizon that will affect the future of OEM practice. The dominant forms of health-care delivery for OEM are at the moment freestanding community occupational health centers and hospital-based or group-based occupational medicine clinics. Both models predominantly serve employees of companies in their local area, varying from a very small to very large catchment area from which cases come. In-plant and corporate health services may provide only minimal care and may prefer to refer the injured worker to a local hospital or occupational health practitioner. It was in large part the prospect that employers would offer comprehensive health care at the place of employment that panicked general practitioners in the 1950s and led to the backlash against occupational medicine. Recently, some large employers have become involved again in this model, with on-site "company clinics" (urgent care or primary-care clinics for employees), and several large corporations, notably Walgreens, have explored models of branded health care in the community. At present, most of these health services do not emphasize occupational medicine.

OEM has not been well served by the health-care system in general, and that needs to change. Hospitals, which control much of the actual delivery of occupational health services in the United States, are designed for diagnosis and treatment; they are not geared for routine and screening (surveillance) tests such as chest x-rays and hearing tests or for prevention. Current hospital and multispecialty electronic medical record systems are grossly deficient for the purposes of occupational medicine and do not allow easy interface with software that is better suited. Billings for workers' compensation are generally treated like any other form of insurance despite reporting and case management expectations. Medical records for occupational cases are mostly kept together with those of other patients, although there are different retention requirements and confidentiality issues. These are mostly technical issues, however, and are likely to be resolved eventually as occupational medicine becomes better accepted as a service that every health-care system is expected to offer. Progress will also be accelerated if a few health-care facilities get dropped as preferred providers.

Some of the practical and business issues, such as record-keeping and billing, will likely be solved by emerging technologies, as they will be across all fields of medicine. More fundamentally, the practice of prevention and wellness that is so important in OEM is already moving ahead rapidly from advances in genomics, bioindicators, individualized medicine, and exposure science. OEM will continue to emphasize the health of workers, in their personal life (and that of their families), in occupational health, in the environment, and in the community in which they live. This broad sweep is increasingly supported by major employers, who are willing to pay to maintain a healthy workforce through wellness programs.

It is always dangerous to predict that the future will be like the past, but the big changes in occupational health services for this generation have probably already occurred. Progress in the short term will probably be the result of incremental improvement in quality, adoption of new technology, and analysis of big data sets, much like the rest of medicine. There is always the likelihood of unanticipated disruptive innovation, of course. A few changes already seem likely to have a disproportionate effect on the practice of occupational medicine, such as artificial intelligence for assessment of causation, online and remote health care (already common in settings such as offshore oil drilling platforms and greatly expanded during the COVID-19 pandemic), and wearable and ingestible sensors for monitoring as well as online medicine. New and better biomarkers based on epigenetics, particularly related to chemical exposure, are likely to play a big role in monitoring disease risk, both in particularly hazardous work environments and in much more refined and sensitive risk assessment for communities in environmental medicine.

OEM as Public Health and Prevention for the Worker

A former president of the American College of Occupational and Environmental Medicine (ACOEM), Kathryn Mueller, once defined the field by saying, "We protect the health of the people who make our world and keep it running." OEM physicians are engaged in all aspects of workers' health and the workplace and now spend more time addressing issues in healthy workers, workers groups, employers, or companies, with less than half their time spent addressing injured or ill patients' issues. Yet another past president of ACOEM, Warner Hudson, a former public health director himself, has defined occupational medicine as "public health for the employed population," environmental medicine as public health brought down to the individual level, and their union in OEM as the synthesis of public health and medicine.

OEM has always existed in dualities as both a clinical specialty for injured workers and a population-based practice for health management, with work injury care financed primarily by workers' compensation. This sense of always facing in two directions is reflected in the history of the specialty, which at times has been a powerful engine for progressive reform and workers' rights and at other times may have reflected the paternalistic and potentially repressive policies of some employers.

Increasing awareness that the OEM physician can impact overall worker health, workers' families, and their environment has resulted in an expanded breadth of this medical specialty. NIOSH has recently established a program on Total Worker Health, of which ACOEM is an affiliate. The program promotes a comprehensive approach to worker well-being by protecting safety and enhancing health and productivity for the benefit of workers, employers, and the nation. OEM physicians are increasingly asked to optimize all aspects of a worker's health.

The World Health Organization (WHO) also advocates for safe, healthy, and decent work for all workers and for the protection of their families from loss. WHO stresses the importance of a healthier and safer workplace to prevent disease and as a prerequisite to attain some of their sustainable development goals such as ensuring healthy lives and promoting well-being, sustainable economic growth, and decent work for all. Important occupational issues that need to be addressed include working conditions; the built environment; and chemical, biological, physical, and psychosocial hazards.

ACOEM represents OEM specialists who champion the health of workers, safety of workplaces, and quality of the environment even as the workplace changes. Increased use of automation and a shift from manufacturing to service-based workers has coincided with downsizing of traditional corporate medical departments. Recently, only 15–26 percent of ACOEM members list corporations as their primary work setting. The majority of OEM physicians work in clinical settings (52%–57%), while others work in government jobs (9%), academic settings (7%–9%), consulting (5%–11%), and other settings (<2%). ACOEM physician members are highly trained with 43–47 percent board certified in occupational medicine and 65–71 percent board certified in another specialty. ACOEM publishes numerous guidance documents, position statements, and evidence-based guidelines, including guidance for treatment and evaluation of law enforcement officers. ACOEM also develops evidence-based guidelines (*ACOEM Practice Guidelines*) addressing treatment for a variety of work-related conditions.

In 2019, the National Academy of Medicine recommended adopting work system changes that create healthy, positive work environments for healthcare workers to lessen burnout. This initiative, originally focused on healthcare workers, could serve as a model for managing the workplace going forward, and OEM physicians are well suited to lead the way based on their training, prior experience, and expertise.

Where OEM Goes from Here

OEM does not exist in isolation. American society is changing, and with it, so is the future of OEM in this country.

All of medicine is facing a crisis. Treatment and hospital care are too expensive, hospitals and health-care system managers have a louder voice than physicians and nurses, prevention is pushed to the sidelines, the public is confused over basic issues (such as vaccination), and medical practice is undergoing a technological revolution, although it lags in other sectors. The COVID-19 pandemic and the opioid crisis both revealed how fragile the American health-care system really is. The spectacle of health-care workers and essential workers struggling and sacrificing to do their job and risking their own health and possibly lives to do so, often in the absence of basic protection, was the most vivid possible image of the importance of occupational health. The exodus of health-care professionals from frontline medicine imperils health care and small hospitals in rural areas and is, in part, a direct response to the perception by frontline health-care workers that their work is not valued or respected, given the behavior of some community residents. On the other hand, the Affordable Care Act demonstrated the enormous value of near-universal health insurance. The SARS-CoV-2 vaccine showed what biomedical science is truly capable of achieving in prevention. Environmental issues will go from urgent to critical even as the challenges of global climate change, and its accompanying local disasters such as wildfires, together with the rising frequency of innumerable local issues involving air and water pollution and issues of environmental justice, loom larger than ever. Less developed than the occupational medicine side of OEM, environmental medicine is lagging and needs to catch up quickly.

OEM does include a variety of regulatory examinations and roles, from which some OEM providers earn a substantial proportion of their income. The OEM physician will need to collaborate with government officials to continue to evaluate the value of these exams and modify the requirements as necessary. They could use traditional data-driven research tools but also more recent applications of artificial intelligence and so-called big data. In some cases, such exams may become moot or even obsolete, as in the case of commercial driver or pilot exams, should vehicles no longer require human drivers and pilots—a very real prospect with current technology.

It is not fantastical to think that as medicine itself changes, there will be new openings to contribute and new opportunities for what OEM has to offer. A prevention-oriented, evidence-based, primarily outpatient, outward-looking medical specialty in the mold of a critical science, capable of handling complicated issues on an individual and community basis, is powerfully attractive as a model for medicine as a whole.

The concept of sustainability may be key to redefining the mission of OEM. Sustainability means managing the economy, protecting the environment, and allowing society to develop in an optimal way for the long term, generation to generation. The opportunity is to connect health with social, economic, and environmental sustainability, doing what OEM does best. The means to do this is to protect workers, their families, and community residents from harm during a time of unpredictable change; to protect the workforce and its essential productivity; and to protect communities from being harmed by environmental hazards and disruption. OEM is doing all these things now, but it has the capability to do much more.

Not coincidentally, this expanded mission is a logical step from OEM's historic role in "critical science" (see chapter 10), consistent with the drive to achieve global and national sustainability (in all sectors of the economy, society, and environment) and the United Nations (UN) Sustainable Development Goals. To do this on an expanded scale requires that OEM receives support beyond the health sector alone, grows in number and scale as a medical and public health profession, and develops greater capacity and leadership in environmental medicine. That this can be done is demonstrated by how far OEM has come since the 1950s, despite opposition and misunderstanding.

The intellectual tools to achieve the "critical science" function of OEM (see chapter 10) are the same, but the practical tools are different for occupational medicine and environmental medicine. The field of OEM practice is primarily driven by the occupational medicine side because there is much less clinical activity on the environmental side. It would be hard to make a living practicing strictly environmental medicine in a clinic, if done ethically within mainstream medicine based on the best current scientific evidence, even in academia. As a consequence, it is difficult to envision environmental medicine becoming a separate field of practice, and it will probably continue to be subsumed by occupational medicine in medical practice.

The continuous emergence of new chemical, infectious, and environmental hazards; advances in manufacturing and technology; pollution; climate change; substance use issues; and other events that impact the environment and workplace have increased the need for trained OEM physicians who can meet these demands. OEM practice continues to respond to new technology, work organization changes such as the increased use of artificial intelligence and automation, changing regulations, and demographic trends such as the aging of the workforce. As OEM physicians respond to future challenges, the specialty will need to continue to keep up with new developments and continue to be the champions at the forefront of worker health and the environment. OEM practice will continue to expand its scope in prevention while maintaining its role in the care of injured workers.

The footprint of OEM is huge: everyone works in some form or impacts those who do not. The value and benefit of work transcends more than simply the worker's financial security, as employment is an economic engine for society and also an integral component that makes an individual unique and purposeful. For example, the parent working in a chemical plant can bring something home to the children. The inability to return to work may financially destroy an entire family. Thus, OEM protects the worker, protects families, makes the workplace more sustainable, manages risk, supports productivity, adds resilience and reduced vulnerability to disruption and disaster, and prevents economic loss to society as well as to the enterprise. It contributes to all three elements of enterprise sustainability and sustainable development: the economy (by protecting workers and preventing loss), the environment (both in general and in the microenvironment of the workplace and built environment), and society (not least by protecting the health of communities as well as individuals).

OEM, more than most other medical specialties, is driven by society, the economy, and technology rather than new drugs, biomedical research, and health-care innovations. It is a unique field of medicine, uniquely positioned to be responsive to a changing world. The field is good medicine, good medical care, a good means of achieving fairness and health protection, and a good future-risk management strategy. On a deeper level, it is an ongoing dialogue between the world of medicine and the world of everyday life.

Acknowledgments

The authors thank Dr. Douglas W. Martin, medical director of Unity Point Health—Saint Luke's Occupational Medicine, Sioux City, Iowa, and incoming president of the American College of Occupational and Environmental Medicine, for review and valuable comments.

Some of the material in this chapter originally appeared in Baker B., Kesler D., Guidotti T. Occupational and environmental medicine: public health and medicine in the workplace. *Am J Pub Health*. 2020;110(5):636–637. Used by permission.

Bibliography

Chapter 1. A Brief History of Occupational and Environmental Medicine in the United States

Aldrich M. History of Workplace Safety in the United States, 1880–1970. EH.Net Encyclopedia, edited by Robert Whaples. August 14, 2001. Accessed October 4, 2021. http://eh.net/encyclopedia/history-of-workplace-safety-in-the-united-states-1880-1970/.

Gochfeld M. Chronological history of occupational medicine. *J Occup Environ Med*. 2005;47(2):96–114.

Gochfeld M. Occupational medicine practice in the United States since the industrial revolution. *J Occup Environ Med*. 2005;47(2):115–131.

Guidotti TL. Occupational and environmental medicine. In: *The Handbook of Occupational and Environmental Medicine*. Santa Barbara, CA: Praeger/ABC-CLIO; 2020.

Hunter D. *Diseases of Occupations*. 6th ed. London: Blackwell; 1978. [Hunter was a distinguished professor in London. This edition of his textbook remains the single most accessible source for historical material.]

Mock HE. *Industrial Medicine and Surgery*. Philadelphia: WB Saunders; 1919.

Ramazzini B. *On the Diseases of Occupations*. Modena: Antonio Capponi; 1700. There are many editions of this medical classic, ranging from inexpensive paperbacks to special editions with ornate bindings. For the serious reader, it is recommended that the first purchase be a cheap version with wide enough margins to write notes, because so much remains relevant today, and this book should be read, not just admired.

Selleck HB. *Occupational Health in America*. Detroit: Wayne State University Press; 1962.

U.S. Department of Labor. Annals of the Department. History. Accessed August 25, 2021. https://www.dol.gov/general/aboutdol/history/dolchp01.

Walsh DC. *Corporate Physicians: Between Medicine and Management*. New Haven, CT: Yale University Press; 1987.

Chapter 2. Schools of Thought in Occupational and Environmental Medicine

Guidotti TL. *The Handbook of Occupational and Environmental Medicine: Principles, Practice, Populations, and Problem-Solving.* 2nd ed. Santa Barbara, CA: ABC-CLIO; 2020.

Guidotti TL. Knowing. In: *Health and Sustainability.* New York: Oxford University Press; 2015. pp. 41–72.

LaDou J, Harrison R. *Current Diagnosis & Treatment: Occupational and Environmental Medicine.* 6th ed. New York: Lange/McGraw Hill; 2021.

Levy B, Wegman DH, Baron SL, Sokas RK. *Occupational and Environmental Health.* 7th ed. New York: Oxford University Press; 2017.

Smith KF, Smith HJ. *Occupational and Environmental Medicine: Board Review and Clinical Synopsis.* Beverly Farms, MA: OEM Press; 2021.

Chapter 3. Theory and Practice of Occupational and Environmental Medicine

Boulton ML, Wallace R. *Maxcy-Rosenau-Last Public Health and Preventive Medicine.* 16th ed. New York: McGraw Hill; 2022.

Friedman DJ, Starfield B. Models of population health: their value for US public health practice, policy, and research. *Am J Pub Health.* 2003;93:366–369.

Guidotti TL. *Health and Sustainability.* New York: Oxford University Press; 2015.

Gunning-Schepers LJ, Barendregt JJ, van der Maas PJ. Population interventions reassessed. *Lancet.* 1989;333:479–481.

Hobson J, Smedley J, eds. *Fitness for Work: The Medical Aspects.* 6th ed. London: Oxford University Press; 2019.

Leavell HR, Clark EG. *Textbook of Preventive Medicine.* New York: McGraw Hill; 1953. Original description of the levels of prevention.

Methorn JM, Talmage JB, Ackerman WE, Hyman MH. *AMA Guides to the Evaluation of Disease and Injury Causation.* Chicago: American Medical Association; 2013.

Rose G, Khaw K-T, Marmot M. *Rose's Strategy of Preventive Medicine.* New York: Oxford University Press; 2008. A classic, essential reading.

Talmage JB, Methorn JM, Hyman MH. *AMA Guides to the Evaluation of Work Ability and Return to Work.* 2nd ed. Chicago: American Medical Association; 2011.

Chapter 5. Profiles: Practitioners in Action

Hobson J. *Why I Became an Occupational Physician and Other Occupational Health Stories.* London: Oxford University Press; 2020.

Chapter 6. Corporate Sector and Private Practice

Felton JS. *Occupational Medical Management: A Guide to the Organization and Operation of In-Plant OHSs.* Boston: OEM Health Information; 1989.

Guidotti TL, Arnold S, eds. *Occupational Health Services: A Practical Approach.* 2nd ed. New York: Routledge; 2012.

Hartenbaum NP. *The DOT Medical Examination: An Unofficial Guide to Commercial Drivers' Medical Certification.* 7th ed. Beverly Farms, MA: OEM Press; 2020.

Hartenbaum NP, Baker BA, Levin L, Saito K, Sayeed Y, Green-McKenzie J; Work Group on OEM Competencies. ACOEM guidance statement: ACOEM OEM core competencies. *J Occup Environ Med.* 2021;63(7):e445–e461. https://doi.org/10.1097/JOM.0000000000002211.

Moser R Jr. *Effective Management of Health and Safety Programs: A Practical Guide.* 3rd ed. Beverley Farms, MA: OEM Press; 2008.

Smith I. *Occupational Health: A Practical Guide for Managers.* London: Taylor and Francis; 2007; 6th ed., Beverly Farms, MA: OEM Press; 2021.

Swotinsky RB. *The Medical Review Officer's Manual: MROCC's Guide to Drug Testing.* 6th ed. Beverly Farms, MA: OEM Press; 2021.

Tao X, Kalia N, Bernacki EJ. *Workers' Compensation Claims Management: An Evidence-Based Approach to Measuring, Predicting, and Controlling Costs.* Beverly Farms, MA: OEM Press; 2019.

Chapter 7. Practice Settings

De Hart RL. *Guidelines for Establishing an Occupational Medical Program.* Chicago: American Occupational Medical Association; 1987.

Gaydos JC. Military occupational and environmental health: challenges for the 21st century. *Mil Med.* 2011;176(suppl 7):5–8. https://doi.org/10.7205/MILMED-D-11-00097.

Guidotti TL, Kuetzing BH. Competition and despecialization: an analytical study of occupational health services in San Diego, 1974–1984. *Am J Ind Med.* 1985;8:155–165.

Harber P, Rose S, Bontemps J, Saechao K, Liu Y, Elashoff D, Wu S. Occupational medicine practice: activities and skills of a national sample. *J Occup Environ Med.* 2010;52(7):1147–1153.

Harber P, Rose S, Bontemps J, Saechao K, Liu Y, Elashoff D, Wu S. Occupational medicine practice: one specialty or three? *J Occup Environ Med.* 2010;52(7):672–679.

Krahl PL, Malone TM, Thomas RJ, Gaydos JC. Military Occupational and Environmental Medicine and the Training of Occupational and Environmental Medicine Residents at the Uniformed Services University. 2019. Accessed September 1, 2021. https://apps.dtic.mil/sti/pdfs/AD1108031.pdf.

Mallon TM, ed. *Occupational Health and the Service Member.* Government Printing Office; 2019. Accessed November 21, 2022. https://medcoe.army.mil/borden-occupational-health-and-the-sm.

Rest K, ed. How to begin an occupational health program—administrative and ethical issues (entire issue). *Semin Occup Med.* 1986;1(1):1–96.

Chapter 8. Academic Occupational and Environmental Medicine

For current information on individual training programs and training program requirements, please use current online information sources, such as the following:

https://www.theabpm.org/become-certified/specialties/occupational -medicine/. ABPM. OM.
https://www.theabpm.org/2021/03/10/the-american-board-of-preventive -medicine-announces-updates-to-the-special-complementary-and -alternative-pathways-for-certification-in-the-specialties-of-aerospace -medicine-occupational-medicine-an/.

Accreditation Council for Graduate Medical Education (ACGME). *Preventive Medicine—Occupational Medicine Milestones.* 2020. Accessed October 4, 2021. https://www.acgme.org/globalassets/pdfs/milestones/preventivemedi cineoccupationalmedicinemilestones.pdf.

American Medical Association. *AMA Green Books.* Accessed October 4, 2021. https://www.acgme.org/About-Us/Publications-and-Resources/AMA -Green-Books/.

Green-McKenzie J, Emmett EA. Characteristics and outcomes of an innovative train-in-place residency program. *J Grad Med Educ.* 2017;9(5):634–639. https://doi.org/10.4300/JGME-D-16-00689.1.

Green-McKenzie J, Savanoor U, Duran H, Jones C, Vearrier D, Malak P, Emmett EA, Shofer FS. Outcomes of a survey-based approach to determine factors contributing to the shortage of occupational medicine physicians in the United States. *J Public Health Manag Pract.* 2021;27(suppl 3):S200– S205. https://doi.org/10.1097/PHH.0000000000001315.

Hartenbaum NP, Baker BA, Levin JL, Saito K, Sayeed Y, Green-McKenzie J; Work Group on OEM Competencies. ACOEM guidance statement: ACOEM OEM core competencies. *J Occup Environ Med.* 2021;63(7):e445–e461. https://doi.org/10.1097/JOM.0000000000002211.

Howard J. NIOSH: a short history. *Am J Pub Health.* 2020;110(5):629–630. https://doi.org/10.2105/AJPH.2019.305478.

MacLaury J. The job safety law of 1970: its passage was perilous. *Mon Labor Rev.* 1981;104:18.

Meiklejohn A. Industrial health: meeting the challenge. *Br J Ind Med.* 1959;16(1): 1–10. https://doi.org/10.1136/oem.16.1.1.

National Institute for Occupational Safety and Health (NIOSH). Extramural Workforce Development: Training Project Grants. 2021. Accessed October 4, 2021. https://www.cdc.gov/niosh/oep/trainprojgrnts.html.

National Institute for Occupational Safety and Health (NIOSH). NIOSH Total Worker Health® Program. Accessed October 4, 2021. https://www.cdc .gov/niosh/twh/default.html.

National Institute for Occupational Safety and Health (NIOSH). The Team Document: Ten Years of Leadership Advancing the National Occupational

Research Agenda. 2006. Accessed October 4, 2021. https://www.cdc.gov /nora/pdfs/NORA1Team-document_2006-121.pdf.

National Institute for Occupational Safety and Health (NIOSH); Lechliter J. 50 Years of NIOSH. Accessed October 4, 2021. https://www.cdc.gov/niosh /pdfs/NIOSH-50-Year-Timeline2021.pdf.

National Institute of Environmental Health Sciences. Research Training. 2018. Accessed November 21, 2022. https://www.niehs.nih.gov/careers/research /index.cfm.

National Research Council. *Addressing the Physician Shortage in Occupational and Environmental Medicine: Report of a Study.* Washington, DC: National Academies Press; 1991. https://doi.org/10.17226/9494.

Occupational Safety and Health Administration. OSHA Celebrates 40 Years of Accomplishments in the Workplace. Accessed October 4, 2021. https:// www.medph.org/apha/wp-content/uploads/2014/10/OSHATimeline .pdf.

Sappington CO, Marbaker ND. The industrial physician and the general practitioner. *JAMA.* 1930;95(26):1955–1957. https://doi.org/10.1001/jama.1930 .02720260001001.

WGBH Educational Foundation. Deadliest Workplace Accidents. 2011. Accessed October 4, 2021. https://www.pbs.org/wgbh/americanexperience/features /triangle-fire-deadliest-workplace-accidents/.

Chapter 9. Case Studies

Guidotti TL. *The Handbook of Occupational and Environmental Medicine.* Santa Barbara, CA: Praeger/ABC-CLIO; 2020.

Chapter 10. Core Controversies

Guidotti TL, ed. *Global Occupational Health.* New York: Oxford University Press; 2011.

Guidotti TL. *The Handbook of Occupational and Environmental Medicine.* Santa Barbara, CA: Praeger/ABC-CLIO; 2020.

Chapter 11. Classic Research in Occupational and Environmental Medicine

Checkoway H, Pearce N, Kriebel D. *Research Methods in Occupational Epidemiology.* 2nd ed. New York: Oxford University Press; 2004.

Hunter D. *Diseases of Occupations.* 6th ed. London: Blackwell; 1978.

Levy BS, Wegman DH, Baron SL, Sokas RK. *Occupational and Environmental Health.* 7th ed. New York: Oxford University Press; 2017.

Mendelsohn ML, Peters JP, Normandy MJ, eds. *Biomarkers and Occupational Health Progress and Perspectives.* Washington, DC: Joseph Henry Press; 1995.

Morabia A. *A History of Epidemiologic Methods and Concepts.* Basel: Springer; 2004.

National Academy of Sciences, Committee to Review the NIOSH Respiratory Disease Research Program. *Respiratory Diseases Research at NIOSH: Reviews of Research Programs of the National Institute for Occupational Safety and Health*. Washington, DC: National Academies Press; 2013.

Chapter 12. Contemporary Research and Looking Ahead

Sources for emerging research in OEM include the websites of funding agencies and sponsoring organizations, which usually include lists of current projects. These include but are not limited to the following:

National Institute of Environmental Health Sciences (https://www.niehs .nih.gov/research/index.cfm)
National Institute of Occupational Safety and Health (https://www.cdc .gov/niosh/programs.html)
National Toxicology Program (https://ntp.niehs.nih.gov/). NTP is formally a part of NIEHS.

For an overview of contemporary research in occupational and environmental medicine, the reader is directed to current and recent issues of the following publications:

Journal of Occupational and Environmental Medicine
Archives of Environmental and Occupational Medicine
Occupational and Environmental Medicine (UK)
Occupational Medicine (UK)
Environmental Research
Environmental Health
Scandinavian Journal of Work Environment and Health
Environmental Health Perspectives
American Journal of Industrial Medicine
SH@W: Safety and Health at Work (Korea)

These are the principal research journals in OEM. There are many other journals with related content in occupational health and industrial hygiene, environmental health, and specific subjects relevant to OEM. There are also many national, regional, and local journals in OEM and related fields that publish research, but the coverage of these journals may not be representative of global developments.

The remainder of this bibliography annotates the studies mentioned by Dr. How-Ran Guo in the chapter.

American Psychiatric Association. *Diagnostic and Statistical Manual of Mental Disorders*. 4th ed. Washington, DC: American Psychiatric Association; 2000.
Anastas PT, Warner JC. *Green Chemistry*. New York: Oxford University Press; 1998.
Asante-Duah K. *Public Health Risk Assessment for Human Exposure to Chemicals*. 2nd ed. Basel: Springer; 2017.

Becerra TA, Wilhelm M, Olsen J, Cockburn M, Ritz B. Ambient air pollution and autism in Los Angeles County, California. *Environ Health Perspect*. 2013; 121:380–386. https://doi.org/10.1289/ehp.1205827.

Bentley J, Toth M. *Exploring Wicked Problems: What They Are and Why They Are Important*. Bloomington, IN: Archway; 2020.

Biddle J, Roberts K. More evidence of the need for an ergonomic standard. *Am J Ind Med*. 2004;45:329–337.

Figueiro MG, White RD. Health consequences of shift work and implications for structural design. *J Perinatol*. 2013;33:S17–S23. https://doi.org/10.1038/jp .2013.7.

Guo H-R. Working hours spent on repeated activities and prevalence of back pain. *Occup Environ Med*. 2002;59:680–688.

Guo H-R, Tanaka S, Cameron LL, Seligman PJ, Behrens VJ, Ger J, Wild DK, Putz-Anderson V. Back pain among workers in the United States: national estimates and workers at high risk. *Am J Ind Med*. 1995;28:591–602.

Hiyama T, Yoshihara M. New occupational threats to Japanese physicians: karoshi (death due to overwork) and karojisatsu (suicide due to overwork). *Occup Environ Med*. 2008;65:428–429. https://doi.org/10.1136/oem.2007 .037473.

International Agency for Research on Cancer. The carcinogenicity of outdoor air pollution. *Lancet Oncol*. 2013;14:1262–1263. https://doi.org/10.1016/S14 70-2045(13)70487-X.

International Labour Organization. *ILO List of Occupational Diseases*. Rev ed. Geneva: International Labour Organization; 2010.

Iwasaki K, Takahashi M, Nakata A. Health problems due to long working hours in Japan: working hours, workers' compensation (Karoshi), and preventive measures. *Ind Health*. 2006;44:537–540.

Kakiashvili T, Leszek J, Rutkowski K. The medical perspective on burnout. *Int J Occup Med Environ Health*. 2013;26:401–412. https://doi.org/10.2478/s13 382-013-0093-3.

Ke DS. Overwork, stroke, and karoshi-death from overwork. *Acta Neurol Taiwan*. 2012;21:54–59.

Lalloo D, Macdonald E, Figueroa SV-P, Germeni E, McIntosh E. The value of occupational health research. London: Society of Occupational Medicine; 2019.

Lavandero R. Nurse burnout: what can we learn? *J Nurs Adm*. 1981;11:17–23.

Lioy P, Weisel C. *Exposure Science: Principles and Applications*. Cambridge, MA: Academic Press; 2014.

McMenamin TM. A time to work: recent trends in shift work and flexible schedules. *Mon Labor Rev*. 2007;12:3–15.

National Institute for Occupational Safety and Health. *Progress toward Safe Nanotechnology in the Workplace: A Report from the NIOSH Nanotechnology Research Center*. Atlanta: Centers for Disease Control and Prevention; 2013.

Nel A, Xia T, Mädler L, Li N. Toxic potential of materials at the nanolevel. *Science*. 2006;311:622–627. https://doi.org/10.1126/science.1114397.

Nemmar A, Holme JA, Rosas I, Schwarze PE, Alfaro-Moreno E. Recent advances in particulate matter and nanoparticle toxicology: a review of the in vivo and in vitro studies. *Biomed Res Int*. 2013;2013:279371. https://doi.org/10.1155/2013/279371.

Parent-Thirion A, Fernández Macías E, Hurley J, Vermeylen G. *Fourth European Working Conditions Survey*. Dublin: European Foundation for the Improvement of Living and Working Conditions; 2007.

Podila R, Brown JM. Toxicity of engineered nanomaterials: a physicochemical perspective. *J Biochem Mol Toxicol*. 2013;27:50–55. https://doi.org/10.1002/jbt.21442.

Sharifi S, Behzadi S, Laurent S, Forrest ML, Stroeve P, Mahmoudi M. Toxicity of nanomaterials. *Chem Soc Rev*. 2012;41:2323–2343. https://doi.org/10.1039/c1cs15188f.

Sigurdardottir LG, Valdimarsdottir UA, Fall K, Rider JR, Lockley SW, Schernhammer E, Mucci LA. Circadian disruption, sleep loss, and prostate cancer risk: a systematic review of epidemiologic studies. *Cancer Epidemiol Biomarkers Prev*. 2012;21:1002–1011. https://doi.org/10.1158/1055-9965.EPI-12-0116.

Smith L, Folkard S, Poole CJ. Increased injuries on night shift. *Lancet*. 1994;344:1137–1139.

Uehata T. Long working hours and occupational stress-related cardiovascular attacks among middle-aged workers in Japan. *J Hum Ergol*. 1991;20:147–153.

United Nations. Take Action for the Sustainable Development Goals. 2021. Accessed October 1, 2021. https://www.un.org/sustainabledevelopment/sustainable-development-goals/.

Volk HE, Lurmann F, Penfold B, Hertz-Picciotto I, McConnell R. Traffic-related air pollution, particulate matter, and autism. *JAMA Psychiatry*. 2013;70:71–77. https://doi.org/10.1001/jamapsychiatry.2013.266.

Vyas MV, Garg AX, Iansavichus AV, Costella J, Donner A, Laugsand LE, Janszky I, Mrkobrada M, Parraga G, Hackam DG. Shift work and vascular events: systematic review and meta-analysis. *BMJ*. 2012;345:e4800. https://doi.org/10.1136/bmj.e4800.

Whysner J. *The Alchemy of Disease: How Chemicals and Toxins Cause Cancer and Other Illnesses*. New York: Columbia University Press; 2020.

World Heart Federation. World Heart Day 2009: "Work with Heart." Heart Beat. February/March/April, 2009. Accessed January 3, 2023. https://world-heart-federation.org/wp-content/uploads/2017/08/Annual_Report_2010.pdf.

Chapter 13. The Future of Occupational and Environmental Medicine

Baker B, Kesler D, Guidotti T. Occupational and environmental medicine: public health and medicine in the workplace. *Am J Public Health*. 2020;110(5):636–637. https://doi.org/10.2105/AJPH.2020.305625.

Green-McKenzie J, Khan A, Redlich C, Rivera A, McKinney Z. The future of occupational and environmental medicine. ACOEM Presidential Task Force on the Future of OEM. *J Occup Environ Med.* 2022;64(12):e857–e863 Accessed November 21, 2022. https://acoem.org/acoem/media/News-Library/Future -of-OEM.pdf.

About the Editor and Contributors

Editor

Tee L. Guidotti, MD, MPH, DABT, is a physician, international consultant, and retired professor. He helped shape the modern field through his teaching for more than 35 years at the University of Alberta and George Washington University; his mentorship of many leaders in the contemporary field; his leadership in American, Canadian, and international organizations in OEM; his prolific writings on broad topics as well as specific issues; and as an editor of books and journals. He has been president of the American College of Occupational and Environmental Medicine and the Association of Occupational and Environmental Clinics.

Contributors

Ifeoma Margaret Ama, MD, MPH, is a physician in family practice and occupational medicine in the Houston area and the author of *Choose Health*, a book on self-care.

Manijeh Berenji, MD, MPH, FACOEM, is chief of Occupational Health at the VA Long Beach Healthcare System, Long Beach, California.

Robert Bourgeois, MD, MPH, FACOEM, is medical director of the Bourgeois Medical Clinic in Morgan City, Louisiana, and former president of the American College of Occupational and Environmental Medicine.

Bill Bruce, MBA, CAE, was at the time of writing this chapter chief executive officer of the American College of Occupational and Environmental Medicine.

William G. Buchta, MD, MS, MPH, FACOEM, is former president of the American College of Occupational and Environmental Medicine. He directed the occupational medicine practice at the Mayo Clinic for 11 years and is now chief medical officer for Logistics Health, Inc., and also provides consulting services for several large corporations.

Wayne N. Burton, MD, FACOEM, after a career of more than 30 years in corporate occupational medicine, is now a consultant on health and productivity and broader issues in health care. He trained in internal medicine at Northwestern Memorial Hospital in Chicago.

Judith Green McKenzie, MD, MPH, FACOEM, is executive director for Health, Safety and Environment at the Johns Hopkins University and the Johns Hopkins Health System.

How-Ran Guo, MD, MPH, ScD, FACOEM, is director of the Occupational Safety, Health and Medicine Research Center of the Department of Environmental and Occupational Health, College of Medicine, National Cheng Kung University, Tainan, Taiwan.

Philip Harber, MD, MPH, FACOEM, is currently professor at the Mel and Enid Zuckerman College of Public Health at the University of Arizona and professor emeritus at UCLA, where he led occupational and environmental medicine for many years. He trained in occupational and pulmonary medicine at Johns Hopkins.

Natalie P. Hartenbaum, MD, MPH, FACOEM, is president and chief medical officer of OccuMedix, Inc, an occupational medicine consulting firm located in Dresher, PA, through which she serves as medical director or advisor to numerous clients including the Federal Reserve Bank of Philadelphia; she is a former president of ACOEM. She is past-president of the American College of Occupational and Environmental Medicine and a former member of the Board of Trustees of the American Board of Preventive Medicine.

Clarion E. Johnson, MD, MPH, FACOEM, retired as global medical director of ExxonMobil. He trained in cardiology and occupational medicine at Yale.

Denece Kesler, MD, MPH, FACOEM, is professor in the Department of Internal Medicine at the University of New Mexico, program director of Public Health and Preventive Medicine, and former board member of both the American Board of Preventive Medicine and the American Board of Medical Specialties.

Paula A. Lantsberger, MD, MPH, FACOEM, is currently in consulting practice in Spokane, Washington. She was president of Occupational Medicine Associates for 26 years, serving clients in eastern Washington. She trained in internal medicine and occupational medicine at the University of Pennsylvania.

Ernest C. Levister Jr., MD FACP, FACPM, retired from a referral-based consultant practice in San Bernardino, California (serving the Inland Empire region), specializing in cardiopulmonary and other physiologically based evaluation.

Zeke J. McKinney, MD, MHI, MPH, FACOEM, is program director of the HealthPartners Occupational and Environmental Medicine Residency at the University of Minnesota School of Public Health and affiliate assistant professor in the Division of Environmental Health Sciences.

Robert K. McLellan, MD, MPH, FACOEM, is professor emeritus at Dartmouth University and former chief of the Section on Occupational Medicine of the Dartmouth-Hitchcock Medical Center and former president of the American College of Occupational and Environmental Medicine.

Raúl Alexander Mirza, DO, MPH, MS, former army major, is director of Clinical Public Health and Epidemiology at the U.S. Army Public Health Center.

Chang Rim Na, MD, MPH, is chief of Service, Kaiser Permanente Occupational and Environmental Health. She trained in internal medicine and in occupational medicine at Yale University.

J. Brent Pawlecki, MD, MMM, FACOEM, is the chief health officer at Wells Fargo Bank, and formerly at Goodyear Tire and Rubber. He also previously held corporate medical director positions at other major corporations. He trained in occupational medicine, internal medicine, and pediatrics at Yale and Bridgeport Hospital and obtained a master's degree in medical management at the University of Southern California.

Pouné Saberi, MD, MPH, trained in occupational and environmental medicine and in family medicine at the Hospital of University of Pennsylvania. She practices OEM at the VA Medical Center in Philadelphia. She has served as national president of Physicians for Social Responsibility.

Tanisha Taylor, MD, MPH, FACOEM, is chief medical officer of Robert Wood Johnson Barnabas Health's Corporate Care with clinical duties out of the Monmouth Medical Center–Southern campus in Lakewood, New Jersey. She trained in internal medicine and occupational medicine at Yale University.

Index

Note: Page numbers followed by *t* indicate tables and *f* indicate figures.